Pl. 1

Stanhopea Devoniensis.

Pub.d by J. Ridgway & Sons, 169, Piccadilly, Sept.r 1, 1837.

Printed by P. Gauci.

John Lindley

1799–1865

FRONTISPIECE: John Lindley at the age of thirty-five. Portrait by Charles Fox, 1834.
British Columbia Archives and Records Service, Crease Collection

John Lindley
1799–1865

*Gardener – Botanist
and
Pioneer Orchidologist*

BICENTENARY CELEBRATION VOLUME
Edited by William T. Stearn

Antique Collectors' Club in association with
The Royal Horticultural Society

ISBN 1 85149 296 8

British Library Cataloguing-in-Publication Data
A catalogue record for this book is available from the British Library

Printed in England
by the Antique Collectors' Club Ltd., Woodbridge, Suffolk
on Consort Royal Satin paper
supplied by the Donside Paper Company, Aberdeen, Scotland

To
Robert Morris Hamilton
and
Lawrence Duttson
in Appreciation of
their Major Contributions
to
Knowledge of
JOHN LINDLEY
and his Family

ACKNOWLEDGEMENTS

It is a pleasant duty to thank the institutions and individuals who have graciously provided illustrations for this tribute to John Lindley. The frontispiece and Figures 3, 7, 12 and 16 are reproduced here by courtesy of the British Columbia Archives and Record Service; Colour Plates 5-42, Figure 15 by courtesy of the Royal Botanic Gardens, Kew; Colour Plate 1, Figures 4-6, 10,. 11, 13, 17-20, 24-29 by courtesy of the Lindley Library; Colour Plates 2-4 by courtesy of a private individual. The help of Kathryn Bridge, Phillip Cribb and Marilyn Ward is gratefully acknowledged, as is also proof-reading by Eldwyth Ruth Stearn and Primrose Elliott.

CONTENTS

PREFACE

This volume commemorates the bicentenary of the birth of John Lindley (1799–1865), one of the most eminent, industrious, versatile and productive of nineteenth-century botanists, a gardener-botanist, teacher, journalist and, above all, orchidologist. He was born on 5 February 1799, the son of a Norfolk nurseryman. Remembered today by botanists for his fundamental achievement in the classification, description and naming of orchids, Lindley also served botany as a professor, as an author and as the editor for many years of *The Botanical Register*. He served horticulture as a diligent administrator of the affairs of the Horticultural Society of London (now Royal Horticultural Society), as the author of *The Theory and Practice of Horticulture* and as the editor of *The Gardeners' Chronicle*. His forthright report on the Royal Botanic Garden at Kew saved it from destruction and provided a view of its potentialities leading ultimately to the development of the Royal Botanic Gardens, Kew into a world-important institution. For that alone its myriad visitors owe gratitude.

To the general horticultural public the name Lindley brings to mind only the superb Lindley Library of the Royal Horticultural Society, vastly expanded from his extensive private library bought after his death. The present volume's intent is to provide a wider view of Lindley's life and his manifold achievements, a view of a man much more dynamic than the aged bearded Lindley of the portrait in the Lindley Library which was painted when all his work was done (Colour Plate 1).

The first chapter 'The Life, Times and Achievements of John Lindley' sketches his career as a whole. Subsequent chapters deal with aspects of his work deserving more detailed treatment, that is, as an orchidologist, as a palaeobotanist and as a horticulturist. Each is self-contained. There is accordingly of necessity some overlap and repetition.

The name of John Lindley occurs many times in my *Botanical Latin*, because I made much use therein of his publications. To indicate the length of my association with Lindley, going back to about 1930 and in appreciation of his work I wrote in 1965 in the preface to *Botanical Latin*. 'As a young man I became familiar with the Lindley Herbarium at the Botany School, Cambridge, curiously enough at about the same age as Lindley was when he became assistant librarian to Sir Joseph Banks and acquainted with the Banksian Herbarium. Later, as librarian of the Lindley Library of the Royal Horticultural Society of London, which Lindley also served for many years, I came to know his numerous publications and to admire the industry, tenacity and ability with which he undertook successfully so many different things. In writing this book *[Botanical Latin]* I have been particularly impressed by the great contribution that Lindley made to exactness and clarity of terminology, notably in his *Introduction to Botany* and *Elements of Botany,* which represent, however, but small parts of his activity, and, like Daydon Jackson and other makers of glossaries, I have taken his work as a foundation. Lindley's books were written vigorously and with good sense, drawing upon extensive reading and experience, and they still repay consultation. In the year of his centenary [1965] I am happy indeed to take this opportunity of expressing gratitude both for the example of his life and for his achievements.' Written a hundred years after Lindley's death, it still remains an appropriate tribute two hundred years after his birth.

When I contributed a short biography of Lindley to the *Dictionary of Scientific Biography* in 1973 and a longer one to Sprunger's *Orchids from the Botanical Register* in 1991, a treasure trove of Lindley letters, memoranda, portraits, illustrations etc. lay unrevealed and unsuspected in the Archives of British Columbia, Victoria, B.C., Canada, until in 1994 Mr Robert Morris Hamilton of Richmond, B.C. made known its existence by publishing transcripts of Lindley letters reposing in the Crease Family Collection of the B.C. Archives. His continued painstaking transcription of Lindley's often hasty abominable handwriting has vastly extended knowledge of Lindley and his family, his activities and the financial difficulties haunting him. Particularly welcome has been ample hitherto unknown information about Miss S.A. Drake, described in Jack Kramer's *Women and Flowers* (1996) as 'one of the most elusive of all Victorian botanical artists'. The enquiries of Mr Lawrence Duttson into local records in Suffolk and Norfolk have made a notable contribution to this, supplementing Mr Hamilton's work. The new biographical information in the present volume is entirely due to the enthusiasm and diligence of him and Mr Hamilton. I thank them both, as also the Archives of British Columbia, for graciously making a selection of this copyright Lindley material available for use here. My thanks similarly go to University College, London for permission to publish Miss J.M. Allford's list of Lindley's publications and to the contributors who have dealt here with a diversity of matters relating to Lindley's legacy to us: Mr Christopher D. Brickell, Mrs Kathryn A. Bridge, Dr Phillip Cribb, Professor William G. Chaloner, Dr Brent Elliott and Mr William L. Tjaden. To the ever obliging librarians of the Lindley Library and of the Herbarium Library, Royal Botanic Gardens, Kew, I likewise express my gratitude for their generous help.

W.T. Stearn
Royal Botanic Gardens, Kew, Surrey, England

COLOUR PLATES

FIGURES

Part I

The Life, Times and Achievements of John Lindley 1799-1865

William T. Stearn

Introduction

Abundant creative and productive energy characterised so many great men prominent in the Victorian era, even if born earlier than Queen Victoria's reign, as to mark it as a distinctive Victorian feature. Thus William Morris (1834-1896), story teller, poet, designer, printer, business man and socialist, was described by his doctor as having done the work of ten men. Much the same could be said of John Lindley (1799-1865), honoured nowadays as the foremost British orchidologist of the nineteenth century, indeed by some as 'the father of orchidology'. However, if Lindley had never interested himself in orchids, he would nevertheless stand out among the scientists of that century for his other achievements. As said elsewhere (Stearn, 1973), he was 'a man endowed with an extraordinary capacity for work and a restless, aggressive untiring intellect, who attained distinction in all his activities. Lindley was among the most industrious, many-sided and productive of the nineteenth-century botanists. As administrator, professor, horticulturist, taxonomist, editor, journalist and botanical artist he used to the full his time, his abundant energy and his remarkable talents, with lasting beneficial results in many fields of botany and horticulture'. Orchids were, however, his great botanical love. He established more than 120 genera of Orchidaceae and his publications on the family are still necessarily consulted by botanists concerned with its nomenclature and classification. In the *Index Kewensis* 8, 252 entries relate to Lindley's publications. The maintenance of the Horticultural Society of London (since 1861 the Royal Horticultural Society) during a period of crisis, as also the saving of the Kew botanic garden, stand to his credit. Indeed the Royal Botanic Gardens, Kew, would probably not exist as a botanical institution and possibly not even as a garden of international repute but for Lindley's forthright report of 1838 on 'the management of the Royal Gardens', which led to its salvation and scientific development. He gave the name *Victoria regia* (now *V. amazonica*) to the gigantic Amazonian waterlily, now a feature of the Kew and other botanic gardens.

COLOUR PLATE 1. John Lindley, aged sixty-three. Portrait by E.U. Eddis, 1862, in Lindley Library

Linnaeus and Lindley

In many ways Lindley's varied achievements in the nineteenth century paralleled those of the Swedish naturalist Carl Linnaeus (1707-1778) in the eighteenth century. Both grew up in countries recovering from long impoverishing wars; both became influential esteemed professors and produced numerous works of lasting importance within a creative span of about forty years. By precept and example, both gave effective attention to botanical terminology and nomenclature. Obviously the two owed much genetically and educationally to devoted parents with limited financial means, but, well endowed with self-esteem and self-confidence, never doubting their capacity for any task, they made their way in the world by attracting attention to their ability and justifying by fruitful endeavour the support and encouragement they received. In 1829 Lindley said of Linnaeus, that he was 'a person exactly adapted to the state of science of the time in which he lived… Nature had gifted him with a logical accuracy of reasoning, and a neatness and perspicuity of expression'. Obviously Lindley most appreciated in Linnaeus the qualities he himself possessed. He, like Linnaeus, crammed his life with unceasing activity; their many important publications testify to that. Unfortunately loss of memory and mental deterioration marred the last years of both men.

The gardening interests of their fathers strongly influenced them both; Linnaeus' father was a Swedish country clergyman with a well-stocked garden in Småland, southern Sweden, Lindley's a skilled but commercially unsuccessful nurseryman in Norfolk, East Anglia. All their lives they combined botany and horticulture in their work and the diversity of orchids fascinated them. These extraordinary plants require for their study an understanding of their floral structure only to be gained initially from living material. Linnaeus' travels, particularly in Lapland and on the Baltic islands of Öland and Gotland which possess twenty-nine species of orchids, acquainted him with European species; thus on 2 June 1741 he found on Öland, much to his surprise, *Ophrys insectifera, Orchis militaris, O. morio, O. sambucina, O. maculata, O. incarnata* and *Gymnadenia conopsea*. However, exotic species he knew only from herbarium specimens and illustrations (cf. Stearn, 1975). Lindley was more fortunate; abundant living material of tropical orchids continually came into his hands.

Unlike Linnaeus, John Lindley worked during a period notable for improvements in glasshouse heating, for massive importations of orchids from the seemingly inexhaustible moist tropics without regard to conservation of wild stocks, and for their successful cultivation in England, notably by the nursery firm of Loddiges and Sons at Hackney and by Joseph Paxton at Chatsworth. Orchid growers needed names for their new plants. Lindley was one of the few botanists happy and competent to study, classify and name such plants. Whereas Linnaeus complained that he lacked in Sweden the means of illustrating the new plants in the Uppsala botanic garden, Lindley fortunately controlled a periodical, *The Botanical Register,* entirely devoted to portraying new and little known plants in colour. These included numerous orchids.

Moreover, Lindley's temperament accorded with the prevailing belief of his period in the virtue of hard work, economically necessary and morally right, for high achievement essential. As Samuel Smiles later made evident in his *Self-Help* (1859) by example after example of 'sedulous attention and painstaking industry', these qualities opened the way upward for talented ambitious young men equipped with extraordinary staying-power. Thus Lindley's contemporary, William MacGillivray (1796-1852), who became Professor of Natural History at Aberdeen, in 1819 (the year Lindley came to London) walked from Aberdeen to London in order to see the collection of birds in the British Museum. As David Elliston Allen noted in his *The Naturalist in Britain* (1976), 'This extreme physical doggedness was matched by astonishing displays of intellectual stamina. In virtually every field of study the Victorian age produced figures of such many-sided energies and accomplishments as to leave us open-mouthed in wonderment and make us feel weak merely reading about them. Natural history has its full share of these. Beside a Pugin or a Paxton it could set a Lindley or a Loudon: men of equally prodigious output and quite invincible in their dynamism. Lindley until the age of fifty never knew what is was to feel fatigue and never took a holiday before he was fifty-two'. As Allen also remarks, 'Work for such men was more than just an interest that absorbed them; it was a compulsive discharge of effort. Brought up to feel guilt at idleness and an utter abhorrence of sloth, recreation for them could never mean relaxation'. Such was the social context for Lindley's monumental achievements. Fortunately Mrs Lindley, with their three children, from time to time escaped from it.

Early Years

John Lindley was born on 5 February 1799 at Catton near Norwich, the capital city of Norfolk in eastern England and long a prominent cultural centre. His parents were George Lindley (c.1769-1835) and Mary Lindley (neé Moore). George Lindley, despite his great horticultural knowledge, particularly as a pomologist, ran somewhat unsuccessfully a nursery at Catton. He came from Yorkshire but his wife was probably a Norwich woman. They married at Catton on 4 October 1796 and had four children. The venerable Norwich Grammar School (now Norwich School), which received a royal charter in 1547, gave their son John a sound classical education. Here he acquired a good knowledge of Latin and Greek and must have been instructed in the writing of clear English. From a French refugee in Norwich he learned French and drawing; to these he later added German, of much value to him as it was to Robert Brown. Work as a boy in the nursery under his father's expert eye gave him a practical experience in horticulture and fruit-growing valuable indeed for his future career, as was also his collection and study of the wild flowers around Norwich. He left school in about 1814-1815. George Lindley's debts prevented him from giving John a university education at Oxford or Cambridge, then the only two English universities, or buying him a commission in the army, which he particularly wanted at the age of eighteen. For this botanists should be grateful. A warrior at heart, John Lindley waged battle after battle on such issues as the tax on glass, the mismanagement of royal forests and the artificial Linnaean 'sexual system' of plant classification; he was reputed to be even more forceful in speech than writing! As an army officer he would never have had the time or opportunity for so much botanical research, especially on orchids, and he would certainly not have produced so many important publications.

Even when a famous professor, Lindley drilled at weekends as a volunteer in the south Middlesex militia; apart from weekend gardening and archery, this seems to have been his major recreation! His son Nathaniel recorded that 'all his life, however, he took the greatest interest in military operations and read military histories and followed the movements and battles in Hungary, the Crimea and India with the greatest keenness'. On leaving school he went to Belgium for a short time as the representative of an English seedman.

Unfortunately Lindley lost the sight of one eye in childhood, as did later the celebrated horticulturist and *Crocus*-expert Edward Augustus Bowles (1865-1954). They both saw more detail in plants with their one eye than most people ever do with two eyes. Artistically gifted, they portrayed plants skillfully, beautifully and accurately, their monocular vision fortunately no impediment.

George Lindley's debts

The cost of running his large Catton nursery much exceeded George Lindley's income from it and his debts mounted. To save his father from bankruptcy, John Lindley some time in the 1820s gallantly and courageously stood surety for him. Regarding this encumbrance John's son Nathaniel, a lawyer, stated: 'It was a generous act but an unwise one. My Father had no means of his own, nor had any expectations from any one. The millstone thus early hung round his neck caused him trouble throughout life. He strongly advised me not to make the same mistake. He saw when it was too late that he should not have made himself legally responsible for more than he could possibly pay himself'. Editing and publishing George Lindley's *Guide to the Orchard and Kitchen Garden* (1831), an excellent work, can be regarded as part of John Lindley's efforts to pay off debt. He moved among men of wealth as an intellectual equal but was never one of them. For most of his life financial anxiety was probably never far from his thoughts. With a wife, a son and two daughters, all long dependent and needing allowances, a cook, other domestic staff, a gardener and a large house to maintain, Lindley's income then can never have exceeded outlay to produce a comfortable reserve of savings. He wanted and merited a Civil List pension but did not receive one. Despite a life of unceasing toil Lindley died heavily in debt.

Friendship with W. J. Hooker

William Jackson Hooker (1785-1865), classically educated like Lindley at the Norwich Grammar School, was, again like Lindley, a prodigious worker and self-educated botanist with marked artistic talent. Before moving to Glasgow in 1820 to become professor of botany, he lived at Halesworth, Suffolk, being there a somewhat unsuccessful brewer. He soon learned of young Lindley's ability and invited him to Halesworth. Hooker had a good private botanical library which included a copy of Louis-Claude Richard's *Démonstrations botaniques, ou Analyse du Fruit considéré en général* (Paris, 1808); Richard said he had produced this in seven days. Desirous of owning a copy Lindley, in 1818, translated his work into English at one sitting, working at it continuously for nearly three days without going to bed. It was published in 1819 as *Observations on the Structure of Fruits and Seeds,* with notes and six plates from drawings by Lindley (Figure 1). Particularly notable in the preface is his rejection of the Linnaean 'sexual system' of classification then widely accepted and his advocacy of 'the natural orders of the great Jussieu' as opening 'the way to the most interesting fields of observation. By it the mind is kept perpetually in action'. His mind certainly was! Evidently already aware of the value to a young man of making himself known, he sent copies to Robert Brown, L.C. Richard, A. Richard, A.P. De Candolle, du Petit Thouars, A. de Jussieu, Kunth, Charles Lyell and others. On another occasion, when Lindley was a guest of the Hookers at Halesworth, the housekeeper noted suspiciously that his bed had not been slept in. Discreet enquiry revealed that young Lindley, ambitious to become a plant collector and botanical explorer, had slept on the bedroom floor to accustom himself to sleeping later on the planks of a ship! His ambition was to go to Madagascar or the East Indies. In fact he never travelled further than Belgium, Ireland and France. Hooker gave him a recommendation to the great Sir Joseph Banks (1747-1820), whose herbarium and library constituted the botanical centre of London.

In January 1819 Lindley left Norwich for London. His sister Mary (1800-1887) stayed in Norfolk and earned her living as a family governess. His other sister Anne (b.1804) died when at Christmas 1831 an attack of scarlet fever (scarlatina) tragically ravaged the Lindley household. From his father he received a small allowance which supported him in London until he became a paid employee of Banks in October. Thus began a new momentous chapter in his life.

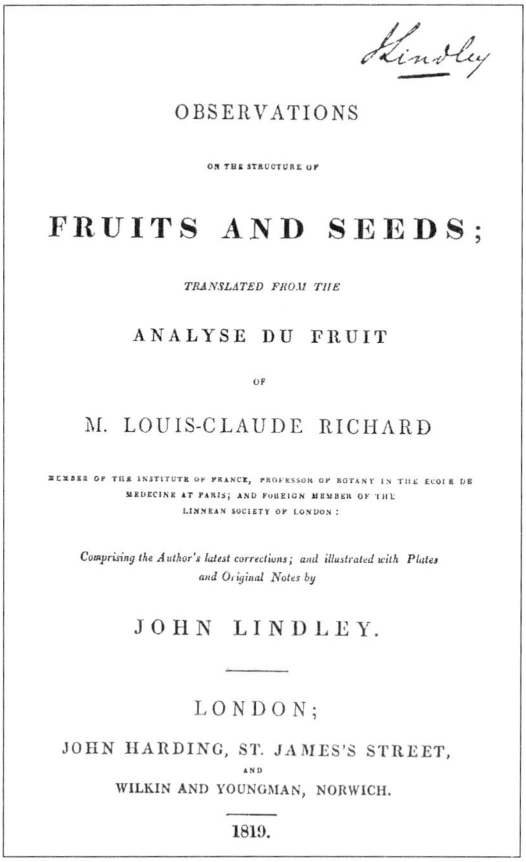

OBSERVATIONS

ON THE STRUCTURE OF

FRUITS AND SEEDS;

TRANSLATED FROM THE

ANALYSE DU FRUIT

OF

M. LOUIS-CLAUDE RICHARD

MEMBER OF THE INSTITUTE OF FRANCE, PROFESSOR OF BOTANY IN THE ECOLE DE
MEDECINE AT PARIS; AND FOREIGN MEMBER OF THE
LINNEAN SOCIETY OF LONDON:

*Comprising the Author's latest corrections; and illustrated with Plates
and Original Notes by*

JOHN LINDLEY.

LONDON;

JOHN HARDING, ST. JAMES'S STREET,
AND
WILKIN AND YOUNGMAN, NORWICH.

1819.

FIGURE 1. Title-page of Lindley's first book, 1819

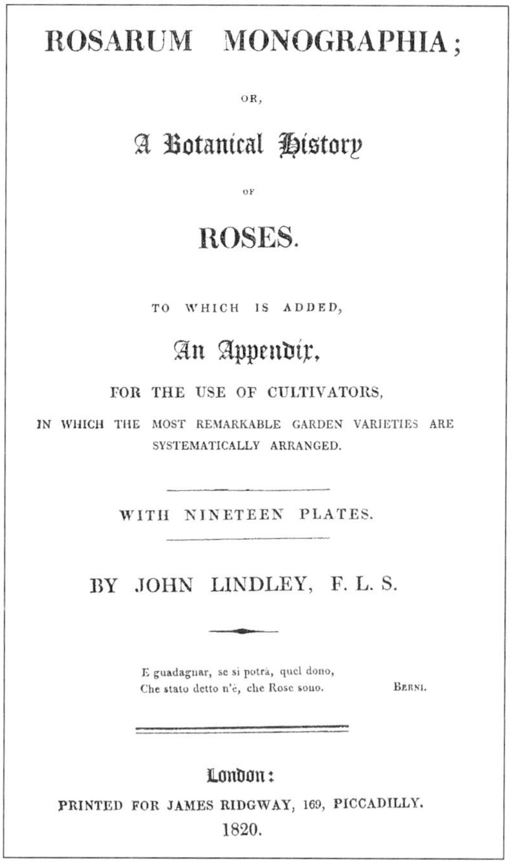

ROSARUM MONOGRAPHIA;

OR,

𝔄 Botanical History

OF

ROSES.

TO WHICH IS ADDED,

An Appendix,

FOR THE USE OF CULTIVATORS,

IN WHICH THE MOST REMARKABLE GARDEN VARIETIES ARE
SYSTEMATICALLY ARRANGED.

WITH NINETEEN PLATES.

BY JOHN LINDLEY, F. L. S.

E guadaguar, se si potrà, quel dono,
Che stato detto n'c, che Rose sono.   BERNI.

London:
PRINTED FOR JAMES RIDGWAY, 169, PICCADILLY.
1820.

FIGURE 2. Title-page of Lindley's monograph of roses, 1820

Work in the Banksian Herbarium

At Banks' house in Soho Square, of which Robert Brown (1771-1858) was the botanist and librarian, Lindley had access to the richest botanical library and herbarium in Britain. Here he worked diligently on the genus *Rosa,* the genera of Rosaceae, and the genus *Digitalis.* The astonishing results were his *Rosarum Monographia; or A Botanical History of Roses* (xii + 156 pages; 1820, Figure 2 and Colour Plates 2 to 4) with nineteen engraved plates, eighteen beautifully and accurately drawn by himself, in which he distinguished seventy-six species, thirteen described for the first time, and a survey of the Rosaceae subfamily Pomoideae in *Transactions of the Linnean Society of London* 13:88-106 (1821) in which he established the genera *Chaenomeles, Osteomeles, Eriobotrya, Photinia, Chamaemeles* and *Raphiolepis,* all now accepted. This was followed by *Digitalium Monographia xxx penes Gulielmum Cattley* (1821) and *Collectanea botanica* (1821-1826, Colour Plates 5 to 7). There is nothing immature about any of these works, which were remarkable achievements indeed for a botanist aged only twenty-two. All manifest detailed and acute observation, often microscopical,

Tab. 3

rdley.   id.   Pub as the Act directs by J. Ridgway 170 Piccadilly. 1820.   J. Watts sc.

COLOUR PLATE 2. *Rosa laxa* Lindley. Coloured engraving by Lindley in Lindley, *Rosarum Monographia*, pl. 3 (1820)

COLOUR PLATE 3. *Rosa carolina* Lindley. Coloured engraving by Lindley in Lindley, *Rosarum Monographia*, pl. 4 (1820)

22

COLOUR PLATE 4. *Rosa macrophylla* Lindley. Coloured engraving by Lindley in Lindley, *Rosarum Monographia*, pl. 6 (1820)

COLOUR PLATE 5. *Reseda mediterranea* Jacquin. Coloured engraving by Lindley in Lindley, *Collectanea botanica* pl. 22 (1821)

Tab.23.

J.Lindley del.   *Papaver bracteatum?*   Weddell sc.

COLOUR PLATE 6. *Papaver bracteatum* Lindley. Coloured engraving by Lindley in Lindley, *Collectanea botanica* pl. 23 (1821)

together with judicious survey of relevant literature. At the age of twenty-one in 1820 he had been elected a Fellow of the Linnean Society of London and in 1821 C.G. Nees von Esenbeck dedicated to him a genus of Theaceae as *Lindleya;* that name has been rejected in favour of *Lindleya* Kunth (nomen conservandum 3328) given in 1824 to a Mexican genus of Rosaceae. More astonishing was his election to membership of the venerable Academia Caesarea Leopoldino-Carolina Naturae Curiosorum then located in Bonn, now the Deutsche Akademie der Naturforscher Leopoldina located in Halle (Saale), the German equivalent of the Royal Society of London. Thus he began early to acquire international recognition.

In London, Banks, ever a shrewd judge of men and their potentialities, obviously recognised the ability of this forceful, ambitious young man just as he had earlier recognised the ability of Francis Masson, Robert Brown, George Caley, Matthew Flinders and others, and he employed him as an assistant to Robert Brown in his library and herbarium at Soho Square. Banks, however, died on 19 June 1820. This period of eighteen months in the celebrated Banksian library not only furthered Lindley's botanical education; there he met people influential in botany and horticulture who were important for his subsequent career.

In the preface, dated 'March 31st, 1820', to his *Rosarum Monographia* he stated 'To the noble library and inexhaustible Botanical Treasures of the Right Honourable Sir Joseph Banks, with that unexampled liberality for which their illustrious possessor has been ever celebrated, I have been allowed the freest access'. This preface also reveals that he was already well acquainted with Joseph Sabine, who grew a large collection of cultivated roses and was Secretary of the Horticultural Society of London; Sir James Edward Smith, owner of the Linnaean collections; Aylmer Bourke Lambert and Charles Lyell, to whom he dedicated the *Rosarum Monographia,* being much indebted to 'his liberality and to his intimate knowledge of the genus'. Lyell rewarded him with £100, enabling him to buy a microscope and a small herbarium. The death of Banks deprived Lindley of his livelihood, but he had gained the friendship of William Cattley (1787-1835), a wealthy merchant who was a keen botanically minded horticulturist (cf. Hetherington, 1994) and paid him to draw and describe new plants in his garden at Barnet. He also paid for the publication of Lindley's *Digitalium Monographia* (1821), although a deterioration in his business affairs obliged him to cease his support in 1821. That patronage had, however, been for Cattley a good investment. The orchidaceous genus *Cattleya,* which Lindley gratefully named in his honour with *C. labiata* as the type-species, comprises about fifty species in South and Central America and over 4,000 hybrid cultivars, which have made *Cattleya,* 'Queen of Orchids', a popular florist's orchid, even for button-holes. In 1820 the Horticultural Society of London employed him to draw roses. Thus began Lindley's association with the Society (later the Royal Horticultural Society) which extended to forty-three years.

Tab. 33

Cattleya labiata.

COLOUR PLATE 7. *Cattleya labiata* Lindley. Coloured engraving by J. Curtis in Lindley, *Collectanea botanica* pl. 33 (1821)

FIGURE 3. Bedford House, Acton Green, the Lindley family residence. Drawing by Sarah or
Barbara Lindley, c.1845

Employment by the Horticultural Society of London.
The Lindley Family

On 25 February 1822, shortly after Lindley's twenty-third birthday, he was
appointed Assistant Secretary of the Garden of the Horticultural Society at
Turnham Green, Chiswick, Middlesex, to superintend the collection of plants
and to help lay out the garden, with many other duties but little authority,
which remained in the hands of Joseph Sabine. The Society's historian, Harold
R. Fletcher, rightly stated in 1969 that 'as Assistant Secretary, Vice-Secretary, and
for the last five years of his working life as Secretary, he was the backbone of
the Society and possibly the greatest servant it has ever had'.

His income assured, he married on 11 February 1823 Sarah Freestone (1797-
1869), from South Elmham, Suffolk. Their first child was born in December in
1823 but died soon after. Asa Gray described Mrs Lindley in 1839 as 'a quiet
lady of plain manners and apparently very domestic habits'. They had necessarily to live near the Horticultural Society's garden at Turnham Green,

Chiswick. At first they rented a small house on the south side of Acton Terrace. Later the family moved into Melbourne House, then (seemingly in 1834) into an adjacent house, Bedford House (built about 1793), a large Georgian house with large windows, both on Acton Green, then a completely rural area. At the back of the house stretched a long and wide garden and beyond that there were fields as far as Acton village. In this capacious house Lindley accommodated his herbarium and library; here came distinguished visitors; here the artist Miss S. A. Drake illustrated orchids and other plants for the *Botanical Register;* here his two daughters spent most of their time drawing. Several of their sketches portray the house as it was then. Lindley never owned it, although he lived there until his death in 1865. Evidently Mrs Lindley's family, the Freestones, bought the house and, as a married woman could not then own property independently of her husband, they placed it in the hands of trustees, so that Lindley's creditors could not seize and sell it. This house still stands, named Bedford House and converted into thirteen flats, but so altered that only half of the front, together with only half of the coadstone ornamented pediment, shown in Sarah's drawing (Figure 3), is now visible. A building and shops occupy what was the Lindleys' front garden. Within twenty years of Lindley's death the garden, arboretum and fields of his time had been replaced by the roads and houses of the Bedford Park garden suburb near Turnham Green station.

John and Sarah had three surviving children, Sarah (1826-1922), nicknamed 'Totty', Nathaniel (1828-1921), nicknamed 'Natty', and Barbara (1830-1927), nicknamed 'Dunny'. Both daughters were accomplished artists, having inherited their father's talent and been taught drawing by his friend the Norwich-born painter and engraver Charles Fox (1794-1849). Sarah contributed botanical line-drawings to her father's publications, notably *The Vegetable Kingdom* (1846) and early volumes of *The Gardeners' Chronicle* (Figures 11 to 14); these are simple, clear and accurate, with the minimum of shading. She married in 1853 Henry Pering Pellew Crease (1823-1905), a barrister who became in 1861 Attorney General in British Columbia; to her we owe the preservation of the Lindley material now in the Crease Collection, British Columbia Archives, Victoria, B.C., Canada. Her life in British Columbia with its hardships was very different indeed from the sheltered life she had had in the Lindley home, as Kathryn Bridge's detailed full-length biography of this remarkable woman, *Henry & Self. The Private life of Sarah Crease 1826-1922* (1996) describes. She had seven children. Her sister, Barbara, married a clergyman, Edward Thompson. The longevity of the three Lindley children (ninety-three to ninety-seven years) contrasts with their father's sixty-six years and their mother's seventy-four years. Their aunt, Mary Hastings, John Lindley's sister, lived to eighty-five. The Lindleys' firstborn son, George, died of scarlet fever in 1832.

The family correspondence preserved in British Columbia makes evident that they were an affectionate closely united family. Nathaniel became a distinguished lawyer, ultimately Master of the Rolls, was knighted in 1875 and made a life peer in 1900. His reminiscences of his father provide much personal information about Lindley's career (cf. Lindley, N., 1911). Lord Lindley's eldest son, Major General John Edward Lindley (1860-1925), served in the South African War and the First World War. Another son, Walter Barry Lindley (1861-1944), was a distinguished lawyer. A third son, Sir Francis Oswald Lindley (1872 1950), had a varied diplomatic career. Thus the Lindley family attained eminence in three generations. Lindley's great granddaughter, Alice Lindley (Lady Morland), wrote about him in 1965, on the centenary of his death.

The 'Collectanea botanica'

In April 1821 Lindley began publication of a sumptuous folio work with coloured plates mostly by himself, some plants coming from Cattley's garden, *Collectanea botanica or Figures and botanical Illustrations of rare and curious exotic Plants,* which ultimately comprised forty-one plates, sixteen illustrating orchids. Plate 2 (1821) depicts a new genus and species of Orchidaceae from Trinidad which he named *Trizeuxis falcata.* The accompanying text proclaims the fascination for him of the Orchidaceae which thereafter became his dominant botanical interest: 'If we were requested to select the most interesting from the multitude of vegetable tribes, we should, on the whole, perhaps, be willing to give the preference to the natural order of ORCHIDEAE. Whether we consider general elegance of individuals, durability of blossoms, splendid colours, delicious perfume, or extraordinary structure, it would be difficult to select any order superior to Orchideae in these respects, and few even equal to them. To the cultivator, who esteems plants for their beauty only; to the botanist, who, rejecting outward attractions, is chiefly captivated by anomalous structure, or intricate organisation; or to the amateur, who wisely prefers to have these requisites combined; to all, or any of these, we conceive that accurate figures of foreign Orchidaceous plants cannot fail to be particularly acceptable. We therefore propose to publish one species of this family in each succeeding number; and we hope to be able soon to add such important information with respect to the treatment of Orchideae, as will entirely remove the present difficulty of cultivating them, and as may enable any one to manage them as readily as the most common plants of our hot-houses.' The last part (1826) of the *Collectanea botanica* contains an 'Orchidearum Sceletos', a classified list of the orchid genera then known, 154 instead of the twenty-eight listed by Olof Swartz some twenty years earlier. Of these forty-three had been published by Robert Brown, twenty-one by Lindley himself, twelve by Swartz, ten by L.C. Richard, four by Kunth. The family is now (1996) estimated to comprise about 800 genera.

Loudon's 'Encyclopaedia of Plants'

About 1822 Lindley met a lowland Scot, like Robert Brown a welcome emigrant into England, as ambitious, methodical, enterprising, tenacious and hard-working as himself and likewise devoted to horticulture and botany, John Claudius Loudon (1783-1843). They were certainly birds of a feather. Loudon intended to compile an encyclopaedia of plants, having completed an *Encyclopaedia of Gardening* (1822). There already existed Robert Sweet's *Hortus suburbanus Londinensis* (1818) and James Donn's *Hortus Cantabrigiensis,* 9th ed. (1819) listing plants in British gardens, but Loudon planned a more elaborate and comprehensive work ultimately having nearly 10,000 little woodcut illustrations by James De Carle Sowerby (1787-1871). He enlisted Lindley's collaboration. The title-page of *An Encyclopaedia of Plants* (1829), a work of 1,159 closely-printed pages dealing with 14,649 species of flowering plants and ferns, states 'The specific characters by an eminent botanist'. The preface reveals this botanist to be 'Professor Lindley, F.R.S., L.S., G.S. &c.' According to Loudon, he 'determined the genera and the species to be arranged under them; prepared the specific characters, derivations, and accentuations; he either wrote or examined the notes; and he corrected the whole while passing through the press'. In other words, Lindley was responsible for virtually the whole of the massive work. It stands comparison with Linnaeus' *Systema Vegetabilium* (1774). Most botanists would be proud to have achieved as much in a lifetime. Lindley had accomplished it by the age of thirty in addition to all his other time-consuming tasks; it reveals an astonishing wide acquaintance with plants, as well as with Latin and Greek.

The genera of *Orchidaceae,* which were or had been in cultivation in Britain, here number 61 arranged in eight tribes, of which Lindley had proposed six. He concisely described 214 species. His account of the family is as follows: 'Of all tribes of plants, this is the most singular, the most fragrant and the most difficult of culture. The flowers are often remarkable for their grotesque configuration, which has been likened to heads and bodies of animals, and for the strange character of their stems which are sometimes attenuated into a degree of gracefulness scarcely equalled even among grasses and sometimes contracted into a clumsy goutiness of figure such as is known no where else. The species are found inhabiting the mountains and meadows of the cooler parts of the globe, or adhering by their tortuous roots to the branches of the loftiest trees of the tropical forest, to which their blossoms often lend a beauty not their own [i.e. not that of the trees themselves]. Vulgarly this last description of plants is called parasitic; they are, however, not so, deriving no support from the juices of the plants on which they grow, but on the contrary are epiphytes, merely adhering to other plants for support and vegetating in the rich black soil. It is very singular that the pollen of these plants has no parallel, except among the very different and distinct order of Asclepiaceae.'

The Years 1826–1840

Lindley, of course, depended upon the Horticultural Society for his livelihood. Sabine's autocratic management of the Society's affairs worried him as leading to disaster but he could do nothing except protest personally to Sabine. Expenditure, at Sabine's optimistic instigation, on projects that, although worthy, were too many and too costly for the Society's means, by 1826 had brought it near ruin, especially as John Turner, the Society's Assistant Secretary, had embezzled part of its funds. The Society dismissed Turner in 1826. In 1827 it appointed Lindley as Assistant Secretary of the Society as well as of the Society's Garden, but insisted that he provide a security for £1,000. With the Society's affairs in so perilous a state and worsening in 1829, Lindley must have felt his own position insecure, even though he had protested to Sabine about the latter's actions. Obviously he would have welcomed a new, even if only supplementary, appointment. It came in 1828.

Meanwhile, in 1825, Protestant dissenters, many wealthy, excluded on religious grounds, as were Jews and Roman Catholics, from the only two English universities Oxford and Cambridge, together with other liberal-minded men, had been trying to establish a non-sectarian university in London. Their success resulted in the foundation of London University (later renamed University College) in 1826, for which professors were needed. Lindley's friend William Jackson Hooker, now happily a professor in Glasgow, declined accepting the new university's Professorship of Botany; Lindley accordingly applied for it in March 1828 and received notice of his appointment in May 1828; he retained his post with the Horticultural Society. His emoluments, like those of the other London professors, depended on the fees paid by students, supplemented by a meagre salary. The fledgling university lacked the wealth of Oxford and Cambridge colleges in money and land. In the same year he was elected a Fellow of the Royal Society of London on the recommendation of Robert Brown, Thomas Andrew Knight and Joseph Sabine, three distinguished sponsors.

Lindley's inaugural lecture to the University of London on 30 April 1829 set forth clearly his views on the nature and objects of botany and its utility in relation to medicine, horticulture and geology. Linnaeus' so-called 'sexual system' of classification received short shrift as 'not fitted for the present state of natural science', as did the mystical systems of the German nature-philosophers such as Lorenz Oken, being 'really little better than romantic speculations'. His approach was essentially practical. The basis of classification he maintained should be based on study of the vegetable kingdom 'in all its forms and bearings', both external and internal, including physiology, and finally chemical and medicinal properties. Such manifold study of plants was fundamental to his teaching, and many of his publications. With this address Lindley initiated the broad-based botanical instruction and research which by the end of the century had become traditional for University College.

Lindley delivered five university lectures a week from eight to nine in the morning during the spring term but six to seven in the evening during the autumn term. To reach his classroom at University College he had for some years to ride on horseback from Turnham Green, presumably on a hired horse. 'He is constantly in his lecture-room at University College, both in Winter and Summer courses at the appointed time. On these occasions he forms a remarkable contrast to the pupils by whom he is surrounded. He is a fresh, ruddy, hale-looking man, and after his morning's ride, in the midst of fresh-plucked plants, presents an appearance entirely different from that of the pale students, who have generally been but a few minutes before roused from their too scanty slumbers'. (Anon. 1839). Teaching over, he had to ride back to Turnham Green, attend to the work in the Society's garden or else stay overnight in London for much of the week to attend to the Society's business at 21 Regent Street, the Society's office and library. Later he travelled there by horse-drawn omnibus. Surprisingly he also found time for writing, editing and the study of orchids and other plants.

Lindley, when appointed professor in London, like Hooker in Glasgow, had never heard an academic lecture in his life. Unhampered by tradition, both lectured well. Maxwell Tylden Masters (1833-1907), Lindley's successor (with Thomas Moore) as editor of *The Gardeners' Chronicle,* stated that a lecture by Lindley was among the most interesting he heard when a student. Fortunately Lindley's son Nathaniel wrote an account of his father's procedure. 'He took infinite pains with his lectures. He never read them; but he prepared notes for the subjects to be attended to and arranged these with care, and against each heading he made a note of the time he should dwell upon it. He did this in order to avoid spending too much time on the first subjects and crowding the subsequent ones into too short a space of time towards the end of his discourse. Further than this he prepared large coloured drawings to illustrate his lecture and hung these up on a frame near where he stood. I have often seen him prepare these. He had one or more large sheets of paper which he put on the floor; then on his hands and knees he first sketched and afterwards coloured what be wanted. The drawings looked very rough and coarse when seen at a short distance; but they were most effective when hung up in the theatre in which he lectured. He lectured in the large theatre in University College during the summer at 8 a.m. for an hour four days a week; and in the Apothecary Society's Garden in Chelsea on two days a week. At the end of each lecture he invited the students to come and tell him anything they did not understand and he gave them any flowers not previously distributed in order that they might take them home and examine them. He did all he could to encourage those pupils who were in earnest and took a real interest in their botanical studies. I attended a course of his lectures at University College myself and speak from what I myself saw and heard.'

As stated elsewhere.'the years 1805 to 1830 saw the triumph of the view that the retention of the admittedly artificial Linnaean "sexual system" of classifying plants according to the number of their stamens and styles was an anachronism and that it should be replaced by more "natural" systems based on A.L. de Jussieu's and utilising a wider range of associated characters' (Stearn 1989). This was very much Lindley's viewpoint; indeed he helped Hooker with the 'natural method' of his *Flora Scotica* (1821). Sir James Edward Smith's scholarly *The English Flora* (4 vols., 1824-1828) adopted the obsolescent Linnaean system. For student use Lindley therefore published in 1829 *A Synopsis of the British Flora, arranged according to the Natural Orders* (Figure 4), of which a second edition appeared in 1835 and a third in 1841, for which his early botanizing in Norfolk provided the basis. The first two editions are nomenclaturally important on account of new species, e.g. *Rubus fissus,* Lindley therein described. He had, however, other works on hand. Among these was the first part of *The Genera and Species of Orchidaceous Plants (1830-1840, Figure 5).*

'Students', the new Professor stated, 'are particularly requested not to furnish themselves with any introductory work by the late Sir James Edward Smith or Dr Thornton', both Linnaean devotees. He had therefore to provide them with text-books of his own. Accordingly in 1830 he published *An Outline of the First principles of Botany,* which was later translated into German and Italian, and *An Introduction to the Natural System of Botany.* The same year he began the publication in parts of two important works on orchids. The great Austrian-born resident botanical artist at Kew, Franz Andreas Bauer (1758-1840), had by 1830 produced some of the finest illustrations of the floral structure of orchids ever made, accurate, remarkably detailed and aesthetically pleasing. He and Lindley, both expert microscopists, were friends living not three miles apart. Accordingly Lindley, with customary enterprise, provided the text to these *Illustrations of Orchidaceous Plants by Francis Bauer — with Notes and Prefatory Remarks by John Lindley,* with thirty-five lithographed folio plates (part 1 in 1830; 2 in 1832; 3 in 1834; 4 in 1838; cf. Stewart & Stearn, 1991). Much less sumptuous was the octavo *The Genera and Species of Orchidaceous Plants* (1830-1840 in seven parts). This provided a basic classification of the family and short diagnoses and descriptions in Latin of all the orchids then known, many being new to science as herbarium specimens from botanical collectors and living specimens from orchid growers continuously came into his hands for identification and naming.

In 1829 Lindley took over the editorship of *The Botanical Register* to which he had contributed in August 1819 'a most ingenious and elaborate description' of *Maranta zebrina,* now *Calathea zebrina* (5:t.535), followed by descriptions and his own illustrations of *Rosa kamchatica* (t.419), *R. ferox* (t.420), *R. alpina* (t.425) and *R. multiflora* (t.425) in December 1819 and January 1820. Like the contemporary and rival *Curtis's Botanical Magazine,* it portrayed in colour a

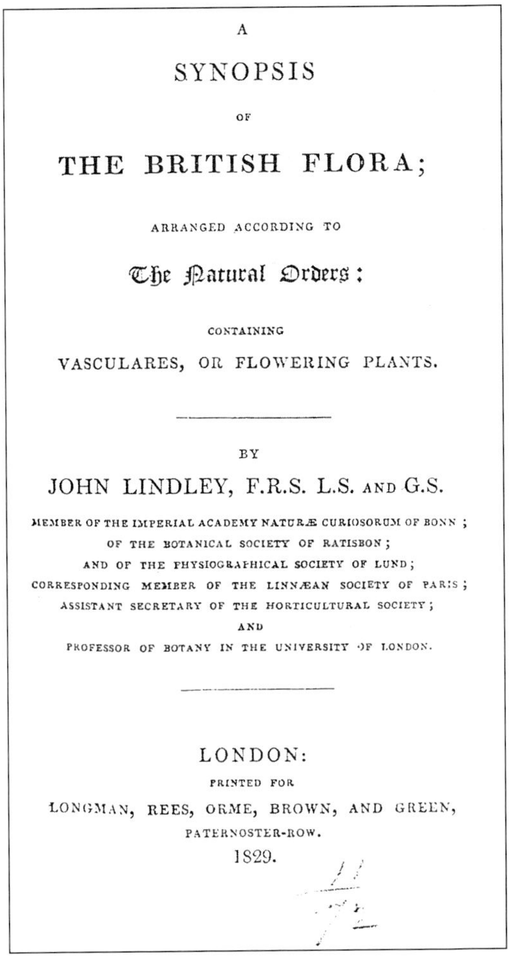

A

SYNOPSIS

OF

THE BRITISH FLORA;

ARRANGED ACCORDING TO

The Natural Orders:

CONTAINING

VASCULARES, OR FLOWERING PLANTS.

BY

JOHN LINDLEY, F.R.S. L.S. AND G.S.

MEMBER OF THE IMPERIAL ACADEMY NATURÆ CURIOSORUM OF BONN ;
OF THE BOTANICAL SOCIETY OF RATISBON ;
AND OF THE PHYSIOGRAPHICAL SOCIETY OF LUND ;
CORRESPONDING MEMBER OF THE LINNÆAN SOCIETY OF PARIS ;
ASSISTANT SECRETARY OF THE HORTICULTURAL SOCIETY ;
AND
PROFESSOR OF BOTANY IN THE UNIVERSITY OF LONDON.

LONDON:

PRINTED FOR

LONGMAN, REES, ORME, BROWN, AND GREEN,

PATERNOSTER-ROW.

1829.

FIGURE 4. Title-page of Lindley's British flora, 1829

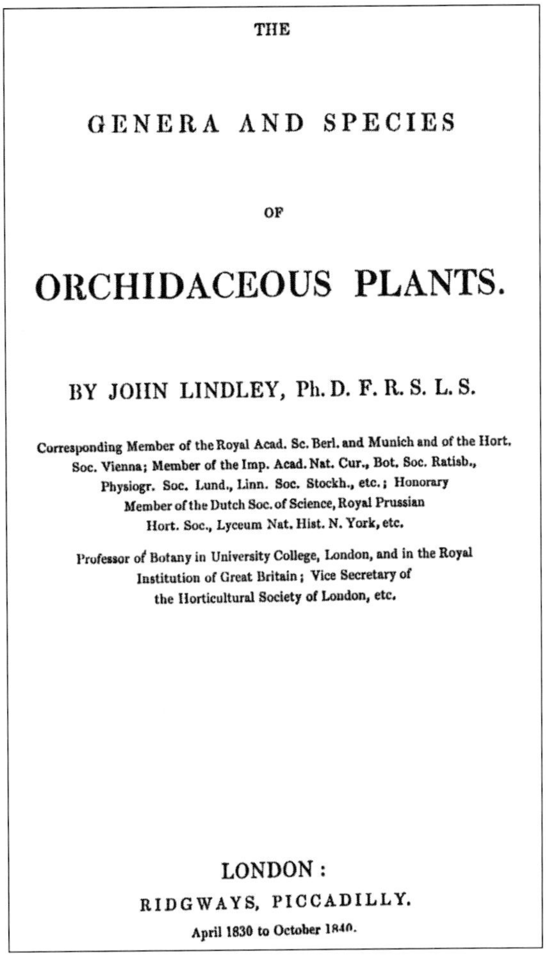

THE

GENERA AND SPECIES

OF

ORCHIDACEOUS PLANTS.

BY JOHN LINDLEY, Ph. D. F. R. S. L. S.

Corresponding Member of the Royal Acad. Sc. Berl. and Munich and of the Hort.
Soc. Vienna; Member of the Imp. Acad. Nat. Cur., Bot. Soc. Ratisb.,
Physiogr. Soc. Lund., Linn. Soc. Stockh., etc.; Honorary
Member of the Dutch Soc. of Science, Royal Prussian
Hort. Soc., Lyceum Nat. Hist. N. York, etc.

Professor of Botany in University College, London, and in the Royal
Institution of Great Britain; Vice Secretary of
the Horticultural Society of London, etc.

LONDON :

RIDGWAYS, PICCADILLY.

April 1830 to October 1840.

FIGURE 5. Title-page of Lindley's first major work on Orchidaceae

diversity of plants. Lindley now controlled an excellent medium for graphically recording new orchids. Illustrations of orchids are scattered through its volumes. *The Botanical Register* was not financially so successful as the older *Botanical Magazine* when invigorated by Hooker and it ceased publication in 1847, by which time Lindley, who had edited vols. 15-53 (1829-1847), was actively involved in editing *The Gardeners' Chronicle* (1842 et seq.) as well as the *Proceedings and Transactions* of the Horticultural Society of London. Fervently interested in popular education and much needing money, he contributed a large number of botanical articles, up to the letter R., to *The Penny Cyclopaedia of the Society for the Diffusion of Useful Knowledge* (28 vols.; 1833-1843); this was an excellent authoritative work packed with information. Lindley's contributions are unsigned but his hand is very evident in articles such as, for example, that on *Bambusa* (3: 355-357; 1835), wherein he published eight new specific names, and that on *Orchidaceae* (16: 476-479; 1840). Of like educational intent were his *An Introduction to Botany* (1832; 4th ed., 1839), *Flora Medica* (1838), *School Botany* (1839; 12th ed., 1862) and *The Theory of Horticulture* (1840), of which a revised and extended new edition appeared in 1855, as *The Theory and Practice of Horticulture,* wherein he gave reasons for the whole range of best horticultural practice. He regarded this as one of his very best works and it was translated into Dutch, German and Russian.

Lindley wrote in a clear direct manner, which makes his works still readable, conveying much information with precision. He gave especial attention to botanical terminology. The language of botany, 'from one cause or another, whether accident, ignorance, pedantry, over-fastidiousness, vanity or careless-ness', he wrote, was 'marvellously in want of reformation'. This he sought to effect by providing a logical and comprehensive glossary of botanical Latin terms, with their English equivalents and definition, in his *Introduction to Botany;* it formed the basis of botanical terminology in English-speaking countries. Being permanently valuable, it is reprinted in W.T. Stearn's *Botanical Latin,* 313-357 (1966; 4th ed., 1992) from the *Introduction to Botany,* 3rd ed. (1839). He proposed that the names of *all* botanical families should end in -*aceae;* accordingly he replaced the name *Compositae* by *Asteraceae, Cruciferae* by *Brassicaceae, Labiatae* by *Lamiaceae, Leguminosae* by *Fabaceae, Orchideae* by *Orchidaceae* and *Umbelliferae* by *Apiaceae.* Many family names accepted now were introduced by Lindley in 1846 although some had already been published by P.F. Horaninov in his little-known *Primae Lineae Systematis Naturae* (1834).

Lindley, however much he had on hand, seems never to have recoiled from accepting another onerous task. One such was the *Fossil Flora of Great Britain* (3 octavo vols; 1831-1837) in collaboration with the geologist William Hutton (1797-1860) of Newcastle upon Tyne. A summary of what was then known, with descriptions also of fossil plants hitherto unknown, this owed much of its value to plates drawn by William Crawford Williamson (1816-1895), then a medical apprentice aged about seventeen, later a celebrated palaeontologist and botanist. A catalogue of known extant specimens figured has been published by A. Newman and I. Chatt-Ramsey in 1985. When Williamson arrived at University College in 1840 to further his medical education, Lindley, who had been so precocious himself, was surprised that his collaborator had begun so young. Another unexpected task of this period was the completion of Sibthorp and Smith's *Flora Graeca,* the most costly and certainly one of the most beautiful of British botanical works. When Sir James Edward Smith (1759-1828) died, he had published volumes 1-6 (1806-1827) and had prepared the text for volume 7 fasc. 1 (1831) which his friend Robert Brown saw through the press. There remained the preparation of three and a half volumes to complete the planned ten volumes of this great work with its superb plates by Ferdinand Bauer. In 1831 Thomas Platt (d.1842), one of Sibthorp's two executors, the other being Sibthorp's cousin John Hawkins (1761-1841), turned for help to Lindley,

Smith's critic and opponent. Lindley, who was much surprised, then had relatively little knowledge of the Mediterranean flora but that did not deter him and, with the publication in November 1840 of volume 10 fasc. 2, he ended a project which had begun some fifty years earlier. For this he received £350, a large sum then, equivalent to one year's salary, and very welcome because of his having so naïvely undertaken to pay his father's debts. It is of interest that this great work was written from start to finish by two Norwich botanists and elegantly printed by a printer from Norwich, Richard Taylor.

Honorary Doctorate

Apart from election to Fellowship of the Royal Society of London 1828 and the award of its Royal Medal in 1857, Lindley received no British honours in his long and productive career. The celebrated Bavarian botanist Carl F.P. Martius (1794-1868) on a visit to England had been very hospitably received by Mr. and Mrs. Lindley and he was obviously much impressed by Lindley's character and publications. Accordingly he enquired in 1832 if Lindley would accept the degree of Doctor Philosophiae from the university of Munich. The diploma came in 1833. This German degree had then no British academic equivalent, the nearest being Magister Artium (M.A.) with which it was earlier synonymous. Henceforth Lindley was designated Dr Lindley, if not Professor Lindley, thanks to this enterprise of the University of Munich in conferring such a degree on a foreigner. He may well have been the first British subject to have been thus honoured. Only those without a university degree can imagine the emotional impact of receiving such foreign academic recognition.

Later honours from abroad were election to the Institute de France as a corresponding member and to the American Academy of Science and Arts as a Foreign Member. In 1839 the University of Basel also gave him an honorary doctorate.

Crisis in the affairs of the Horticultural Society

Sabine's mismanagement of the Horticultural Society's affairs, above all its mounting debts, became by 1830 a matter of public concern and of outspoken angry comment in the press. A Member of Parliament and Fellow of the Society, Robert Gordon, accordingly headed a Committee appointed by the Fellows to enquire into the Society's income and expenditure, debts and assets. Sabine, the Honorary Secretary who had worked hard but not always wisely for the Society over fourteen years, resigned. Lindley had now to defend himself. A letter of his to Sabine came before the Committee in which, among much else, he stated 'You know perfectly well that I have always protested against the statements by which the Council have frequently been deluded into sanctioning measures and expenditure, which had they known the real state of

FIGURE 6. John Lindley, aged forty. Lithograph from *The Naturalist* 4: 434 (1839)

the Society's affairs, they could not have countenanced … I have never been a party to the exaggeration of the Society's means, and concealment of the Society's debts, by means of which many honourable and excellent men in the Council have unfortunately been induced to believe a ruined Society to be in a state of prosperity'. It left him securely in charge to work with George Bentham (1800-1884), the new Honorary Secretary, in restoring the Society's fortunes. Among other innovations he started in 1831 a series of lectures to Fellows on botany in relation to horticulture, forerunners of the lectures at Royal Horticultural Society flower shows. Moreover at his instigation the Council decided in 1830 that it would recommend no student gardener for employment unless he had passed a Society examination in literacy and horticulture, probably the first such examination anywhere, but later adopted at Kew, Edinburgh, and elsewhere, He also identified the plants introduced by the Society's collectors, notably those of David Douglas from North America.

The 'Sertum Orchidaceum' and Miss S.A. Drake

These administrative duties in no way abated Lindley's study of orchids or the acceptance of other responsibilities. He continued to publish revisions of orchid genera as parts of his *The Genera and Species of Orchidaceous Plants,* the last part appearing in 1840. By then he had begun publication of a sumptuous folio work appealing to the increasing number of wealthy people interested in growing orchids, *Sertum Orchidaceum or a Wreath of the most beautiful Orchidaceous Flowers* (1837-1841) with forty-nine coloured lithographed plates (Colour

FIGURE 7. Miss Sarah Anne Drake (1803–1857), aged forty-four, John Lindley's principal botanical artist from 1832 to 1847. Sketch, 1847, by Sarah or Barbara Lindley

Plates 8 to 13 and 16). The chief artist, Miss Sarah Anne Drake (1803–1857), also skilfully portrayed many orchids and other plants for Lindley in *The Botanical Register* (Colour Plates 14 and 15) and other publications, notably in *Ladies Botany,* and she served him industriously and loyally as the botanical artist Robert Hood Fitch (1817–1892) served Lindley's friend William J. Hooker. Unlike Fitch, however, she long remained so obscure that Blunt and Stearn stated in 1994 that of Miss Drake 'almost nothing seems to be known beyond her work' of uniform high quality and Jack Kramer in 1996 described her as 'one of the most elusive of all Victorian botanical artists', who 'apparently led a rather solitary life' (Figure 7). This is no longer true. Robert M. Hamilton's transcripts of Lindley documents, Victoria, British Columbia, and Lawrence Duttson's investigations in Norfolk and London of births, marriages and deaths have brought her career to light. The daughter of a Norfolk farmer, John Drake, Sarah Anne Drake was born in Skeyton on 24 July 1803. Although not related to

John and Sarah Lindley, she and Lindley's sister Anne were friends and schoolmates and she thus had a lifelong association with the Lindley family. Her education included a stay at a school in Paris. About 1830 she came to Acton Green and lived there until 1847 in the Lindley household, affectionately known as 'Ducky' but professionally as 'Miss Drake of Turnham Green.' Under Lindley's supervision she soon became a very accomplished botanical artist particularly esteemed for portraying orchids.

Miss Drake's employment as a botanical artist ended in 1847 when *The Botanical Register* ceased publication. Soon afterwards she returned to Norfolk and lived with an uncle, Daniel Drake, a farmer at Fritton. Here in November 1852 she married a well-to-do farmer, John Sutton Hastings (c.1792-1869) of Longham, Norfolk, a widower. The Rev. T.R. Drake conducted the marriage service and John W. Drake was a witness, both men possibly her brothers. She died at Longham Hall on 9 July 1857, less than a year after Lindley, the cause of death recorded as diabetes, for which no treatment then existed, and was buried in the graveyard of St Andrew's church, Longham. The Australian orchid genus *Drakaea* Lindley commemorates her. An even better memorial is the collection of her 325 orchid portraits reproduced in Sprunger's *Orchids from the Botanical Register 1815-1847* (1991). Painting and drawing were often accomplishments of middle-class young ladies but few could have attained such excellence, such 'crisp, clear style and design', as is manifest in these illustrations by Miss Drake.

Lindley dedicated the *Sertum Orchidaceum* to William Spencer Cavendish, 6th Duke of Devonshire (1790-1858), whose collection of orchids at Chatsworth was probably the finest in Britain, being under the care of Lindley's friend Joseph Paxton (1803-1865). In the text to Plate 1 depicting *Stanhopea Devoniensis* Lindley (now *Stanhopea hernandezii* (Kunth) Schlechter) he quoted Paxton's directions on cultivation and commented: 'The success with which epiphytes are cultivated by Mr Paxton is wonderful' and 'the climate in which this is effected, instead of being so hot and damp that the plants can only by seen with as much peril as if one had to visit them in an Indian jungle, is as mild and delightful as that of Madeira. As to luxuriance of growth, never have they been seen in their native woods in such perfect beauty.' Although Miss Drake drew many illustrations from living plants, she had to base others on drawings sent to Lindley, for example, Plates 2, 5, 7 and 11 on drawings made in Brazil by J. Théodore Descourtilz (not to be confused with the naturalist Michael Étienne Descourtilz, whose *Flore médicale des Antilles* Théodore illustrated), 9, 29 and 40 made in British Guiana by Robert H. Schomburgk, t.8 by William Griffith, t.34 by Miss M.A. Mearns and t. 37 *(Dendrobium nobile)* from a Chinese drawing now in the Lindley Library's Reeves Collection of Chinese plant illustrations.

COLOUR PLATE 8. *Oncidium pectorale* Lindley. Coloured lithograph by S.A. Drake in Lindley, *Sertum orchidaceum,* pl. 39 (1940)

Pl. 39.

Miss Drake, del.

N. Gauci, lith.

Oncidium pectorale.

Pub.ᵈ by J. Ridgway & Sons, 169, Piccadilly, June 1840.

Printed by P. Gauci.

Pl. 35.

Dendrobium macrophyllum.

COLOUR PLATE 9. *Dendrobium anosmum* Lindley *(D. macrophyllum* Lindley). Coloured lithograph by S.A. Drake in Lindley, *Sertum orchidaceum,* pl. 35 (1840)

Pl. 3.

Dendrobium nobile.

COLOUR PLATE 10. *Dendrobium nobile* Lindley. Coloured lithograph by S.A. Drake in Lindley, *Sertum orchidaceum*, pl. 3 (1837)

COLOUR PLATE 11. *Stanhopea hernandezii* (Kunth) Schlechter *(S. devoniensis* Lindley). Coloured lithograph by S.A. Drake in Lindley, *Sertum orchidaceum*, pl. 1 (1837)

COLOUR PLATE 12. *Catasetum saccatum* Lindley. Coloured lithograph by S.A. Drake in Lindley, *Sertum orchidaceum*, pl. 41 (1841)

Lindley's contribution to Australian botany

Although Australian plants cultivated in Britain were illustrated from time to time in *The Botanical Register*, Lindley's unexpected interest in the flora of Australia probably arose from receiving for identification a collection of specimens gathered by Major (later Sir) Thomas Livingstone Mitchell (1792-1855) on surveying expeditions into unknown eastern Australia. For new species he provided names and concise Latin diagnoses published as footnotes at appropriate places in Mitchell's account of his travels, *Three Expeditions into the Interior of Eastern Australia, with Descriptions of the recently explored Region of Australia felix and the present Colony of New South Wales* (1838; 2nd ed. 1839). Lindley's notes were reprinted in *Annales des Sciences naturelles* 15: 56-64 (1841) but to ascertain the precise type-locality of a species one must consult Mitchell's

COLOUR PLATE 13. *Catasetum longifolium* Lindley. Coloured lithograph by S.A. Drake in Lindley, *Sertum orchidaceum*, pl. 31 (1840)

Catasetum longifolium

COLOUR PLATE 14. *Catasetum barbatum* (Lindley) Lindley *(Myanthus barbatus* Lindley).
Coloured engraving by S.A. Drake in *Botanical Register* 21: pl. 1778 (1835)

Miss Drake del.   Pub. by J. Ridgway 169 Piccadilly. Ap.1.1835.   J. Watts sc.

COLOUR PLATE 15. *Catasetum macrocarpum* Richard *(Monachanthus viridis* Lindley). Coloured engraving by S.A. Drake in *Botanical Register* 21: pl. 1752 (1835)

COLOUR PLATE 16. *Catasetum laminatum* Lindley. Coloured lithograph by S.A. Drake in Lindley, *Sertum orchidaceum,* pl. 38 (1840)

COLOUR PLATE 17. *Odontoglossum lindleyanum* Rchb.f. & Warcz. Coloured lithograph by W.H. Fitch in Bateman, *Genus Odontoglossum,* pl. 11 (1866)

narrative and maps. His travels extended from New South Wales into Victoria.

A collection of about 1,000 species growing in the Swan River Colony, Western Australia and communicated by James Drummond, James Mangles, Robert Mangles, Andrew Toward and Nathaniel Bagshaw Ward also came into Lindley's hands. There existed a work by the Austrian botanist Stephan Ladislaus Endlicher (1804-1849), *Enumeratio Plantarum quas … ad Fluvium Cygnorum … collegit Carolus Liber Baro de Hügel* (May 1837) listing plants collected in the Swan River Colony by Karl A.A. Hügel. Not surprisingly Lindley found among his specimens a number of species not recorded by Endlicher and presumably new to science. With the help of George Bentham (1800-1884), then Secretary of the Horticultural Society, later author of the massive *Flora Australiensis* (1863-1878), Lindley provided diagnoses of 283 species, including eighteen new genera, among them *Drakaea* and *Loudonia,* in 'A sketch of the vegetation of the Swan River Colony'. This formed part of the *Appendix to the first twenty-three Volumes of Edwards' Botanical Register* (part 1, pp i-xvi; November 1839; part 2, pp xvii-xxxii, 1 December 1839; part 3, pp xxxiii, 1 January 1840). The dates of publication of this 'sketch' are important because some names published here conflict with other names published about the same time. Lindley was certainly over-optimistic in assuming that a diagnosis such as 'Asparagus micranthus; caule ramosissimo intricato ramulis divaricatis, floribus minimis solitariis' would suffice to distinguish it from all other species of the genus. In fact the type-gathering of this associated with other specimens makes clear that it belongs not to *Asparagus* but to *Corynotheca*.

This work did not end Lindley's interest in the Australian flora. Together with Bentham, W.J. Hooker and Willem H. de Vriese, he and they identified the specimens collected by Mitchell on a long northern journey through New South Wales and Queensland. This material included fifty-six new species published in footnotes to Mitchell's *Journal of an Expedition into the Interior of tropical Australia in Search of a Route from Sydney to the Gulf of Carpentaria* (1848).

Such work on Australian plants must have been very time-consuming. It is astonishing that Lindley managed to fit this in with his other activities. He never again tackled such general floristic research.

Lindley and Paxton

In ability, enterprise, industry and efficiency, in their rise to eminence from lowly beginnings and their devotion to horticulture, Lindley and Joseph Paxton (1803-1865) were much alike; they were also masterful and authoritative men. Their successful careers, linked by interests in common, notably in orchids, began in the service of the Horticultural Society of London, but Paxton's career by its versatility was even more remarkable than Lindley's. The seventh son of a Bedfordshire farmer, Paxton worked in various gardens until in 1823, at the age of twenty, he became a gardener in the Chiswick garden of the Horticultural Society, to which Lindley had been appointed garden secretary in 1822. There began their life-long friendship. The Society's garden was on land leased from the Duke of Devonshire, William Spencer Cavendish (1790-1858), one of whose residences, Chiswick House, adjoined the garden. Paxton, who cannot have had more than a few years of basic village schooling, had obviously set himself on a rigorous course of self-improvement such as he later commended to young gardeners and, like Lindley, he already manifested that 'energetic individualism which produces the most powerful effects upon the life and action of others' so much praised in Samuel Smiles' inspiring *Self-Help* (1859). They certainly exemplified Smiles' contention that 'self-culture also calls forth power and cultivated strength'. Thus when the Duke, a deaf and somewhat lonely unmarried man, wandered in the Horticultural Society's garden he enjoyed talking to this intelligent self-educated young gardener. He became so impressed by Paxton's ability that in 1826 he appointed him, aged only twenty-three, as head gardener at his vast Chatsworth estate in Derbyshire. This may have been a hasty decision but the Duke had good reason all the rest of his life to be grateful for it.

Never a man to lose an opportunity, Paxton set off by coach from London to Chesterfield, Derbyshire, presumably walked during the night the twelve miles or so from there to Chatsworth and arrived at 4.30 am on 9 May 1826. Naturally he found nobody about. He accordingly, in his own words, 'explored

FIGURE 8. *Victoria amazonica (V. regia* Lindley) flowering for the first time in cultivation, with Annie Paxton, aged seven, standing on a leaf at Chatsworth, November 1849. Engraving in *Illustrated London News,* 17 November 1849.

'On unbent leaf, in fairy guise,
Reflected in the water,
Beloved, admired by hearts and eyes,
Stands Annie, Paxton's daughter'.

the pleasure grounds and looked round the outside of the house. I then went to the kitchen gardens, scaled the outside wall and saw the whole of the place, set the men to work at six o'clock ... and afterwards went to breakfast with poor dear Mrs Gregory and her niece. The latter fell in love with me and I with her, and thus completed my first morning's work at Chatsworth before nine o'clock.' They married nine months later, neither with the slightest premonition that he would later be the wealthy Sir Joseph Paxton, MP, and she the astute and formidable Lady Paxton.

The Duke of Devonshire (later President of the Horticultural Society) at this time had little interest in horticulture but he caught Paxton's enthusiasm, relied on his efficiency, trusted his judgement and whole-heartedly furthered his endeavours as gardener, forester, glasshouse designer and landscape architect. These are well covered in the works of Violet Markham (1935), George F. Chadwick (1961) and John Anthony (1973). The strangeness of *Oncidium papilio (Psychopsis papilio),* a species introduced from Trinidad and described and named by Lindley in 1825, aroused the Duke's interest and led him to assemble a rich collection of orchids at Chatsworth. The Duke's example and Paxton's success in growing orchids, at a lower temperature and with less humidity than had been customary, stimulated others to cultivate them. Among these were the Rev. John Clowes (1777-1846), commemorated by the genus *Clowesia* Lindley, Charles W.W. Fitzwilliam, Viscount Milton (1786-1857), commemorated by the genus *Miltonia* Lindley, whose head gardener Joseph Cooper was esteemed by Paxton as an expert orchid grower, and James Bateman (1811-1897), author of the gigantic *Orchidaceae of Mexico and Guatemala* (1837-1843) and *A Monograph of Odontoglossum* (1864-1874) commemorated by the genus *Batemannia* Lindley (Colour Plate 17); the doubling of the 'n' was an accepted linguistic procedure for keeping the preceding vowel 'a' short. The commercial growing of orchid plants expanded to meet the increasing public demand, as did the introduction of epiphytic species from the moist tropics of America and Asia, collected on so vast a scale by their often unscrupulous collectors as to exterminate some species or endanger their survival. Many of these came into the hands of Lindley for description and naming and Paxton for cultivation. During their early years the celebrated nurserymen Conrad Loddiges and Sons of Hackney, a firm created by Conrad Loddiges (c.1739-1826) and maintained by his son George (1784-1842), together with William Rollison (c.1765-1842) and his son George (1796-1879) of Upper Tooting, were the leading commercial growers of orchids. Thus Loddiges and Sons listed in 1839 more than 1,600 named orchids, none of them artificial hybrids, grown in their nursery. Later the firms of James Veitch, which acquired Rollison's orchids, Hugh Low, Benjamin S. Williams and Henry F.C. Sander rose to eminence. Lindley's orchidological successors, Heinrich Gustav Reichenbach (1824-1889) and Robert Allen Rolfe (1855-1921), profited from their collections.

In 1831 Paxton started the *Horticultural Register and general Magazine* (5 vols., 1831-1836); then, in 1833, *Paxton's Magazine of Botany and Register of Flowering Plants* (16 vols., 1833-1849), followed, in collaboration with Lindley, by *Paxton's Flower Garden* (3 vols., 1850-1853). In 1841 he and Lindley with two supporters founded *The Gardeners' Chronicle*. Paxton's interests by then had extended beyond simple gardening to the design of glasshouses and dwelling houses; in 1836 he began for the Duke the Great Conservatory at Chatsworth, completed in 1840 and demolished in 1920, and in 1838 to rebuild on a new site the village of Edensor. He was already investing in railways. Paxton was the first to flower, in 1849, the giant Amazon Waterlily, named *Victoria regia* by Lindley in 1837; its huge leaves, up to eight feet across, supported Paxton's daughter Annie, aged seven (Figure 8); turning one over he admired the architecture of the girder-like large radiating veins and smaller transverse veins beneath which together upheld its wide relatively thin upper surface (Figure 9). Later he used this

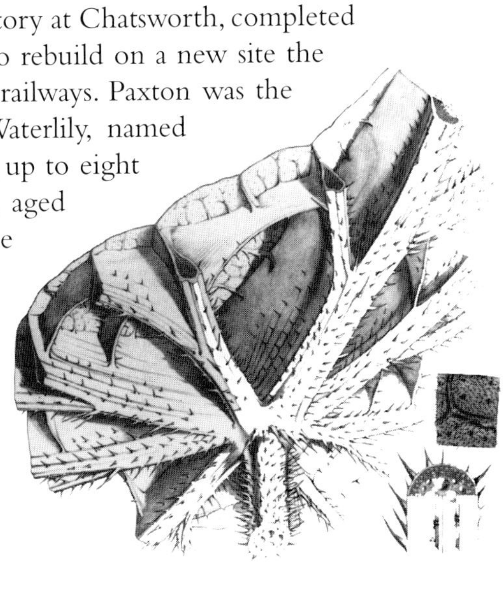

FIGURE 9. *Victoria amazonica.* Part of underside of leaf. Lithograph by W.H. Fitch in W.J. Hooker, *Victoria regia* (1851) [cf. Blunt and Stearn, *Art of Bot. Illust.* p. 269]

very type of construction, as he admitted, in his remarkable design for the Crystal Palace, a gigantic glasshouse, to house the Great Exhibition in 1851. This was accepted in 1850 and Queen Victoria knighted him in 1851 for his work on it. After the death of the Duke in 1858 Paxton resigned all his offices at Chatsworth, which is hardly surprising in view of his many other commitments as a Member of Parliament for Coventry since 1854, as an architect and as a director of the Midland Railway since 1849. He also became Chairman of the Select Committee on the Thames Embankment.

Paxton's capacity for sustained unceasing work, like Lindley's, had limits which he, also like Lindley, refused to recognise until it was too late. His health failed in 1865, as Lindley's had done earlier, and they both died that year, as did their friend W.J. Hooker at Kew. Their joint endeavours had included the saving from destruction of the Royal Botanic Gardens, Kew, as detailed below, and the compilation of *A Pocket Botanical Dictionary* (1840). It is fitting that their joint interest in orchids should be commemorated by the genus *Paxtonia* Lindley and joint authorship of *Arhychium, Ornitharium and Sarcopodium* Lindley & Paxton.

The Chelsea Physic Garden

The Apothecaries Act of 1815 legalised the standing of apothecaries as general practitioners of medicine provided they had been licensed by the Society of Apothecaries in London, a qualification abbreviated to L.S.A. To obtain this, an apprentice apothecary had to serve not less than five years under an approved apothecary and then six months at least in the medical practice of a public hospital (cf. Bishop, 1953). The rigorous examination tested, among much else, a knowledge of materia medica which included medicinal plants. For these the Society of Apothecaries maintained their Chelsea Physic Garden, founded in 1673. In 1835 the Society appointed Lindley as their Professor of Botany and he lectured there regularly early morning, presumably riding over from Turnham Green on horseback, until the abolition of the professorship in 1853. A resulting publication was his *Flora medica* (1839) which may have prompted the University of Basel to confer on him the honorary degree of Doctor of Medicine in 1839. The Chelsea work was in addition to his duties as Assistant Secretary of the Horticultural Society, Professor of Botany in the University of London and editor of *The Botanical Register,* then of *The Gardeners' Chronicle,* and his private study of orchids.

Saving of the Kew Botanic Garden

After the death in 1820 of Sir Joseph Banks, the Royal Botanic Gardens at Kew declined and its management no longer had 'the dynamism, the sense of purpose and direction that his presence had bestowed upon Kew', as stated by the Garden's historian, Ray Desmond. With the death of George III, also in

1820, there was no longer royal patronage; biting criticism of its neglect and invidious comparison with other botanic gardens mounted, notably by George Glenny and the more influential J.C. Loudon (see page 31). The Lords of the Treasury objected in 1837 to the expense of maintaining the garden at Kew and would probably have been glad to get rid of it. They needed an expert report from a committee but their hands were tied as its membership. By 1837 Lindley had become a prominent figure in British botany and horticulture while Paxton had become known as one of the country's most efficient and enterprising head gardeners with his status enhanced by the Duke of Devonshire's appreciation of his managerial ability and devoted service. The two made a formidable strong-minded pair whose authority could not be disputed; moreover they were good friends. The Lords of the Treasury accordingly had no alternative to appointing Lindley backed by the Horticultural Society of London and Paxton backed by the Duke of Devonshire, the Society's President, but they added a more acquiescent practical gardener, John Wilson, head gardener of the Earl of Surrey, the Lord Steward and Treasurer. They were required to make recommendations on the garden's future. The three thoroughly inspected Kew Garden in February 1838, a good time for seeing it at its worst, and in March 1838 Lindley produced a cogent and lucid critical report, which was two-edged. He set out practical and patriotic reasons for not abandoning the Kew Botanic Garden as the Government may have intended but, on the contrary, advocated that it should 'be at once taken for public purposes, gradually made worthy of the country and converted into a powerful means of promoting natural science', a national botanic garden which would be a botanical and horticultural centre for the British colonies, with herbarium and library. Such a seemingly unwanted report might have passed into obscurity but for the fact that Lindley had it copied and put copies into the hands of the Duke of Bedford who wanted 'a great National and Royal Botanic Garden' at Kew, the Duke of Devonshire who was both Paxton's master and President of the Horticultural Society, and other far-sighted influential men. However, in February 1839, the Secretary of the Treasury offered the plants of Kew to the Horticultural Society for its garden at Chiswick. Lindley and Bentham acted promptly to thwart this proposal, which would have ended the Kew Garden as a botanic garden, by calling a meeting of the Society's Council. They rejected this destructive proposal. Ignoring the political power of Lindley's ducal allies, Lord Surrey then over-played his hand by ordering the destruction of the Australian and South African plants in the Kew glasshouses so that these could be converted into vineries, even though giving general approval to Lindley's report. He was evidently unaware that Queen Victoria, who had in 1839 favoured giving up the garden, had now learned of its founding by Augusta, Princess of Wales (after whom the present Princess of Wales House is named) and with Prince Albert had become more interested in its maintenance. On 11 February 1840 Lindley learned that the Government intended to abolish the botanic garden, demolish the glasshouses and get rid of its plants. He then told the Prime Minister that he would have the matter raised in Parliament. This Lord Aberdeen did and was assured that the Government had never had any intention of abolishing the garden! This lie indicated that the garden had been saved. Public indignation was such that Lindley's report could no longer be officially ignored. It was laid before Parliament in May 1840. The Kew Botanic Garden and pleasure grounds passed to the Commissioner of Woods and Forests, thereby becoming public property. Thus ended what Lindley described as 'the barbarous Treasury scheme of destroying the place' and he more than any other individual had brought about its salvation.

Lindley and his old Norwich friend, Sir William Jackson Hooker, since 1820 Professor of Botany in Glasgow, were both suitable candidates for the directorship of the nationalised Kew Botanic Garden. The Duke of Bedford supported Hooker, the Duke of Devonshire supported Lindley, who had now a secure position. Hooker was very anxious to return to England; although fifty-four, only six years off the age when present directors, whatever their energy and experience, are obliged to retire, Hooker faced no such restrictions. He had in fact twenty-four years of creative endeavour at Kew ahead of him. In 1838 with the Kew directorship in mind he had already written to Lindley from Glasgow that 'though I have nothing to complain of here yet, I have reason to believe that my income is much less than yours and because I am willing to make some sacrifice to be enabled to return and spend the rest of my days among my friends and connections in England'. Lindley stood down and in March 1841 Hooker learned that he had been appointed as director: 'Having no instructions for my guidance I determined to follow the suggestions of Dr Lindley's report'. Thus two Norwich men, both educated at the Norwich Grammar School, shaped the future of what was to become a world-famous institution, the Royal Botanic Gardens, Kew. Both died in 1865.

The Potato Blight and Irish Famine

The Kew episode by no means ended Lindley's association with the Government. In 1845 a mysterious potato-destroying disease, already known in eastern North America, afflicted the potato crop all over western Europe with sudden devastating effect. It appeared first in Belgium into which potato varieties evidently disease-carrying had recently been imported from North America for breeding purposes. Thence in 1845 it quickly reached England, then Ireland, which by high fecundity had become the most densely populated country in Europe and more dependent that any other on a dangerously vulnerable mono-culture, that of the potato. The high yield of the potato grown in Ireland on the efficient 'lazy-bed' system with little labour had made this the peasant's mainstay for food, even though in some years adverse weather conditions caused failures of the crop. According to Bourke and Lamb (1993), 'an analysis of the weather data for the growth season of 1845 shows that conditions were indeed favourable for the development of the disease to epidemic level that year'. No one knew anything then about the widespread dispersal of fungal spores by wind. People, however, suspected or believed there was a connection between the weather and the disease. The unexpected rotting of potatoes throughout Ireland so alarmed the British Government that it immediately set up a scientific commission consisting of Lindley, Lyon Playfair, a well-known chemist, and Robert Kane, an Irish Roman Catholic scientist, to investigate. In Ireland they soon became aware that news of the devastation was not a customary Irish exaggeration; they found there a large-scale tragic calamity which they spent three weeks surveying, but every recommendation for saving the crop proved useless. The rot in potatoes was associated with a fungus, now known as *Phytophthora infestans,* believed by Lindley to be a consequence of the decay, thus an epiphenomen, being secondary to the effect of the weather, but rightly held by the Rev. Miles Joseph Berkeley and other mycologists to be the cause. Despite his disbelief, Lindley made Berkeley's opinion widely known by publication in *The Gardeners' Chronicle.* There was no doubt whatever of the terrible distress of the peasantry of Ireland and, much less publicised, of the Western Highlands and Islands of Scotland (where 150,000 people were affected) and the report in November 1845 by Lindley, Kane and Playfair led to the repeal of the 1815 Corn Laws restricting the importation of cheap American wheat into Britain and Ireland, for which the Anti-Corn-Law League had fought for so long, with far-reaching political consequences. Kept well informed from Ireland, Lindley corresponded between 18 February 1846 and 22 June 1849 with Sir Robert Peel, Prime Minister, Sir James Graham, Home Secretary, Sir Charles E. Trevelyan, Treasury Head, Sir George Gray, Home Secretary, and Sir Robert Kane, about the disastrous potato situation. From the beginning in 1845 he had kept the public well informed by *The Gardeners' Chronicle.* Woodham-Smith's *The Great Hunger* (1926) vividly portrays the plight and suffering of the starving destitute Irish peasants and the efforts of the British Government, the Quakers and others to relieve their distress. The literature relating to the Irish famine of 1845-1847 is very extensive; Bourke and Lamb (1993) and Nelson (1995) list the most important works and papers. 'The main reason', as stated by Bourke and Lamb, 'why the impact of the disease on the crop was abnormally great was that many of the most popular potato varieties grown at the time proved to have no resistance whatever to the new disease'. Of this genetical background to the disaster, understandably Lindley and his contemporaries had no inkling; they knew only its tragic effect. The Irish famine revealed the danger to a prolific people of reliance on a monoculture.

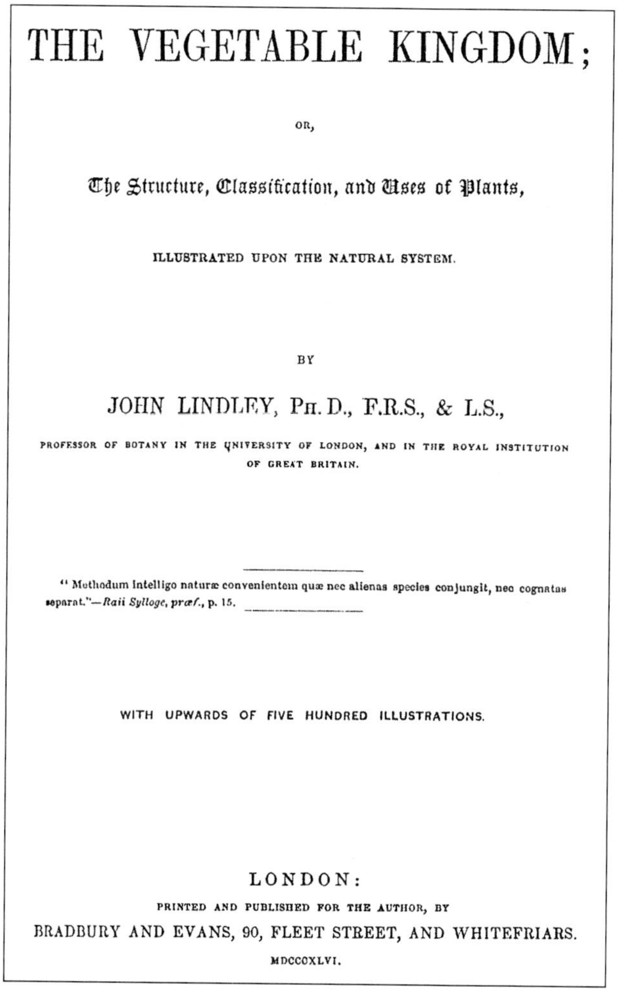

THE VEGETABLE KINGDOM;

OR,

The Structure, Classification, and Uses of Plants,

ILLUSTRATED UPON THE NATURAL SYSTEM.

BY

JOHN LINDLEY, PH. D., F.R.S., & L.S.,

PROFESSOR OF BOTANY IN THE UNIVERSITY OF LONDON, AND IN THE ROYAL INSTITUTION OF GREAT BRITAIN.

"Methodum intelligo naturæ convenientem quæ nec alienas species conjungit, nec cognatas separat."—*Raii Sylloge, præf.*, p. 15.

WITH UPWARDS OF FIVE HUNDRED ILLUSTRATIONS.

LONDON:

PRINTED AND PUBLISHED FOR THE AUTHOR, BY

BRADBURY AND EVANS, 90, FLEET STREET, AND WHITEFRIARS.

MDCCCXLVI.

FIGURE 10. Title-page of first edition of Lindley, *The Vegetable Kingdom* (1846)

'The Vegetable Kingdom'

In 1846 Lindley published his most ambitious work, *The Vegetable Kingdom, or the Structure, Classification and Uses of Plants* (lxviii + 908 closely-printed pages with 526 illustrations, many by his daughter Sarah), the culmination of his many years of detailed study of plants and their literature (Figures 10 and 11). It remains an encyclopaedic work too rarely consulted, for it brings together a wealth of firsthand information not so readily available elsewhere. Lindley begins with a judicious historical survey of plant classification from John Ray onwards, then sets out his own detailed accounts of all the families of plants, and provides a key to the families; in these he paid attention to a much wider range of characters than had his predecessors. Originally he had intended to produce a *Genera Plantarum,* a task so vast that he could have achieved it only by relinquishing his manifold other activities. Thus the preparation of Bentham and Hooker's *Genera Plantarum* (1862-1883) took twenty-five years. Obviously much information collected for such a work found publication in *The Vegetable Kingdom*. Lindley learned, however, that the Austrian botanist Stephan Ladislaus Endlicher (1804-1849) had such a work in preparation. Endlicher published in nineteen parts between 1836 and 1841 a *Genera Plantarum secundum Ordines naturales disposita* (lx + 1483 pages, with four supplements between 1842 and 1850), with which Lindley's intended work would have unnecessarily competed. Endlicher recognised 367 genera of Orchidaceae, of which 117 had been established by Lindley.

The Vegetable Kingdom was arranged according to what Lindley considered a 'natural system'. He regarded the characters of plants as 'the living Hieroglyphics of the Almighty which the skill of man is permitted to interpret. The key to their meaning lies enveloped in the folds of the 'Natural System'. He never succeeded, as he continually changed his own system, in devising one that he found wholly satisfactory, especially because he believed 'physiological characters are of greater importance in regulating the natural classification than structural'. Honestly accepting the charge of inconsistency, he vigorously defended the propriety of such changes: 'The Author may now be equally charged with inconsistency in not adhering to his former plan of classification after having promulgated it. But he is not conscious of having ever pretended that it even approached permanency. – See *Natural System,* p xiii. In fact there is no such thing as stability in these matters. Consistency is but another name for obstinacy … The Author cannot regard perseverance in error as commendable, for the sake of what is idly called consistency; he would rather see false views corrected as proof of their error arises. His object has not been to establish a system of his own, which shall be immutable, but to contribute to the extent of his ability … All that we can do is to throw our pebbles upon the heap.'

Owing to its faulty premises Lindley's classification was never accepted as a whole. Julius von Sachs in his *Geschichte der Botanik* (1875; English translation, *History of Botany,* 1890) described it as 'one of the most unfortunate ever attempted … We find this opposition between theory and practice much more strongly marked in Lindley than in De Candolle … De Candolle laid down correct principles for determination of affinities but in some cases did not follow them, whereas Lindley deduced quite incorrectly the rule of system from existing and long established natural affinities'. Lindley took the view that the character of an organ becomes more and

FIGURE 11. *Eriostemon myoporoides.* Engraving by Sarah Lindley in Lindley, *The Vegetable Kingdom,* 3rd ed. (1853)

FIGURE 12. John Lindley reading galley proofs of *The Gardeners' Chronicle*. Drawing by Sarah or Barbara Lindley c.1845

more important in classification to the degree that its physiology serves for the preservation and propagation of the individual. Sachs remarked that 'by this principle he judges of the systematic value of anatomical characters, those of the embryo and endosperm, of the corolla and the stamens, everywhere laying stress on their physiological importance ... This mode of proceeding on the part of Lindley, compared with his own system, which with all its grave faults is still always a morphologically natural system, proves that like many other systematists he did not literally and habitually follow the rules he himself laid down ... The success which was really obtained in the determination of affinities was due chiefly to a correctness of feeling, formed and continually being perfected by constant consideration of the forms of plants'. From this Sachs rightly concluded that men like Lindley were never quite clear about the rules by which they worked. Lindley had great artistic ability and he sought a pattern in nature; thus like John Hutchinson, also of great artistic ability, he perceived correlations which did not necessarily tally with the theoretical justification he gave them. The lasting value of Lindley's great work lies not at all in his discarded general system but in the detailed accounts of individual families. Peter F. Stevens (1994: 105-10) has discussed Lindley's views on the natural system.

A second edition, little altered, appeared in 1847, the third and last in 1853, within ten years of his breakdown in health. As he stated, this third edition, having extra inserted pages, contained much new matter; moreover, better illustrations replaced many of those in the original edition. Here were his final opinions on the definition and content of families. For that reason the account of Orchidaceae provides a summary of his conclusions on its classification.

'The Gardeners' Chronicle'

Another of Lindley's ventures was the founding with Joseph Paxton, Charles Wentworth Dilke and William Bradbury of *The Gardeners' Chronicle* in 1841, of which the horticultural part was edited by Lindley (Figures 12 to 14). Then, as

FIGURE 13. *Ceratostigma plumbaginoides* Bunge *(Plumbago larpentae* Lindley). Engraving by Sarah Lindley in *The Gardeners' Chronicle* 1847: 732

for more than a century later, it met the need of gardeners for a weekly journal that provided practical and scientific information on a diversity of horticultural matters. Indeed at the beginning it was far more diverse in content than later. The *Chronicle* summarised the proceedings of horticultural and botanical societies, provided foreign and domestic political news, together with market prices of fruit, garden memoranda, entomological articles, records of new plants etc, and forthright editorials in which Lindley campaigned successfully, for example, against the tax on glass and its excessive high cost, which impeded glasshouse development. The tax was repealed in 1845 and during the next ten years the cost of glass fell to a quarter of its former price. The *Chronicle* also advertised plants and sundries for sale and situations of employment wanted and vacant. There were such surprising items as the trial at the Guildhall of two women snowballing at what they described as 'the shocking sight of a black man going to be married to a white woman, although the wife was no great shakes'. In the course of time it became the most convenient periodical for the quick publication of new species and was so used by Kew botanists such as J.G. Baker and N.E. Brown. H.G. Reichenbach described many new orchids in *The Gardeners' Chronicle.* Lindley's editorship for twenty years ensured the maintenance of a high standard which earned it international repute. It attained in British horti-cultural matters the standing which *The Times* had in matters social and political.

In 1850 Paxton and Lindley started a periodical with hand-coloured lithographed plates, *Paxton's Flower Garden,* which ran only to three volumes and ended in 1851. Long after the death of the two authors, Thomas Baines published a revised edition, likewise in three volumes, between 1880 and 1885.

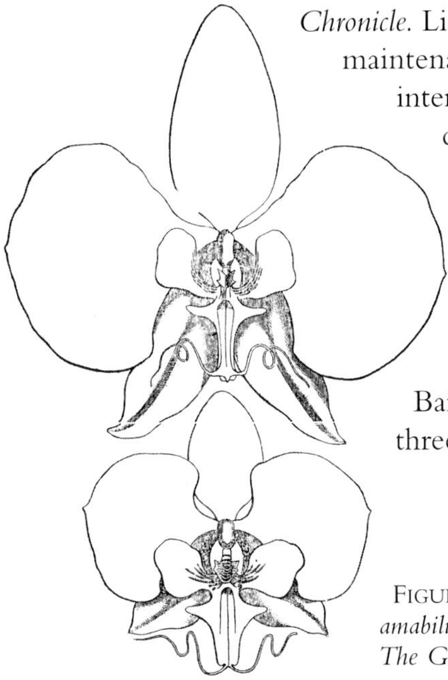

FIGURE 14. *Phalaenopsis grandiflora* Lindley (above), *Ph. amabilis* (L.) Blume (below). Engraving by Sarah Lindley in *The Gardeners' Chronicle* 1848: 32

Darwin and Lindley

In May 1862 Charles Darwin published a book of 176 pages entitled *On the various Contrivances by which British and foreign Orchids are fertilised by Insects and the good Effects of Intercrossing,* which dealt with their floral morphology in detail. Although Darwin's correspondence reveals J.D. Hooker at Kew as his greatest helper, he gratefully acknowledged other assistance: 'Dr Lindley has sent me fresh and dried specimens and has in the kindest manner helped me in various ways'. Their association seems to have begun in 1843 and continued off and on until 1862. Much of their correspondence seemingly no longer exists but Darwin's interest in orchids was, like Lindley's, of long standing. Darwin even told Lindley that 'orchids have interested me more than anything in my life', even though their intricacy led him to say to Hooker 'I was a fool ever to have touched orchids'! The erratic floral behaviours of the genus *Catasetum* puzzled them both. In November 1832 Lindley published two genera, *Myanthus* and *Monachanthus.* By 1837 he was astonished to find, as recorded in *The Botanical Register* (23:t. 1951), 'a plant of *Myanthus* changing into a *Monachanthus,* related to *Monachanthus viridis,* and combining in its own proper person no fewer than three supposed genera, *Myanthus, Monachanthus* and *Catasetum*'. It led him to state in 1853 that 'such cases shake to the foundation all our ideas of the stability of genera and species'. In 1861, when Darwin was completing his book *On the various Contrivances,* he provided Lindley with an explanation of this unexpected transformation: '*Catasetum tridentatum* is male and never seeds according to Schomburgk, *Monachanthus viridis* is female. *Myanthus barbatus* is the hermaphrodite form of the same species'. Robert Schomburgk collecting in British Guiana had reported that in British Guiana one species of *Catasetum,* identified as *C. tridentatum,* produced three kinds of strangely different flowers, i.e. female, male and hermaphrodite. This caused Darwin to publish a paper 'On three remarkable forms of *Catasetum tridentatum,* an orchid in the possession of the Linnean Society' (*Journal of Proceedings of Linnean Society, Botany* 6: 151-157; November 1862, but read 5 April 1862). Unfortunately, according to R.A. Rolfe (1891), Darwin and Schomburgk had misunderstood the situation. Under the name *C. tridentatum* two species with female flowers much alike but male flowers very different were being confused. Thus Darwin's female flower was a female flower of *C. barbatum,* his supposed hermaphrodite flower a male flower of *C. barbatum,* his male flower a male flower of *C. macrocarpum* (syn. *C. tridentatum).* Writing of *Catasetum* Oakes Ames (1945) remarked: 'Few genera of plants have played greater havoc with human pride; few genera of plants have so humbled men of science as *Catasetum* deceived Darwin and *Catesetum* deceived Lindley'. Previous experience had prepared neither for such fantastic sexual dimorphism.

George Glenny's attacks on Lindley

Despite his notorious hot temper, his lack of tact in dealing with humble gardeners, his vigorously expressed opinions and resentment at opposition, Lindley was a warm-hearted and generous man on good terms with most of his botanical and horticultural contemporaries but certainly not with George Glenny (c.1793-1874). A horticultural journalist as forceful and fearless in giving offence as Lindley himself and quick with stinging comment, hence Tjaden's apt description of him as a 'horticultural hornet', Glenny obviously enjoyed controversy. He had even told the mighty W.T. Aiton at Kew to 'reform or quit'. For many years he attacked Lindley in his periodicals, first the *Horticultural Journal,* then the *Gardener's Gazette,* and though he exaggerated, there must have been some foundation for his scurrilous remarks. Glenny nursed a long-standing grievance against the Horticultural Society of London and in particular the Society's employee, Lindley, responsible for shows, because his exhibits of plants did not receive the awards he considered they deserved. He publicly accused the Society of deliberately treating him unfairly. In 1836 Glenny stated in his *Horticultural Journal* that 'we cannot say that we suspect the sapient doctor who sits like a nightmare on the affairs of the Society of doing anything in a business-like manner'. Lindley habitually discussed various plants at the Society's shows and his seemingly presumptuous remarks made him vulnerable to criticism by gardeners with different opinions and greater knowledge. Glenny accordingly praised Mrs. Louisa Lawrence (d.1855), wife of the surgeon (later Sir) Trevor Lawrence, for taking Lindley to task; he 'having fairly tried everybody's patience, Mrs Lawrence gave him as neat a set-down'. He noted, 'Doctor Lindley well named a *professor* of botany, is more garrulous, and more foppish, and more foolish than any of the whole race of dandies and danglers. The grossness and indecency of the Council can only be equalled by the impertinence, flippancy and vanity of their paid assistant, or paid master, whichever they please.'

Year in, year out, Glenny's publications kept up their fire, Sarcastically he asked in the *Gardener's Gazette* (1837): 'Has a certain well-respected gentleman at Regent Street and Turnham Green the title and distinction of M.D. (which being translated is Mad Doctor)? The politeness with which the learned doctor bullies the exhibitors, the discretion with which he awards the most conspicuous place to the productions of his friends...' – so Glenny continued to rile Lindley. Unfortunately resentment against Glenny's insults led Lindley into an ungracious and impolite act. Exhibitors at a Chiswick Show in July 1837 resolved that, 'differing as many persons may upon different subjects from Dr Lindley, there is but one opinion upon the fact of his gentlemanly conduct and uniform kindness towards exhibitors' and accordingly as a mark of respect they proposed to present him with a piece of plate valued at thirty guineas. The subscribers were respected nurserymen and gardeners obviously genuine in their regard for Lindley, but

Glenny was associated with organising its presentation. Hastily Lindley refused to accept their generous gift; for him it was too closely associated with Glenny and the *Gardener's Gazette,* 'one of those unprincipled newspapers which are the disgrace of a civilised people'. Glenny joyfully printed Lindley's letter. It provided yet further ammunition against the arch-enemy: 'Dr Lindley is in a towering passion at the success of the *Gardener's Gazette* … and he has been silly enough to show it.' Glenny mockingly pretended that his *Gardener's Gazette* had been *'doctored to death,* like the orchideous plants were at Chiswick, and fallen victim to the Lindleyan system.'

Glenny's attacks on Lindley continued off and on until about 1850. They possibly had as salutary and stimulating effect on the Horticultural Society as the fleas on a hedgehog but did no good to either opponent. Glenny became bankrupt in 1839; ultimately, as stated by Tjaden (1986), he was 'forced to do what he could do very well, write on horticulture for other publishers. It was on this writing for thirty years from 1841, that he relied for most of his income and on which his modern reputation has rested.' Born a little earlier than Lindley, he outlasted him by eight years.

A horticultural show interlude

Edward Beck (c.1804-1861) was a Quaker nurseryman at Isleworth, Middlesex, only about five miles from the Horticultural Society's garden at Chiswick, with which he was undoubtedly familiar. About 1850 Beck published anonymously a pamphlet *A Packet of Seeds saved by an old Gardener,* purporting to be the recollections of one James Gregory but giving an authentic picture of a country gardener's life then. Here Gregory recalls his visit to the horticultural show at Chiswick organised by Lindley: 'When I went up to London, the squire got me an order so that I might go to Chiswick early on the show-day and see the plants put up in their places; and I never could have believed anybody that had told me all I saw with my eyes that day. I seemed lost in a wood of plants, as I walked about the tents, where the gardeners put them down before they began to stage them:- and such a set of men, too; why, their helpers were better dressed and better mannered than the head men in our parts; and yet, when I asked a question now and then of some of 'em, they didn't seem to want for conceit. As good luck would have it, I met a gardener that lived once not far from Birdwood, and had left to go into a London nursery. I should not have known him, but he made me out; and very kind he was. After all the plants were staged, and it wasn't till just before ten – and I'd got to Turnham Green by six – my friend said; 'I wish I could get you a ticket for breakfast; but I have got so little here, I know Doctor Lindley won't give me one for you.' 'Oh', said I, 'I'll ask him myself'. 'You'd better not', said he; 'for you'll get no ticket, and like enough something from him that'll serve you instead of breakfast.' Says I, 'There's not a man's face on earth that I'm afraid of. I've often heard of the Doctor, and read

FIGURE 15. John Lindley, aged fifty. Portrait by I.H. Maguire in Ipswich Museum Portrait series

a deal more in Glenny and the Journal; and now I'll have a look and a word for myself, if you'll just shew him to me.' 'Come along', says he, and away we went. After a longish hunt, he shewed me a gentleman sitting on a stool under a tree, with a walking-stick in his hand, a and a pair of spectacles on his nose; and said he, 'That's the Doctor.' 'Thank you,' said I; 'and now wait a minute for me.' So I went up, and lifted my hat, breaking ground, as my poor father, when he was soldering, would have called it. 'Well,' said he, 'what do you want?' 'I should thank you, sir,' said I, 'for a breakfast-ticket, for I'm a stranger, and a long way from home.' 'What have you brought, gardener?' 'Nothing, sir,' said I, 'but myself; but I have sent something,' said I, 'before to-day; but not to these shows:' and I shewed him a silver medal I had had sent me, through my master, for a basket of fruit. 'These breakfast-tickets,' said he, 'are for exhibitors and helpers only; but I will give you one:– and there,' said he, handing me another, 'that will admit you after one o'clock; for it is not often I see so much of the country as you have brought with you.' He looked me all over; at my knee corduroys, my leather gaiters, and at my canary waistcoat, and long blue coat with metal buttons, and then into my face, as if he'd have burnt a hole in it; all the while asking me questions, and wetting his fingers at his lips, and then running them over the cards in his hand. As soon as he stopped, I lifted my hat, thanked him, and bid him good morning; but not before I'd heard him refuse tickets to two gardeners running; one, because his plants were not all in their places, or all to rights; and to the other, because he was so dirty and untidy.'

Lindley as an orchidologist

Lindley's devotion to the study of orchids made him from 1830 onwards the leading botanical authority on orchids, building upon, revising and largely changing the pioneer work of Olof Swartz (1760-1818) and Robert Brown (1773-1858). Swartz, a Swedish botanist, spent the years 1784 to 1786 in Jamaica, which has above 155 orchidaceous species, and in Hispaniola; thus he knew many orchids in a living state. He distinguished twenty-eight genera in his 'Genera et species Orchidearum' (Schrader, *Neues Journ. Bot.* 1 (1): 1-108; 1800). Robert Brown, a Scot who sailed on Matthew Flinders' voyage to Australia as naturalist, with Ferdinand Bauer as artist, became acquainted with many species there and then others in cultivation at Kew. These he described in his *Prodromus Florae Novae Hollandiae*, 209-333 (1810) and Aiton's *Hortus Kewensis,* 2nd ed. 5: 188-222 (1813). He established twenty-nine new genera, among them, *Listera, Goodyera, Lissochilus, Eulophia, Vanda* and *Pleurothallis.*

As newly introduced orchids came into Lindley's hands, his first task was to try and fit them into the genera dealt with by Swartz and Brown. Soon it became evident that the majority represented unnamed genera and species. He was not content to describe them as new but gradually to revise the family as a whole and place them within a system of which the final version appeared in the third edition of his *Vegetable Kingdom* (1853) as noted above. In this he was more successful than in some other parts of the vegetable kingdom in following John Ray's procedure, which he quoted, of trying not to associate like with unlike species and not to separate like from like: 'Methodum intelligo Naturae convenientem, quae nec alienas species conjungit, nec cognatas separat' (Ray, *Stirp. Europ. Sylloge,* Pref.; 1694). The classification of the family in R.L. Dressler's *The Orchids; Natural History and Classification* (1981) has much in common with Lindley's. Thus a considerable part of his orchid system has survived into modern classifications of the Orchidaceae.

Lindley's sound appreciation of generic limits within the family led Bentham and Hooker with their wide generic concept in 1883 to accept 114 Lindley genera; these include such genera as *Ada, Aspasia, Cattleya, Cochlioda, Coelogyne, Galeandra, Laelia, Miltonia, Schomburgkia* and *Sophronitis.* Pfitzer in 1889 accepted 127 of Lindley's genera; with the narrower modern generic concept, even more have now found approval.

The naming of genera

With regard to the naming of plants Lindley held strong opinions as did Linnaeus. 'Since the days of Linnaeus, who was the great reformer of this part of Natural History', he stated in 1841, 'a host of strange names, inharmonious, sesquipedalian, or barbarous, have found their way into Botany, and by the stern but almost indispensable laws of priority are retained there. It is full time, indeed, that some stop should be put to this torrent of savage sounds, when we find such words as Calucechinus, Oresigenesa, Finaustrina, Kraschenninikovia, Gravenhorstia, Andrzejofskya, Mielichoferia, Monactineirma, Pleuro-schismatypus, and hundreds of others like them, thrust into the records of Botany without even an apology. If such intolerable words are to be used, they should surely be reserved for plants as repulsive s themselves, and instead of libelling races so fair as flowers, or noble as trees, they ought to be confined to Slimes, Mildews, Blights, and Toadstools'. These censorious remarks echo Linnaeus' condemnation in his *Critica botanica,* precept 249 (1737) of generic names 'an ell-long, or difficult to pronounce or unpleasant'.

On the formation of generic names Lindley wrote in 1839: 'So impossible is it to construct generic names that will express the peculiarities of the species they represent, that I agree with those who think a good, well-sounding, unmeaning name as good as any that can be contrived. The great rule to follow

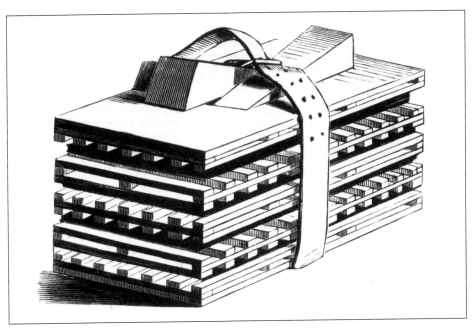

FIGURE 16. 'Papa's plant press'. Drawing by Sarah Lindley, 1852

is this: In constructing a generic name, take care that it is harmonious and as unlike all other generic names as it can be.' Providing such names for the many new genera of Orchidaceae he distinguished cannot have been an easy task. Obviously he sought to indicate some feature of the genus, whenever possible, e.g. *Cirrhopetalum* (from *cirrhus,* curl of hair, tendril, *petalum,* petal) referring to the twisted lateral sepals, *Eria* (from *erion* wool) referring to the woolly flowers, *Herpysma* (from *herpysmos,* creeping) of creeping habit, *Holothrix* (from *holos,* whole, *thrix,* hair) referring to its extensive hair-covering, *Micropera* (from *mikros,* small, *pera,* pouch) referring to the small saccate lip, *Ommathodium* (from *omma,* eye) with eye-like spots on the lip. The intent of some names, e.g. *Abola, Ania* (from *ania,* trouble), *Apaturia, Ate, Ipsea* and *Oecoclades* (from *oikeious,* private, *klados,* branch), is obscure. Existing mythological names, e.g. *Arethusa, Calypso, Disa* and *Norna,* preceded Lindley's adoption of *Acacallis, Empusa, Ione, Lycaste* and *Oberonia.* He commemorated some noted orchid-growers by the genera *Batemannia, Clowesia, Miltonia, Paxtonia* and *Wailesia,* botanical artists by *Alvisia* and *Drakaea,* collectors by *Amellia, Govenia, Hartwegia* and *Schomburgkia,* distinguished scientists by *Burnettia, Herschelia* and *Quekettia,* persons of antiquity by *Ada* and *Aspasia.* Many of these personal names testify to his wide circle of friends and acquaintances gained through his employment by the Horticultural Society and his membership of the Royal Society of London and the Microscopical Society, of which he was once President.

The generic names for orchids published by Lindley are of very diverse origins but conform to his own criteria. He was much aided, as have been other orchidologists, notably C.L. Blume and Rudolf Schlechter, by the richness of the Greek language and the ease with which new compound words can be made from Greek elements; indeed most generic names of orchids, apart from those commemorating persons, have a Greek origin. Of 286 Lindley orchid generic names, 129 come from Greek, eighteen from Latin, twenty-seven from personal names, twelve from mythology.

Lindley described a vast number of new species of orchids and other plants, usually with concise and precise Latin diagnoses, which were adequate for the period but need now to be supplemented. He objected strongly to what he castigated in *The Gardeners' Chronicle* as 'the bad German habit' of providing long descriptions and thereby aroused much controversy in Germany (cf. Sinkora & Short, 1988).

Oakes Ames, for many years the leading American orchidologist, stated that Lindley 'laid the foundations of modern orchidology'. With that verdict there is and has long been unanimous agreement.

Specific Names commemorating Lindley

The esteem in which Lindley's contemporaries held him is evident from the extraordinary large number of species to which they gave the epithets *lindleyi, lindleyanus, lindleyana* and *lindleyanum* in his honour. By no means all of these Lindleyan names have stood the test of time, as have, for example, *Aeonium lindleyi, Begonia lindleyana, Buddleja lindleyana* and *Cotoneaster lindleyi*, to mention only a few of the many that stand. However some have passed into synonymy because they had been described earlier under another name; *Oenothera amoena* (1821), for example, has priority over *Oenothera lindleyi* (1828). Some have disappeared on taxonomic grounds: for example, *Cupressus lindleyi* has long been considered not distinct from *Cupressus lusitanica*. Nevertheless probably no botanist has received more commemorative names than Lindley as the following lists testify.

The epithet *lindleyi* has been published under the following generic names: *Acacia, Actephila, Aeonium, Amydalopis, Anthemis, Arthropodium, Asclepias, Atriplex, Bidens, Bignonia, Bulbophyllum, Calais, Chloraea, Cinnamomum, Clerodendrum, Cordia, Corytholoma, Cotoneaster, Cycnoches, Dampiera, Dendrobium, Eria, Eriochilus, Euonymus, Gesneria, Gloxinia, Grabowskia, Hardenbergia, Hedysarum, Helichrysum, Hibiscus, Ipomoea, Kirschlegeria, Lichterveldia, Megaclinium, Microseris, Mimosa, Neoporteria, Neuwiedia, Oberonia, Odontoglossum, Oeclades, Oncidium, Phreatia, Physosiphon, Pinus, Polemonium, Potentilla, Prunopsis, Pyrus, Rechsteinera, Rhododendron, Rosa, Sempervivum, Siphocampylus, Sphacele, Sporobolus, Styphelia, Uropappus, Verticordia, Vilfa, Zamia*.

The adjective *lindleyanus, -a, -um* has been published under the following generic names: *Alismorchis, Amaryllis, Apaturia, Aporosa, Ardisia, Artemisia, Aspidogyne, Barkeria, Bartholinia, Beadlea, Begonia, Bennettia, Berberis, Bladhia, Bletia, Brumelia, Buddleja, Caladenia, Carex, Cassia, Cattleya, Columnea, Cyrtosa, Desmodium, Disperis, Eria, Erythrodes, Eucalyptus, Eugenia, Eulophia, Galeola, Garrya, Gesneria, Gireoudia, Gyrostachys, Habenaria, Holothrix, Indigophora, Iridorchis, Laelia, Leptochloa, Leptorchis, Listera, Malaxis, Mesodaphne, Mikania, Myrcianthes, Neottia, Nepenthes, Oberonia, Ochavagia, Oecoclades, Oenothera, Ophysis, Pasania, Pentarhaphia, Phragmipedium, Phyllorchis, Pinus, Prestonia, Pseudotsuga, Pultenaea, Quercus, Scepa, Scleria, Sieglingia, Sobralia, Spiranthes, Synaedrys, Trichoneura, Uncaria, Vanda, Willughbya*.

The name *Rubus lindleianus* Lees is apparently the only example of a variant from *lindleyanus*.

Of the generic names above, forty-seven designate genera of Orchidaceae.

For discussion of the generic names *Lindleya, Lindleyella* and *Neolindleya*, see page 69.

Last years

Lindley possessed immense powers of work and of mental concentration, but they had limits which he overstepped. In 1861, against the wishes of his family, he took charge of exhibits from the British colonies for the International Exhibition of 1862 at South Kensington, with all its exhausting work. This he did admirably as is evident from a testimonial of 10 November 1862 signed by twenty-seven Colonial Commissioners representing British colonies. It was Lindley's last public act.

His health had begun to fail (probably due to arteriosclerosis, according to a modern physician), his mental powers and strong memory to decline, and he had a breakdown from which he never fully recovered. He retired from his London professorship in 1861 and from his secretaryship of the Royal Horticultural Society in 1863, much of the work of which from 1861 had been done by Andrew Murray, the Assistant Secretary. This sad decline after some forty years of incessant highly productive intellectual toil has a parallel in that of Linnaeus whose period of creativity (1730-1771) was likewise about forty years. They both served their contemporaries and posterity better than they served themselves.

Lindley went to the spa Vichy in south France in March 1863 to rest and take its anti-rheumatic water, but his wife wrote to their daughter Sarah in July 1863: 'his memory is almost entirely gone … his nerves are shaken and tears are often brought into his eye'. His son's reminiscences confirm this: 'He lost his memory, he could not attend to anything of importance; he could not read for more than a very short time without pain in his head.' He also lost his physical strength but fortunately remained good-humoured. Over the years Lindley had built up a large private herbarium and library. These personally owned tools of research were a necessity for active taxonomic botanists such as J.E. Smith, W.J. Hooker, Lindley, G. Bentham and P.B. Webb during the first half of the nineteenth century. They could also be financial assets. Lindley's orchid herbarium was bought in 1864 by the Royal Botanic Gardens, Kew. Fortunately friends persuaded him to have his portrait painted by Eden Upton Eddis (1812-1901); he chose to hold in his hand not an orchid but a wild rose, recalling his first botanical triumph, the *Rosarum Monographia* of 1820; this (Colour Plate 1) portrays him bearded, because he found the 'cut-throat' razor too dangerous to use in his later years, but for most of his life he was clean-shaven. Lindley died at Acton Green on 1 November 1865, just outlasting two friends of many years, Sir Joseph Paxton who died on 8 June 1865, and Sir William Jackson Hooker who died on 12 August 1865. Their careers had been in many ways linked, particularly as regards the Royal Botanic Gardens, Kew, and contributions to orchidology. Hooker described and illustrated many new orchids in the *Botanical Magazine,* including the genera *Peristeria, Coryanthes* and *Polystachya*. Paxton, by revolutionising the cultivation of orchids, contributed more than any other man to the spread of orchid-growing among the aristocracy and those with newly-acquired wealth seeking to emulate his master the Duke of Devonshire, and thus to the large-scale importation of tropical orchids. Lindley had been for many years the supreme orchidologist.

On 9 November 1865 there died a plant collector, Thomas Bridges (b.1807), who had introduced into cultivation the giant waterlily, *Victoria amazonica (V. regia)*, with which all three were associated. Lindley published the new genus *Victoria* in 1837 in a folio work with a coloured plate, *Victoria regia*, limited to twenty-five copies. Hooker in 1847 published another folio, *Description of Victoria regia or the great Water-lily of South America*, with four superb plates by the celebrated botanical artist Walter Hood Fitch. Paxton, the first to flower the *Victoria*, at Chatsworth in 1849, afterwards stated, as noted above, that the architecture of its leaves with veins of varied size and strength upholding a broad thin surface provided mechanical principles for the construction of the Crystal Palace (Figures 8 and 9).

Another death of 1865 was, on 6 April, that of the politician and economist Richard Cobden, whose Anti-Corn-Law campaign ended successfully with repeal of the Corn Laws in 1846 resulting from the reports by Lindley, Playfair and Kane on the Irish famine. The Duke of Wellington's comment was 'Rotten potatoes have done it'.

After Lindley's death the Royal Horticultural Society bought for £700 his botanical and horticultural library to be the nucleus of a new library replacing the one disastrously sold by the Society in 1859 during a financial crisis (cf. Tjaden, 1987). As a result of that bitter experience the Society vested it in 1868 in a Lindley Library Trust legally separate from the Society. This was a device to safeguard the Lindley Library from a like calamity in the future, the Society, however, maintaining, expanding and housing it (cf. Stageman, 1968; Tjaden, 1993). The Society also instituted, in December 1865, the Lindley Medal commemorative of Lindley's services and awarded now for an exhibit of educational value. It was cast in 1874 (cf. Tjaden, 1994). His prized orchid herbarium rich in type-specimens and drawings had already been sold to the Royal Botanic Gardens, Kew, as noted above. The University of Cambridge acquired the rest of his herbarium, likewise rich in type-specimens, comprising about 58,000 sheets, for £300; it now forms part of the general herbarium at the Botany School, Cambridge.

The American orchidological periodical *Lindleyana* (1986 et seq.), the Mexican rosaceous genus *Lindleya* Kunth (1824) and the orchid nothogenus x *Lindleyana* Garay & H.R. Sweet (1966), covering orchid hybrids with the parentage *Euanthe* x *Renanthera* x *Vanda* x *Vandopsis*, commemorate him. Although seven authors have proposed generic names in his honour, owing to nomenclatural rules only two of their names now stand: *Lindleya* Kunth and *Lindleycladus* Harris, this for a fossil conifer. The first, *Lindleya* Nees (1821), a synonym of *Wikstroemia* Endl. (1821), would invalidate the name *Lindleya* Kunth (1824) as a later homonym had not this been made an officially conserved name, for which *Lindleyella* Rydberg (1908) and *Neolindleyella* Fedde (1940) are accordingly superfluous substitute names. The genus *Neolindleya* Kraenzlin (1899) has been united with *Platanthera* Richard. Unfortunately

Lindleyella Rydberg (1908) invalidates, as a later homonym, *Lindleyella* Schlechter (1914) for a genus of Orchidaceae now renamed *Rudolfiella* Hoehne (1944). Rudolf Schlechter (1872-1925) turned from a detailed and fruitful study of the intricacy of the Asclepiadaceae to an equally detailed and fruitful study of the Orchidaceae and became Lindley's twentieth-century orchidological successor. Thus, although his name *Lindleyella* is no longer tenable, Schlechter's dedication of a genus of Orchidaceae to Lindley, 'Altmeister de Orchideenkunde', fittingly links two extraordinary industrious and percipient students of this vast intricate family.

Some sources of further information

Ames, O. 1945 The strange case of *Catasetum barbatum. American Orchid Society Bulletin* 13: 289-294.

Ames, O. 1948. *Orchids in Retrospect. A Collection of Essays on the Orchidaceae.* Cambridge, Mass.

Anon. 1839. The naturalist's literary portrait-gallery, no. 5. John Lindley, PhD, F.R.S. *The Naturalist* 4 (32): 434-442.

Anon. 1859. [Award of the Royal Medal to Dr. Lindley.] *Proceedings of Royal Society of London* 9: 39-46 [by J.D. Hooker].

Anon. 1865. The late Dr. Lindley. *Gardeners' Chronicle* 1865: 1058, 1059, 1083, 1084.

Anon. 1867. John Lindley. *Proceedings of Royal Society of London* 15: xxx-xxxii.

Anthony, J. 1973. *Joseph Paxton. An illustrated Life of Sir Joseph Paxton. 1803-1865.* Shire Publications, Aylesbury, Bucks.

[Beck, E. 1850.] *A Packet of Seeds saved by an old Gardener.* London

Bishop, W.J. 1953. The evolution of the general practitioner in England. *In:* Underwood, E.A. (Ed.), *Science, Medicine and History: Essays … in Honour of Charles Singer* 2: 351-357.

Boulger, G.E.S. 1893. Lindley, John. *Dictionary of National Biography* 33:27

Bourke, A. & Lamb, H. 1993. *The Spread of the Potato Blight in Europe in 1845-6 and the accompanying Wind and Weather Patterns.* Meteorological Service, Dublin.

Bridge, K. 1996. *Henry and Self. The Private Life of Sarah Crease 1826-1921,* Sono Nis Press, Victoria, British Columbia.

Chadwick, G.F. 1961. *The Works of Sir Joseph Paxton 1803-1865.* Architectural Press, London.

Desmond, R. 1995. *Kew. The History of the Royal Botanic Gardens.* Havill Press, London.

Desmond, R. & Ellwood, C. 1994. *Dictionary of British and Irish Botanists and Horticulturists.* Taylor & Francis, London and Bristol.

Dillon, G. 1957. Development of a system of orchid classification. *American Orchid Society Bulletin* 26: 255-261.

Duttson, L., & Hamilton, R.M. 1998. *Miss Drake the Unknown Orchid Artist* [included in Hamilton, 1998], Victoria, British Columbia, Canada.

Fletcher, H.R. 1969. *The Story of the Royal Horticultural Society 1804-1868.* Oxford University Press, London.

Gardener, W. 1965. John Lindley. *Gardeners' Chronicle* 158: 386, 406, 409, 430, 434, 451, 457, 481, 502, 507, 526.

Green, J.R. 1914. *A History of Botany in the United Kingdom:* 336-353. J.M. Dent & Sons, London.

Hamilton, R.M. 1994-1998. *John Lindley, 'Father of modern Orchidology' a Gathering of his Correspondence.* 4 parts. Robert M. Hamilton, Richmond, British Columbia.

Hetherington, E. 1994. William Cattley, his life and times. 1781-1835. *Proceedings of 14th World Orchid Congress,* 18-22.

Keeble, F. 1912. John Lindley. *In:* Oliver, F.W. (Ed.), *Makers of British Botany:* 164-177. Cambridge University Press, Cambridge.

Lindley, Alice (Lady Morland) 1965. John Lindley, 1799-1865. *Gardeners' Chronicle* 158: 362.

Lindley, N. (Lord Lindley) [1911] Sketch of my father's life. *See* Hamilton R.M. 1995.

Markham, V.M. 1935. *Paxton and the Bachelor Duke.* Hodder & Stoughton, London.

Nelson, E.C. 1995. *The Cause of the Calamity. Potato Blight in Ireland, 1845-1847, and the Role of the National Botanic Gardens, Glasnevin.* Stationery Office, Dublin.

Reinikka, Merla A. 1972. *A History of the Orchid.* University of Miami Press, Coral Gables, Florida.

Rolfe, R.A. 1891. On the sexual forms of *Catasetum*, with special reference to the researches of Darwin and others. *Journal of the Linnean Society, Botany.* 27: 206-220.

Sachs, T. von. 1875. *Geschichte der Botanik.* R. Oldenbourg, Munich [English translation, 1890. *History of Botany,* Oxford University Press, Oxford].

Schultes, R.E. & Pease, A.S. 1963. *Generic Names of Orchids, their Origin and Meaning.* Academic Press, New York and London.

Shteir, A.B. 1996. *Cultivating Women, Cultivating Science, Flora's Daughters and Botany in England 1760 to 1860.* Johns Hopkins University Press, Baltimore and London.

Sinkora, D.M. & Short, P.S. 1988. *'The bad German Habit'. A factual botanical melodrama involving Joachim Steetz.* National Herbarium of Victoria, Melbourne, Australia.

Smiles, S. 1859. *Self-Help.* London

Sprunger, S. (Ed.) 1991. *Orchids from The Botanical Register 1815-1847.* With contributions by P.J.W. Cribb & W.T. Stearn. 2 vols. Birkhäuser Verlag, Basel, Boston, Berlin.

Stafleu, R.A. & Cowan, R.S. 1981. *Taxonomic Literature* 3: 49-60. Bohn, Scheltema & Holkema, Utrecht and The Hague.

Stageman, P.F.M. 1968. Lindley Library Centenary, *Journal of Royal Horticultural Society* 93: 509-515.

Stearn, W.T. 1952. Lindley's Vegetation of the Swan River Colony. *Journal of Society for Bibliography of Natural History* 2: 381-382.

Stearn, W.T. 1961. Two thousand years of orchidology: *Proceedings of the Third World Orchid Conference* (London. 1960): 24-42. London.

Stearn, W.T. 1965. The self-taught botanists who saved the Kew botanic garden. *Taxon* 14: 293-298.

Stearn, W.T. 1967. Sibthorp, Smith, the *Flora Graeca* and the *Florae Graecae Prodromus*. *Taxon* 16: 168-178.

Stearn, W.T. 1973. Lindley, John. *In:* Gillespie, C.C. (Ed.), *Dictionary of Scientific Biography* 8: 371-373.

Stearn, W.T. 1975. The contribution of Linnaeus to orchidology. *Botanical Museum Leaflets, Harvard University* 24: 65-84.

Stearn, W.T. 1976. Carl Linnaeus and the theory and practice of horticulture. *Taxon* 25: 21-31.

Stearn, W.T. 1989. S.F. Gray's 'Natural Arrangement of British Plants. *Plant Systematics and Evolution* 167: 23-34.

Stearn, W.T. 1998. John Lindley's contribution to Sibthorp and Smith's *Flora Graeca*. *Annales Musea Goulandris* 10:

Stevens, P.F. 1994. *The Development of biological Systematics.* Columbia University Press, New York.

Stewart, J. & Stearn, W.T. 1991. *The Orchid Paintings of Franz Bauer.* Herbert Press, London.

Tjaden, W.L. 1983. *The Gardener's Gazette* [edited by George Glenny] and its rivals. *Garden History (J. Garden History Soc.)* 11: 70-78.

Tjaden, W.L. 1986. George Glenny: horticultural hornet. *The Garden (J. Royal Hort. Soc.)* 111: 318-323. [I am indebted to Mr Tjaden for additional information extracted from his unpublished biography of George Glenny and used here.]

Tjaden, W.L. 1987. The loss of a library. *The Garden (J. Royal Hort. Soc.)* 112: 386-388.

Tjaden, W.L. 1993. The Lindley Library of the Royal Horticultural Society 1866-1926. *Archives of Natural History* 20(1): 93-128.

Tjaden, W.L. 1994. The Medals of the Royal Horticultural Society. *Archives of Natural History* 20(1): 77-112.

Woodham-Smith, C. 1962. *The great Hunger, Ireland 1845-9.* Hamish Hamilton, London.

This is a revised and much enlarged version of my earlier biography 'John Lindley (1799-1865). A sketch of the life and work of a pioneer British orchidologist and gardener-botanist' in Sprunger, Cribb & Stearn, *Orchids from The Botanical Register* 2: 15-44 (1991) with new information added from R.M. Hamilton's valuable assembly and transcription of Lindley's correspondence published in 1994-1998 and from Lawrence Duttson's painstaking enquiry into the history of the Lindley family.

Part II

Introductory Lecture

John Lindley

An Introductory Lecture

Delivered in

THE UNIVERSITY OF LONDON

On Thursday, April 30, 1829.

BY JOHN LINDLEY, F.R.S. &c. &c.
Professor of Botany

LONDON:

Printed for John Taylor

Bookseller and Publisher to the University of London,
30, Upper Gower Street
1829

Gentlemen,

In presenting myself before you for the purpose of delivering a course of Lectures upon the science of Botany in this University, I naturally labour under much anxiety; not only as to the success that may attend my efforts at explaining the principles of the science I am called upon to profess, but also as to the opinion that may be entertained by the view I take of its real end and object, and of the mode in which it should be taught. In literature, in physics, in medical science, and even in the sister branch of Natural History,– zoology, the principles upon which those subjects are to be taught are well understood and recognised; and their utility, as sciences or branches of learning, does not require to be insisted on. But in Botany the fundamental principles are still unsettled; the world is much divided about them, and the purpose of the science, except as an accomplishment, is far from being generally understood. I must therefore, on all these accounts, most particularly crave your indulgent and patient attention; an indulgence and patience which it is the more necessary for me to solicit upon this occasion, when I look around me and consider who some of those are that I address, and how slender my pretensions are to instruct them.

I need not explain to you that, by most modern philosophers, all matter is divided into that which has *vitality,* and that which is *destitute of vitality;* the former being called ORGANIC, and the latter INORGANIC. Of these two classes, the former may be said to be merely the latter in a state of life.

ORGANIC bodies are themselves divided into two kingdoms, the *Animal and the Vegetable;* the former is popularly distinguished from the latter by the power of voluntary motion from place to place,– a power, of which vegetables, which are fixed to the soil, are destitute. It is scarcely worth while to enter at this time upon a discussion of the strict value of this character, or to show by what nice gradations these and all other distinctions insensibly melt into each other, as the confines of either kingdom are approached. When you shall have made yourselves acquainted with all the principal forms under which Nature presents herself, and shall have studied the various links by which one kind of matter is connected with another, you will probably arrive at the conclusion, that there is no such thing as a definition in Natural History; and hence you may come to doubt: so insensible, and at the same time so complete, will you find the gradations between *men* and *trees,* between yourselves and those gigantic creations, of which the timbers of this building may be called the bones,– hence I say you may come to doubt whether any one can truly define the boundaries within which the two kingdoms, that these bodies represent, are mutually confined. But with this question we have at present no concern. The ordinary character of locomotion existing in animals, and not existing in plants, is sufficient as a common mark of distinction, without embarrassing the definition with exceptions. The science that treats of the animal kingdom is called ZOOLOGY; that which applies to the vegetable kingdom is called BOTANY.

The objects of Botany, as I understand it, are twofold.

Firstly, to determine the structure, both external and internal, of vegetable bodies, and the laws under which they live, and grow, and propagate. And

Secondly, to acquire the power of distinguishing with precision one kind of plant from another.

This is, in a very few words, Botany properly so called, and is the science, which it is my duty to teach, as distinguished from Materia Medica, to which belongs all that relates to the application of vegetable substances to the purposes of medicine.

At what period of the world Botany first began to be studied as a science, has not been satisfactorily ascertained. By some it has been referred to the highest ages of antiquity: we are assured that Moses and Solomon and other Jewish writers, especially the last, were Botanists, and that traces of much knowledge of the sciences are to be found throughout the Scriptures; Hesiod and Homer are also enlisted in the band of ancient Botanists. But I confess it seems to me difficult to assign the science any such antiquity. That in the most remote ages man had his herbs and his roots; that he was acquainted with the properties of one plant and the uses of another; that he gave them names; and that poets derived many of the beauties of their language from them,– was natural enough; indeed it could not have been otherwise: but this had nothing to do with Botany. The first dawn of that science must have broken from out of the deep investigations of the nature of matter and mind by the philosophers of Greece. How much they knew we have no accurate means of judging; but that they knew a great deal of vegetable physiology is obvious, from their famous paradox, that plants are only inverted animals; a sentiment which, however strangely it may sound, could only have arisen from an extensive knowledge of the vital phænomena of plants. Nor could the doctrine of Aristotle, that all organic matter exhibits a series of successive degrees of development, have possibly been conceived or promulgated, unless the philosophers of his day had possessed a practical acquaintance with vegetation infinitely beyond that of the ages that succeeded.

Happy had it been for them if, instead of retrograding in the path of science, or rather stepping out of it altogether, they had only pursued the course commenced by Theophrastus 350 years before Christ. By that naturalist the beginning was made of applying particular terms to particular modifications of structure: he first named the petiole, which he called $\mu\iota\sigma\chi o\varpi$; he distinguished nut-bearing trees, which he called $\sigma\pi\rho\iota\alpha$, from those of which the fruit is capsular or $\epsilon\lambda\lambda o\sigma\pi\epsilon\rho\mu\alpha\tau\alpha$. He demonstrated the absence of all philosophical distinction between trees, shrubs, and herbs; a distinction upon which his successors were fond of insisting. He speaks clearly of the parenchyma and woody fibre of wood, the former of which he calls the flesh; and he described accurately the difference between Palm wood and that of the trees with concentric layers[*]; so that in point of fact, the discovery of the difference between Dicotyledonous and Monocotyledonous wood was made by

---

[*] Theophr. *Hist.* 1.8

Theophrastus above 2000 years ago, although it was never applied to the purposes of systematic division till about thirty years since. Subsequently to this period Botanists almost disappeared for a long season. Those who have been dignified by historians with that title were either, like Dioscorides, mere *herb-gatherers,* persons whose writings consist of catalogues of names, with imaginary virtues attached to them, or *compilers,* who, like Pliny, knew little themselves, and misunderstood those they copied; or finally *poets,* who, like Virgil, drew much of the beauty of their language from the charms of Nature. This cessation of all philosophical inquiry into the nature of vegetation endured above 1700 years, during the whole of which time scarcely a single addition was made to the stock of knowledge left behind him by Theophrastus. In the room of information books were filled with errors, superstitions, and absurdities, which almost exceed belief. It is not worth while to advert to them particularly in this place, especially as they relate to the history of medicine rather than of Botany; one instance at least may suffice. A certain Nicholas Myrepsicus, one of the last of the Greek physicians, who flourished in the thirteenth century, in compiling from an Arabian writer, mistook the word Dar-sini, which signifies the cinnamon, for $\alpha\rho\sigma\epsilon\nu\iota\chi\sigma\upsilon$, the mineral called arsenic; and in consequence of this blunder, which there was for a long time no one to detect, one of the most useful of all aromatics was held for years to be a dangerous poison.

But with the revival of letters a new direction was given to researches in Natural History. Men ceased to content themselves with blindly copying the writers of antiquity, and set themselves in earnest to examine the objects of Nature that surrounded them. The woods, the plains, the rivers, the ocean, the valleys, and the mountains, were investigated with an ardour that soon made amends for ancient indifference. The first consequence of this was a discovery of the utter worthlessness of the greater part of those writers to whom the world had so long been bound in servile obedience. The spirit of inquiry once excited, men speedily learned to estimate rightly the greater value of facts than of assertions; one discovery produced another, and in a few years a new foundation was laid of that imperfect but beautiful science which constitutes modern Botany. In the early part of the sixteenth century, John Manardi, a native of Ferrara, described the real nature of the anther. He was followed by a long train of writers of various merit, who at first indeed applied themselves exclusively to the collection of new species, but subsequently to an examination of the physiological characters of plants, and to the laws applied by Nature to the government of the vegetable kingdom. Materials soon began to accumulate; and the confusion that had once been caused by ignorance, threatened again to overwhelm the science in consequence of the rapid addition of new matter, which there was no means of keeping in order. Hence *Systematists* sprung up; a race of inquirers to whose labours the present advanced state of Botany is no doubt mainly to be ascribed. That the efforts of the earliest of these writers should have proved unsuccessful, will excite no surprise; with little knowledge of vegetable physiology or anatomy, and with scarcely any notion of the laws of affinity and metamorphosis, they could not be expected to succeed. We should rather wonder at what they did, than at what they omitted to do. Many of them had great merit, especially *Joseph Pitton de Tournefort,* a Professor of Botany at Paris, who flourished in the end of the seventeenth century, and upon whose system the modern arrangement, according to natural orders, is undoubtedly founded. This, however, and all others, was for a time eclipsed by another, better adapted to the circumstances of the times, and emanating from a writer who, having the courage and talent to carry reformation into every branch of Natural History, imparted a lustre to his peculiar system of classification, which is only now, after the lapse of a century, beginning to grow dim.

Charles Linné, or Linnaeus as he is usually called, was a person exactly adapted to the state of science of the time in which he lived. The various departments of natural history had not at that time any thing like their present extensive range, and were without difficulty to be investigated by a single naturalist. They were all equally in need of revision and improvement; they all wanted a settled code of laws to reconcile the fluctuating and jarring opinions which at that time prevailed, and above all things, the nomenclature of Natural History required to be reduced to one uniform standard. For this Linnaeus was peculiarly well adapted. Nature had gifted him with a logical accuracy of reasoning, and a neatness and perspicuity of expression, which carried with them a charm that the world was not slow to appreciate; and these produced the stronger impression, because naturalists had previously been but little accustomed to them. The opinions of Linnaeus were received as if oracular, and their faults were lost in the blaze of light which they cast upon the whole of the organic world.

Most of his labours in other branches of Natural History are now obsolete; but his botanical system being still in use among us, requires that something should be said upon it. Availing himself of the curious discovery that there exist in plants parts analogous to the sexual organs of animals; a question, indeed, of which he has also the merit of having finally demonstrated the truth; and finding that they were very constant in different species, he conceived the idea of employing certain characters derived from those organs as the distinctions of classes and orders. With much skill he reduced all the plants described by his predecessors under these classes, and thus established a system of Botany which was at one time universally adopted, and which, although now superseded by more perfect modes of arrangement, is still fondly clung to by many, to whom, from an acquaintance with it during all their life, it has become endeared. The merit of the Linnaean system was its simplicity; the characters on which the arrangement was made to depend were obvious and easily perceived; and in the early part of Linnaeus's career, the masses of plants grouped under his classes and orders were not inconveniently extensive.

But it was perceived by those who took an enlarged view of the ends of Botany, that however useful this system might have been at the time of its original contrivance, yet that it was by no means such as a more advanced state of science would demand, and that it failed altogether in doing more than collecting, in groups, plants agreeing in one or two unimportant peculiarities, but differing in every other respect. It was found, too, that characters derived from the number of the sexual organs alone, were less certain than was in the beginning believed, that exceptions were extremely numerous, and that cases of doubtful structure were by no means uncommon. And, finally, it was discovered that the principles of Linnaean classification produced the mischief of rendering Botany a mere science of names, than which nothing more useless can be well conceived. The simplicity of the Linnaean system was found to be only a disguise of its superficial character; it was, in short, a positive and serious evil rather than an advantage; for Botanists contented themselves with just as much knowledge as was sufficient to enable them to understand the system, and looked no further. The necessary result of this was to render the science superficial and unworthy of the attention of men of enlightened minds.

In France, in which country the merits of Tournefort, to whom I have already alluded, were best understood, and where the system of Linnaeus was never very favourably received, this feeling struck deep root. The Botanists of that country saw that a system of classification was not the great end of the science, but chiefly the means by which it could be made available to the purposes of mankind; that if plants were to be studied usefully, it must be with reference to their every point of structure, and their every property; that a few vague external peculiarities which had little or nothing to do with the general nature, appearance, or use of vegetables, were the last instead of the first characters that ought to be employed as primary means of distinction. Above all things they blamed the exclusion of physiological considerations from the basis of an arrangement of plants. Let the vegetable world be studied in all its forms and bearings, and it will be found that certain plants agree with each other in their anatomical condition, in the venation of their leaves, in the structure of their flowers, the position of their stamens, in the degree of development of their organs, in their mode of germination, and finally in their chemical and medicinal properties. These then are the characters that ought to serve as the basis of classification; and then scientific nomenclature, instead of being a barbarous and unintelligible jargon, becomes, what it should be, the medium of conveying clear ideas of all the most material modifications of which the vegetable kingdom is susceptible. Let us take an example.– The first of the Linnaean classes and orders is called Monandria Monogynia, and comprehends plants which have one stamen and one style. Now what notion or idea of the nature of the plants comprehended under this Monandria Monogynia can we possibly form, beyond the simple fact that they have one stamen and one style,– a character which has no sort of reference to any one property or peculiarity worth knowing. Contrast with this the natural order called *Scitamineæ*. This name at once conveys the idea of plants with the characters and properties of the *Ginger,* the *Turmeric,* the *Cardamom,* and the *Zedoary;* aromatic herbs, with fleshy roots, and a monocotyledonous foliage and flower, possessing certain peculiarities of structure found in no other plants. The very mention, therefore, of the name *Scitamineæ* conveys to the mind just as accurate and definite ideas as the most laboured definition.

In conformity with these opinions Antoine Laurent de Jussieu published his "Genera Plantarum" in 1789; a work not more remarkable for the excellence of the principles that it advocates, than for the skill and learning with which they are applied to practice. It forms the basis of all more modern systems of a similar kind, and was unquestionably the second great step, as that of Linnaeus was the first, towards the establishment of Botany upon sound philosophical principles.

The system of Jussieu has been much improved by the discoveries and investigations of succeeding Botanists, many of whom, in his own country especially, are deserving of the highest honours that the naturalist can receive. Among these I may more particularly mention the names of the late Louis Claude Richard, and of the present Professor De Candolle. But, far beyond both theses, I must name a living English Botanist*, one of the most illustrious among the naturalists of our day; but to whom, as I think I see him present among you, I cannot more particularly allude.

With the principles of this system I am for my own part satisfied. It appears to me to answer every end that can be expected or desired; to be the most complete analysis of vegetable bodies that can be contrived, and, above all things, to be essentially founded upon theories of structure, the truth of which cannot be disputed.

And what more, let me ask, do we want? A great deal is said about systems; and many people think that Natural History is nothing more than the amusement of shuffling and cutting natural objects, according to the caprices or particular views of different observers. No mistake can be greater than this. Let us, therefore, pause to inquire a little more into the end or use of systems.

A system in Natural History is, in my view of the subject, nothing either more or less than another word for *the mode of studying animated beings;* and it is of importance only so far as it is important to know what is the best mode of studying Nature.

To be perfect it must comply with both of the two following conditions.

It must render the discovery of the name of a given species easy and certain, provided the inquirer is possessed of a thorough knowledge of the structure and properties of that which he is seeking. The importance of this is very great,

---

* Robert Brown Esq., F.R.S. &c, &c.

because without it, it would be impracticable to ascertain the state of recorded knowledge upon any given point.

It must indicate the affinity borne by species to each other, in order that we may judge from analogy of all those circumstances connected with the structure and properties of a newly discovered plant, of which we may be otherwise ignorant. For example, a Botanist ought to be enabled, by the arrangements of his system, to say, from the mere inspection of either the flowers, or the leaves, or the fruit, or any other important part of a plant, what the structure of those parts, which he has not before him, probably is; and this a skilful Botanist will, even in the present imperfect state of our knowledge, be often able to do with considerable accuracy.

Such is, I think, the whole end and use of systems in Natural History; such is the nature of what is called the natural system in Botany; and such are the principles, which it is my intention to inculcate and explain, rather than that superficial mode of study invented by Linnaeus. I am told that in this I shall surely fail; that it is impossible to explain to a Botanical class the mysteries, if they be mysteries, of the natural affinities of plants, and that all experience is against the attempt. But I confess I am not of this opinion. I am ignorant of the insuperable difficulties which are anticipated, and I think that you will never find them. For instance, what difficulty can there possibly be in seeing that the mode of growth of these Palm-leaves, of that Screw Pine, of that Dracæna, or of yonder graceful Bamboo, is extremely different from that of the Rhododendron, and the Azalea, the Rose, and the Pelargonium which stand before me; or to use a more familiar comparison, that the Oak and the Birch and the Pine-tree grow upon quite another plan from the Grass, the Reed, or the Lily. Any one may see that this specimen of *Coniferous* wood is totally unlike that of the *Palm* wood I hold in my hand. In the one case we see that the growth of every year is indicated by a concentric circle, which is necessarily consequent upon the manner in which the trees called Dicotyledonous increase. In this other we find no concentric circles, nor any indication whatsoever of annual growth,– a mode of structure also consequent upon the peculiar mode of development of the trees called Monocotyledonous. In the former we have wood and bark and pith distinctly limited; in the latter the wood and the bark and the pith are all mixed together without any distinct limits. In the leaves of the former, the veins anastomose in various directions, forming a kind of network; in the latter they run parallel with the margin, with no such reticulation. So that the characters upon which this redoubtable system depends, are after all just as obvious and as easily detected, as those of the most superficial mode of study that has ever been invented. Besides this, I cannot do either you or myself the injustice to believe that that which is capable of being explained by me, is not capable of being understood by you; or that difficulties which I, without an instructor, have been able to surmount, cannot be surmounted by you under the auspices of an instructor. Of this, at least, I am well convinced, that if Botany, or any other science, cannot be taught upon philosophical principles, it can neither be taught, nor is worthy of being learned, upon those which are empirical. At all events we will here make the experiment: and in this new Institution we will see whether we cannot do that in Botany, which others find no difficulty in doing in other branches of science; whether we cannot redeem one of the most interesting departments of Natural History from the obloquy which has become attached to it in this country, and whether it is not possible to found a school of Botany in London worthy of being associated with those of Medicine, Zoology, and Natural Philosophy.

I trust that in what I have now been saying of the Linnaean system of Botany, I shall not be misunderstood. For Linnaeus himself, and for the benefits he has conferred upon science, I yield in admiration to no man; but, with regard to his system, it is not fitted for the present state of natural knowledge. I do not object to it because it is artificial,– and this I beg to be particularly observed,– but because it is superficial. A system being artificial is, in my view, no defect at all; the system of natural orders is, in some respects, as essentially artificial as that of Linnaeus; and so will all necessarily be that are to be applied to practice. What I do object to in the sexual, or Linnaean system is, that it teaches nothing, that it goes to nothing, and that it has uniformly had the effect of paralysing the labours of those who have adopted it; and for these reasons I feel justified in rejecting it.

In the remark upon systems which I have now made, I have referred only to what is practical and applicable to purposes of investigation, and not to those others, of very modern invention, which are really little better than romantic speculations. The authors of these latter are not contented with a system fulfilling the conditions which I have just described as all that are required, but they look to something which they call higher and more spiritual. Some pretend that the affinities of natural objects are perfectly indicated, and can be only usefully studied by the aid of certain signs, and marks, and circles, representing abstract notions, and depending upon an assumed, distinctly progressive increase in what is called perfection of structure; a sort of regular, definite, ascending scale of development, from the simple vesicular creatures which cannot be certainly referred to either the animal or vegetable kingdom, up to some unknown point among flowering plants. Others assure you that they can test the accuracy of all the naturalist's divisions, subdivisions, or combinations, of organic beings, by a certain mysterious number, which according to some is 2, to others 3, to some 4, to others 5, or even 7, and finally even 9. It is very difficult to conceive out of what these speculations, upon the potential qualities of numbers, have arisen. The binarists, or those who fancy No. 2 to be the *Lapis lydius,* or touchstone of classification, have, no doubt, mistaken the commonest principles of analysis for some wonderful discovery. Others have been influenced by the notion that all matter is organised under the influence of certain powerful agents or *cosmica momenta,* as they are called;

such as heat, light, earth, or water; and that, *therefore,* at each stage of its development it can never resolve itself into more than the same number of modifications as there are original active agents. I have no intention of entering today into a discussion of these speculative points; and, perhaps, they hardly deserved notice; but I will crave your indulgence for one instant, while I inquire what such hypotheses *go to,* and how they are proved.

We are told that they convey a certain mysterious and indefinable notion of the works of Nature; and that the highest truths in Nature are only intelligible to those who thus study the mysteries of this *Botanical Cabala;* that observation can furnish no abstract idea of Nature and her works, for observation only skims over the surface of things, and conveys ideas as superficial as our powers of vision are confined; but that internal meditation alone will ever elevate the mind to a state capable of contemplating and appreciating the grand principles of nature. Surely all this is very unintelligible. That some good may be gleaned from it I am far from denying; but that mere fancy should be allowed to usurp the place of close observation in Natural History, is scarcely a doctrine to be readily received. And how are these opinions proved, as it is called? Why, gentlemen, I will give you a few instances. Professor Oken of Jena, a man undoubtedly of splendid talents, is one of those who advocate the doctrine of progressive and consecutive development in Nature from one point to another; and in order to prove his theory in Botany, he is forced to declare that the leaves of those Palms, of the Bamboo, and of yonder Screw Pine, are not leaves at all, but (you will scarcely credit it) mere foliaceous dilatations. He further tells us, that the vascular system of such plants is imperfectly developed; that the Palms, the Screw Pines, the New Zealand Flax, the Plantain, and all those tribes, the vascular system of which produces the most powerful cordage, and the most delicate linen fabrics that we know, have their vascular system imperfectly developed. Another of these philosophers, who thinks that the number 4 exercises some magical influence over the mysteries of Nature, informs us that the usual division of organic matter between the two kingdoms of animals and vegetables is inaccurate, and that there are in fact four distinct kingdoms, viz. Fungi, Plants, Animals, and Man★. Surely I need not dwell longer upon this.

But let us turn from the consideration of the use of systems in Botany, to a consideration of the uses of Botany itself.

It has been very much the fashion of late years, in this country, to undervalue the importance of this science, and to consider it an amusement for ladies rather than an occupation for the serious thoughts of man. I hear it said that it is of no use, that the ordinary business of the world could go on just as well as if no

---

★ "Die vier lebenden Naturreiche der Erde nennen wir Pilze, Pflanzen, Thiere, und Menschen." *C.G. Nees von Esenbeck, Handbuch der Botanik,* I.p.12.

such science existed, and that it is in nowise applicable to the wants or necessities of mankind. I will not pay you so bad a compliment as to offer any argument in opposition to those who treat Botany as a mere accomplishment; but I will proceed at once to show you that if it is an accomplishment, it is also a science of no little importance to the world.

We behold the surface of the earth adorned with flowers and leaves of every hue and form; we see the rivers, the lakes, the fields, the woods, the hills, the rocks, the mountains, all clothed with verdure, all invested with a rich robe of vegetation, and each peopled with tribes peculiar to itself; we know that the plants which constitute this vegetation are as various in their forms and habits as the animals that live among them; we see that some have flowers, and leaves, and fruit; that others have none of these; that some have lofty trunks that bear their foliage and fruit aloft in the face of heaven; and that others have none of these; that others lie prostrate upon the ground in damp and shady places, as if to avoid the light of day. We see that the very same laws that regulate the production of the blue mould that is engendered upon cheese, the green slime that clothes shaded walls, and the gray colouring that incrusts our ancient edifices, are the same as those which control the development of the gayest flowers of the field, and the most gigantic timbers of the forest; and more than this,– that not only are these laws identical, but the very materials that Nature uses to form such different creations are nearly identical also,– that the mucor, which is the creation of an hour, born one instant and perishing the next, and the hardest teak wood used in shipping, are formed out of the same materials; that the lofty Palms, the tough and gnarled Oak, and the succulent Potato, the tenacious Grass and the tender Mushroom, scarcely differ, except in the manner in which they are developed, and in the nature of their secretions. Nothing can be more familiar to us than that a strong analogy is maintained between plants and animals in their mode of propagation; that organic beings destitute of locomotive powers, have the same distinction of sexes as those animals in which the locomotive powers are most perfect; and that the embryo of a vegetable undergoes a sort of successive development in many respects analogous to that of man himself, requiring the same kind of fecundation, which is equally effected by animated particles. Finally, according to Baron Humboldt, the forms of plants, in determining the physiognomy of Nature, also influence in a high degree the moral disposition of nations. (P.N.5.52.) We see all these things; we see that they are not the offspring of chance; but that like produces its like, as among animals themselves. And can we doubt that all these things are subject to the influence of certain laws, as wise as those which regulate our own existence? Our daily experience teaches us it would be better for man to be deprived of the aid of the animal world than of that of the vegetable. Our houses, our tables, our dresses, and the very means of communicating to others our thoughts in writing, depend, in a great measure, upon the vegetable world. And if the vegetable world is thus indispensable to our very existence, and if it is really subject to the influence of certain fixed laws, can it be doubted that it is of the utmost importance to the world to be acquainted with these laws? And what is that acquaintance but Botany? I say then, that however interesting a subject it may be, it is a still more important one.

Can the physician dispense with it? All practice and theory answer in the negative. A large proportion of the medicines upon which the physician is compelled to rely for his means of cure, are of vegetable origin; and of them, numerous kinds are not mere vegetable secretions examinable only by the aid of Chemistry, but vegetables, the organic structure of which is unchanged. How are these to be recognised except by a knowledge of Botany, and, let me add, by a kind of knowledge anything but superficial; and how without such a knowledge are adulterations to be detected? The physician necessarily depends very much upon the experience and honesty of the apothecary; but the apothecary must rely upon his own personal skill and knowledge of the true characters of the medicines he prepares: in the first place, to avoid being himself a victim to the fraud or ignorance of those with whom he deals; and in the second place, to be able to protect the professional reputation of the physician from similar malpractices. In what way are medical men to dispense with a knowledge of Botany, on a foreign station? In all countries there are diseases peculiar to the climate; diseases, the remedy for which will usually be found to have been supplied upon the spot by the bounteous hand of Nature. If these remedies are of a vegetable nature, as they most probably will be, in what possible way are they to be detected, supposing the inquirer to be ignorant of the nature of botanical analogies? Let us inquire a little further into this. It has been well observed, that science is very much the art of prediction; that one of the most important ends to which it leads is to be able to foretell with accuracy the property of an unknown body by means of one which is known. Now it is a very old notion, but one which daily experience seems more and more to confirm, that there is some direct analogy between the external forms of plants and their medical properties. This was first distinctly stated by Rudolph Jacob Camerarius, a professor of Botany at Tubingen, who in 1699 published a treatise *"de Convenientiá plantarum in fructificatione et viribus:"* and it has since occupied much of the attention of medical botanists, who with a very few exceptions have adopted the opinion. The apparent anomalies which have led some to take a different view of the subject, are disappearing as science becomes more perfect; and I think the day cannot be far distant when the medical characters of plants will be introduced as an essential part of the definitions of the Botanist. Under circumstances such as those in which a medical man must often find himself on a foreign station, a power of applying his knowledge of Botany in this way must be of the greatest possible importance. He will know how to distinguish between emetic and narcotic, and cathartica and febrifugal plants, by their botanical analogies; and although he may undoubtedly be deceived, yet his disappointment is more likely to result rather from a want of sufficient activity in the herbs he may select, than from any absence of the principles he is seeking. But more than this; he will not only know to what families of plants he may trust with perfect confidence, in what he may be sure of finding no deleterious principles, if no efficient remedies; but he will also be on his guard against the use of plants of those families in which one thing cannot be substituted for another with equal safety. He would unhesitatingly trust himself to any Rubiaceous, or Malvaceous, or Convolvulaceous, or Cruciferous plant, because he would know that he had nothing to fear from them; but he would be very cautious how he employed unknown species of such suspicious families as Solaneæ, or Urticeæ, or Euphorbiaceæ, remembering that among the known plants that they comprehend, are species both wholesome and poisonous to man. I have not unfrequently heard it observed, that if our own indigenous plants are rightly examined, we should find that our native land produces medicines as efficacious as those which we import at great charges from abroad. How this may be, I know not; but this I know, that it is a problem never to be solved without the help of Botany.

Agriculture and Horticulture! Where would these arts be without such aid, especially the latter? Almost every operation that is conducted in them, as far as vegetation is concerned, depends upon the laws of vegetable physiology, and can be explained and understood upon no other. Upon what other principles are we to comprehend the nature of the influence of seasons, of diseases, of heat, of cold, of blights, of mildews, and all the maladies to which vegetation is subject? The gardener knows that one description of plant must be propagated in one way and one in another. Whence was this knowledge derived but from Botany? He knows that the Plum, the Peach, the Apricot, and other Drupaceous fruit-trees require a mode of training and pruning very different from that of the Apple, the Pear, and the Quince. Who told him this? or who in short explained to him the laws of pruning but the Botanist? He finds that the most sterile trees may be compelled to become fruitful, and that this result is to be attained in more ways than one. But how could he have known it unassisted by the Botanist? How could his unassisted reason inform him that decortication in one case, twisting in another, inversion in a third, varying the stock upon which a variety is grafted in a fourth; and, in short, all those simple mysteries upon which Horticulture depends for its very existence, would produce effects, the nature of which could not vary? He knows that he must graft at one season and bud at another; that one description of plant will increase by buds, and another by grafts; a third by cuttings, a fourth by eyes, and a fifth by layers; all operations among those with which he is most familiar. And whence, let me ask, has this familiarity been derived, except from the skilful application on the part of his ancestors, of the laws of vegetable physiology? Nine-tenths of the most important discoveries that have been made in modern Horticulture, especially the art of regulating and adapting artificial climate to vegetation, are due to the botanical knowledge of the most distinguished vegetable physiologist of this kingdom⋆; whose successful attempts at applying science to practice have been recently crowned, if I may so express myself, by the complete subjugation of the unmanageable constitution of the Pine-apple. It is in this way that Botany affects Horticulture, which, without it, would have remained till this day what it formerly was,– the mere act of committing seed to the earth, and of reaping the produce. And who, after this explanation, will dispute the indispensable alliance, the inseparable connection, of Horticulture and Botany?

Even legal decisions are sometimes affected most materially by botanical questions. It is not yet five years since the very existence of one of the most extensive of the mercantile associations of this country depended upon a point of vegetable physiology. A proceeding, most ruinous to its interests, had been taken in the Court of Chancery, which would probably have to this hour remained in operation, had not the Company been extricated from its difficulty by the affidavit of a Botanist.

Look at the artist: he may be thought to have as little concern with the minutiæ of Botany as any class of men; and yet if flower painting is his object, he cannot possibly dispense with a very intimate knowledge of that part of Botany which teaches the theory of vegetable structure. It is undoubtedly true, that from the general ignorance of society upon this subject, the errors of painters in flower and fruit subjects are less generally detected than they would be in other paintings; but this is to excuse the ignorance of the painter by that of the public. What, let me ask, would be thought by an anatomist? and all men are necessarily more or less acquainted with that science:– what, I say, would be thought by an anatomist of a painter, who distorted the muscles of the human body; who drew a foot with four or six toes; who misrepresented the proportion of the limbs; made the hands reaching to the knees; who omitted the joints, making the legs and thighs continuous with the body, without articulation; and who committed an hundred similar absurdities? And yet, in flower painting, nothing is more common than blunders of exactly an analogous kind. We have flowers with too many petals; fruit with the calyx at the apex instead of the base; leaves unarticulated with the stem, inserted in wrong places, opposite when they should be alternate, and alternate when they should be opposite; the veins of one family upon the leaves of another; or, which is more common, such veins as no plants ever possessed; and finally, flowers stuck upon parts where they could no more have grown than a man's head beneath his arms. Surely, it behoves all artists who wish to gain a worthy name in their profession to avoid such blunders; and this nothing but Botany will enable them to accomplish.

⋆ Thomas Andrew Knight, Esq., F.R.S. &c., &c.

Now, let us consider a little the relation borne by Botany to Geology. It is the province of this science to determine the physical history of the globe, from the remains which its crust exhibits at the present day; and form the relics of its great catastrophes to educe some positive evidence of the nature of those catastrophes themselves. You all know how successfully this has been accomplished by the mineralogies, the comparative anatomist, and the fossil zoologist; how interesting the discoveries they have made, and how new a light they have thrown upon some of the most important considerations with which the mind of man can be occupied. But of what avail are all these labours, however meritorious they may be, without the aid of the Botanist? In the most ancient secondary formations with which we are acquainted, even as it is said in the Old Red Sandstone itself, in which the earliest traces are found of organic remains, impressions of plants are distinguished, thus proving that the birth of animals and vegetables was coeval. In the formations that succeed them, that is to say, in the whole district of the coal-measures, deposits which must have been the result of ages, not a trace of land animals is to be seen; while those of plants are beautifully perfect. The whole, therefore, of this long epoch, which is the more interesting as it is so close upon the first creation of organic matter:– the whole of this long epoch, I say, would be a positive blank in the history of the earth, without the aid of Botany; for Zoology and Comparative Anatomy find no materials therein on which to exercise themselves. And onward through all those deposits, which are called supermedial orders, lying above the coal, and extending up to the chalk itself, Botany is of a degree of importance in which it yields to no science. The coal-measures indicate the first traces of organic forms upon dry land: at that period the temperate zone was covered with a vegetation differing in many respects from any thing we now know; but upon the whole, having, as a Botanist can demonstrate, an unquestionable analogy with the modern vegetation of the tropics, not a trace of even a reptile remains, much less of warm-blooded animals; and no other evidence whatever is to be found of the constitution of the atmosphere, or the general condition of the earth's surface at that remote period, than such as is afforded by the study of vegetable remains. And even at a much later period, when an immense variety of monstrous reptiles began to people the earth, the circumstance of no mammiferous animals having even then made their appearance, is perhaps to be explained more satisfactorily upon botanical principles, than upon any others. An accurate knowledge of the nature of the vegetation of all these periods is of an importance to the Geologist which can be scarcely estimated. The study of these is doubtless a matter of great difficulty; but the degree of botanical knowledge, which is indispensable for commencing an investigation of them, is less, I am inclined to think, than is generally imagined. These ancient Floras are so different from those of modern days, that little individual comparison can, in any of the secondary formations, be usefully employed. The Geologist has a Flora of his own, of unknown, but probably not of very great extent; and what he chiefly wants is a clear well defined notion of the fundamental principles of Botany, and of the laws of vegetable structure; for the plan upon which the primitive vegetation of the world was constructed, was, beyond all doubt, exactly the same as that of the present day. With this kind of knowledge to aid him, the Geologist may do much more with his fossil plants than is supposed, or than has yet been done. And what a glorious field for inquiry! What an object for scientific ambition to strike at! A throne by the side of Cuvier is still vacant, and ready to be filled by the first adventurer who shall deserve it.

But whence, it may be asked, are the subjects for a course of Botanical Lectures in this University to be derived; and how, without a Botanical Garden and Museum, are the necessary illustrations to be provided! True it is, there is no botanic garden attached to this Institution; and also true, that no botanical museum yet exists. But let it be remembered, that the principles of a science are to be taught as truly with reference to the commonest forms as to the rarest. And have we not the fields and the rivers? But besides this, is not the whole suburb of this metropolis one magnificent botanic garden? Are not the institutions of London rich in museums, abounding in treasures, which, by the liberality of their possessors, are only amassed for the advantages of science? And to what sources can a botanical Professor look with more confidence than to such as these; and on what can he more certainly depend than on the liberality of those enlightened individuals, whose only object in forming their collections is the diffusion of knowledge? The Council of the Horticultural Society have set a noble example, in placing their garden and museum at the disposal of the University; and the aid which has been furnished by a single private collection, the proprietors★ of which I am proud to call my highly valued friends, is such as no other public or private establishment in this kingdom could have afforded. These, then, are our Botanic Garden, and in these we put our trust.

I have now showed what Botany is, its objects, and its uses. I am, certainly, far from thinking with a distinguished naturalist, now no more, that a course of Botany is the best of all foundations of a perfect education; but I do think it is highly useful to many classes of mankind; that the luxuries and necessaries of civilised life depend very much upon the discoveries that have been made in it; and that it is a kind of knowledge which no person who wishes to receive a finished education can dispense with.

THE END

★ Messrs. Loddiges, of Hackney.

Part III

BOTANY AND MEDICINE
ADDRESS DELIVERED
AT
THE COMMENCEMENT OF
THE MEDICAL SESSION
1834-5
University of London on 1 October 1834

John Lindley

[The close association of John Lindley with horticulture ensured that he kept ever in mind the practical and economic aspects of botany and emphasised them in his lectures and publications. Although not a medical man, he gave the opening address on 1 October 1834 to the Medical Session of London University (now University College) presumably through the absence of Dr Grant, the Professor of Medicine. The Government had set up a Select Committee on Medical Education and to this Lindley alluded at the beginning of his address. Of course he stressed the relevance to a medical man of a knowledge of botany, because plants supplied so many medicaments and also poisons. Augustin Pyramus de Candolle published in 1804 an *Essai sur les Propriétés Médicinales des Plantes companées avec leur formes extérieures et leur Classification naturelle*. A second edition, revised and augmented, appeared in 1816. Lindley possessed this and commented: 'The arguments by which the coincidence of botanical affinity and medical properties is supported have been admirably set out by Professor De Candolle'. By 'affinity' he meant agreement between plants having many structural characters in common. Plants thereby grouped were found to have properties in common, some of medicinal value, some dangerous. For Lindley, as he stated here, 'the structure, function and analogy of organs, and the mutual relations of species, are the really grand subjects of inquiry', and this was not simply of philosophical interest but had implications of practical value, notably for medical men, as he showed by examples – W.T.S.]

UNIVERSITY OF LONDON

ADDRESS

Delivered at the commencement of the
Medical Session 1834-5,
on Wednesday, Oct. 1st 1834,
by

PROFESSOR LINDLEY
Lecturer on Botany at the University

(*Reported in* The Lancet *of October 11th, 1834.*)

You are this day to witness the anomaly of one who is not a medical man, opening the medical session,– an anomaly which I would have wished any one to exhibit other than myself, because, under the most fortunate circumstances, there must of necessity be something in such a position eminently embarrassing. It has, however, frequently happened that Botany, although so closely related, in some respects, to medical science, has been the most assiduously cultivated by men who were not immediately connected with the profession. This has, apparently, happened in consequence of the great extent, the numerous details, and the peculiar difficulties of the science, which demand so much more constant study than men engaged in medical practice can possibly give to it; and hence the Professors at Cambridge and Glasgow are, like myself, entirely unconnected with medicine.

    I am, however, relieved from a part of any embarrassment by two considerations; first, by the peculiar political aspect of the medical world; and, secondly, by the state to which the medical school of the University has now arrived. Now that the whole system of medical education is before one of the three great departments of the highest legislative body of this country, and that we are upon the eve of some important change in the whole frame-work of our medical institutions, it appears to me that a discussion of the defects of existing arrangements, or of the theoretical advantages to be derived from new ones, is better postponed. When we know the course which the government proposes to take in these matters, and the reasons upon which the decision at which it may arrive is founded, we shall be better able to judge upon what points argument or representation may be necessary. Were I, therefore, competent to discuss such a subject, I should purposely abstain on this occasion from doing more than insisting upon the indispensable necessity of a medical education being rendered as *general* as is practicable. Seeing that medical men, from the high, honourable, and confidential position they hold in society, and from the influence they may, consequently, exercise for good or for evil, are continually called upon to form an opinion in matters not immediately concerning their profession, I do think it requires no argument to show that they ought to qualify themselves for so weighty a trust and so responsible a station, by a solid acquaintance with much more than the mere technical course of study prescribed by existing governing bodies, and secured by the ordinary routine of a school education. And, indeed, independently of this duty, such is most obviously their interest. The greatest of all the difficulties that a professional man experiences in starting in the world, is to gain a practice. A practice can only be gained by inspiring the public with confidence, and confidence is far more likely to be inspired by a man whose general attainments are superior to those of other persons in his own station, than by one who, except in what concerns his profession, is not better informed than his neighbours. People naturally suppose that if a man possesses knowledge of a high order in what they themselves understand, he will be pre-eminently skilful in his own profession; and the natural consequence is, their trusting the health of themselves and their families in his hands. Believe me, general information, as well as professional skill, is a prodigious help to a man who has to fight his way in the world. To enable medical students to gain this power by the requisite alterations in the rules of medical corporations is a solemn duty which the rulers of this country owe to the nation,– an act of justice which I feel well persuaded that the present government will not be deterred from performing, either by public clamour or private intrigue.

With regard to ourselves, in the beginning, when the University was young, the plan of instruction untried, the professors in many cases untried also, and the system incapable of being judged by its results, it was indispensable that the session should be opened by a preliminary lecture, in which the views of the professors could be generally explained, the system of teaching pointed out, and a variety of topics connected with medical education in general, insisted on. But this, I trust, has ceased to be called for. The seventh session of the University has opened; your professors are all known by the experience of former years; they have staked their reputation upon the hazard of their previous courses; an account of their stewardship has been rendered; and it is now for the public to judge whether or not it is satisfactory. The connexion of the various subjects embraced in the medical curriculum of the University was explained last year, by my colleague, Dr. GRANT, with, I trust I may be permitted to say, Gentlemen, a rare felicity of expression and being printed, is within reach of all. The results of our system of instruction are already dispersed throughout the empire; that they have not been unsatisfactory is, we flatter ourselves, sufficiently manifest by the gradual advance which has taken place in the numbers of our medical school. In 1831 we entered 248 students, in 1832 294, and in 1833, 353. If, then, we have deserved well of our supporters, if we have indeed fulfilled the expectations entertained of the the medical school of the University of London, no arguments of mine can be necessary to convince you of that fact; but, on the other hand, if we have not redeemed the pledges that have been given to you, and if you have not found that advantage from attending this school which you were taught to expect, no eloquence of mine, if I am gifted with any, could give you confidence for the future; as no arguments, if I could condescend to use them in such a cause, would succeed in satisfying you for the past.

The only point on which I find it really necessary to speak is the *hospital*. Ever since the medical school began to prosper, it has been thought, by those best acquainted with such subjects, extremely desirable that there should be attached to the University an hospital, in which the professors might give *clinical illustrations* of the subjects taught in their lectures. But various obstacles opposed for a time the execution of this project; for you may easily understand that no small degree of energy, and sums of no inconsiderable magnitude, were required to render the University itself fit for your reception, and to fix it upon a solid foundation; and when, before the exhaustion attendant upon such efforts had been supplied, it was proposed to institute an hospital in addition, the difficulty of doing so, which at all times is very great, became unusually severe. The object is, however at last accomplished; a school of *clinical instruction,* that most important of all the departments of a professional education, is prepared by the friends of humanity and of liberal opinions, and the principal part of the appointments to it is filled up. The Council of the University, to whose zeal and perseverance in this good cause I am happy thus to bear testimony, retain in their own hands the right of making all such appointments, in order that they may be sure that the hospital of the University shall always continue what its founders destine it for, a school of *clinical instruction,* in which there may be illustrations, as frequently as possible, by the professors themselves, of the subjects taught within these walls. A list of the appointments, and an explanation of all the regulations connected with the hospital, will be made known as soon as the various arrangements shall be finally completed; and I have the pleasing duty of announcing that this long-desired institution, with accommodation for 125 beds, a greater number than is provided in several of the "recognised" hospitals, will be opened on the 1st of next November. From these subjects I now proceed to what is the proper business of this lecture.

Botany is, in the practice of some writers, if not according to their expressed opinion, the ART of classifying plants according to some artificial method, and of remembering their Græco-Latin names.

Such a study is dignified indeed with the name of science, but to my apprehension it is as much an art as that of recollecting the names of the drawers of a druggist's shop, without knowing anything of their contents. Others would admit what is called vegetable physiology as an essential part of botany, but they cannot dispense with artificial classifications, as a most important, independent, and fundamental subject.

But botany, when considered as a branch of physical philosophy, is subject to no such limitations, and knows of no empirical classifications; its range is wider far, and its character of a much higher order. It embraces not only the knowledge of the structure of all the minute and curious organs of which plants consist, and of the still more singular functions which they perform, and of the important effects which they produce both upon earth and air; but it also demands an examination of the relations which the several organs of plants bear to each other throughout the whole range of the vegetable kingdom; and of the laws which, when the functions of organs are altered or modified, govern the changes in their form from some primitive type. In the animal kingdom there is no example of one organ being employed under new circumstances, to perform a new class of functions in a manner more curious or instructive than we meet with at every step among plants.

Another point of the utmost importance in botany is the study of the mutual relations that plants bear to each other. This is the key-stone of materia medica, so far as the vegetable kingdom is concerned, and is the only safe and practical guide which the practitioner can follow in experimenting upon vegetable productions previously unknown to him; and it is upon this ground in particular that botany is insisted upon in medical studies. The relations of affinity among plants are far less perceptible to the ordinary observer than those of animals, because the structure of plants is so essentially different a one from our own, that analogies are habitually overlooked, until they are pointed out by the finger of science. We readily identify with those of our own bodies the limbs and external organs of the animal kingdom. We can recognise the head, the eyes, the legs, and the abdomen of an insect, as readily as those of an elephant; or can perceive at a glance wherein they are unlike animals of a higher order; the creatures we have been familiar with from our infancy typify in our minds the characters of the principal divisions in zoology. Mammals, birds, fishes, reptiles, insects, molluscous and crustaceous animals, have each their familiar representations even in the minds of children. But in the vegetable kingdom it is quite otherwise; organic beings, whose forms are entirely dissimilar from those of animals, convey no distinct impression to the mind, till they have been carefully studied. Far more simple than animals in their structure, they possess fewer and less obvious signs by which their mutual relationship is to be determined; and yet it is of the highest moment that these should be ascertained before botany can be applied, upon principle, to many most important subjects.

It is *not* names then, nor arbitrary classifications, nor vegetable physiology, considered as an isolated subject, which constitute the science of botany. The structure, function, and analogy of organs, and the mutual relation of species, are the really grand subjects of inquiry. An exact knowledge of structure enables us to understand distinctly how certain functions are to be performed, a comparison of one plant with another leads to the discovery of the analogy of their organs, and by means of such analogies we determine by what degree of resemblance or difference the affinity of species is to be settled. These points ascertained, we are able to proceed, *upon definite principles,* to apply our science to useful purposes, to discriminate, *upon principle,* between the species which yield products important in medicine, or otherwise, to control the operations of the husbandman, to direct the experiments of the colonist, and to arm the world with new powers, the limits of which no one can pretend to estimate.

And this is the great point after all. It is a delightful thing no doubt for the philosopher to find himself able to lift the veil from before the mysteries of the creation; and it will be denied by no one, that to understand, however imperfectly, the design by which we ourselves, and all things material and immaterial which surround us, are constructed, and mutually adapted to the formation of one stupendous and harmonious whole, is one of the highest attributes of man, and one of the loftiest subjects of contemplation in which the human mind can engage. But, gentlemen, the lot of man is not generally cast in such a mould as will enable him to enter profoundly upon considerations of this kind, unless he finds them lead to some practical result, to some valuable end, by which his own condition, or that of his fellow-creatures, may be bettered. Astronomy, with all its glorious truths, is, probably, more valued by the bulk of mankind for its importance in navigation than for its noble philosophical attributes; and in like manner chemistry, by its universal and unlimited application to useful purposes; geology by its interest to miners and agriculturists; and zoology by the power it gives us over the useful or noxious animals that surround us, have acquired the great esteem in which they are popularly held, rather than by atomic theories, speculations in cosmogony, demonstrations of development, or other points of high philosophy.

Let me not be misunderstood. I do not say that you are not to love science for its own sake, without reference to mere utilitarian considerations; I am far from intimating that in theory the charms of science, and its effect in enlarging and liberalising the understanding, ought not to be in themselves sufficient to induce us to devote ourselves to its pursuit. God forbid I should write myself a follower of that cold and repulsive school of which *cui bono* is the chilling motto; on the contrary, I certainly think that those who merely apply themselves to the study of science from motives of cupidity and avarice are unworthy to look upon the glorious thing it will reveal. But it is certain that the great end of science is practical good, and that it is only with reference to such an end that the mass of mankind has leisure to attend to it.

By this test let botany be tried. I need not point out to you that a science which explains the organic laws under which plants are permitted to live and grow, which teaches the manner in which they are influenced by the elements, or how they themselves act upon the earth and atmosphere that surround them, stands in the same relation to the vegetable as physiology to the animal kingdom. When we reflect how considerable a proportion of our food is derived from plants, how large a part of the riches of a country consists in the fruits of the earth, in corn, wine, and oil, dyeing and medicinal plants, timber; or in cattle, which are supported upon various vegetable productions; and when we consider that there is not a blade of grass which springs, nor a fruit which matures, not an ear of corn which ripens, except under the dominion of the laws which botany will teach you; and especially if we remember that there is not one of these productions, the quantity of which may not be increased, or the quality improved, or the very properties modified by artificial means, and that those means can only be furnished by the botanist,– it must be sufficiently obvious how important must that science be, which is connected with matters of such vital consequence, and which leads to such results. Accident, it is true, and blind experiment, and unconquerable perseverance, have conducted the world, in the course of some thousand years, without the aid of science, to a knowledge of many of the processes and facts by which the plants we consume may be multiplied and improved, and applied to human purposes; but through what fatal errors, what lamentable catastrophes, what ruinous destruction of property, has this not been effected! How many thousands of human beings must have perished before the effects of the commonest drugs were empirically ascertained! What incalculable loss of property must have taken place before the present modes of cultivation were discovered! What waste of wealth in colonial speculations might have been averted, had the truths of Botany and her sister sciences been earlier understood! and what a change have they for the last century been producing upon the whole face of the civilised world!

When we speak of agriculture, of horticulture, of arboriculture, or of other arts, upon which botany has a direct bearing, and over which this science exercises a silent, but not on that account a less efficient influence, we are apt to overlook the cause in the effects, and to ascribe to a mere advance in those arts, the improvements we witness, without considering that that cause can be only botany or chemistry, originally applied by some master-hands, and afterwards blindly followed by the community.

When the crops of the potato, the staple food of Ireland, shall have been brought in that country to treble their present quantity, as they surely will be, and when every acre shall yield thrice as much as it now yields, the fact will be known to every one; but the original discoverers of the mode of effecting this most important improvement will probably be forgotten, except in the records of science; and the effect will be ascribed to the improved state of agriculture, without reflecting that it was brought about by a science of which the farmer had scarcely heard.

But if a knowledge of botany leads to consequences thus important, to what evils does not an ignorance of it also lead?

Charcoal is obtained for military purposes from the branches of certain trees; large plantations have been made at much expense to provide such branches. From observations I have made upon charcoal plantations in England, it is extremely doubtful whether more than one-third of the quantity that might be procured from a given space of ground is really obtained. Botany would teach the cultivators better.

Timber, again, is one of the most valuable parts of many estates. It is perfectly certain, that in many of the plantations of this country, enormous losses are sustained by the proprietors not knowing the exact conditions under which the greatest quantity of timber may be obtained in the smallest period of time. Trees are enabled to grow only by the action of light, air, and earth, and their timber will be improved or deteriorated in quality, and augmented or diminished in quantity in proportion to such external agents exercising a favourable or unfavourable influence upon them. What such influences are, it is the proper province of the botanist to elucidate.

The oak, of all our forest trees, is the most valuable. By the ignorance of charlatans, and the counsels of persons of the nominal school of botany, the finest species of English oak has been almost extirpated, and another, of equal value it is true for timber, but of far slower growth and less majestic stature, has been allowed to usurp its place. When Caesar invaded Britain, our oaks were indeed the monarchs of the forest. Trees were then common, from the solid trunks of which the aborigines fashioned canoes which measured thirty-five feet in length. Where are such trees now to be found? Our forefathers felled the choicest of them with that improvidence which is characteristic of semi-barbarous nations, and trusted to Providence for their replacement. Their descendants, when such trees became subjects of tradition, fancied they were chestnuts, and ignorantly endeavoured to supply their place by a species known in a wild state, only in more southern climates, of habits ill adapted to the rigours of our northern station; and by errors which it is impossible now to trace, but which botany might have prevented, the ancient lord of our forests became proscribed, and sentenced to general eradication, contrary to experience, contrary to fact, and, what is more to my present purpose, contrary to theory. The race, indeed, is still preserved, a scattered remnant yet inhabits the land, and, consequently, the error may be retrieved, as it surely will be; but what centuries must now elapse before the like of those which once existed shall be seen again! What losses will have been sustained before that period of their perfection returns!

Are not these instances, taken almost at random, sufficient to establish my case? Let us now turn to the consideration of botany, with reference to its bearing upon the interests of medical men.

I will not attempt to carry you through an investigation of the amount of exact knowledge possessed by the peripatetic philosophers; it is sufficient to know that their botanical science was more theoretical than practical, and that it was soon absorbed by the ignorance of the long dark ages which succeeded them.

The first tangible evidence that we have of a serious attempt to substitute experimental knowledge in botany for an empirical practice which would be perfectly ludicrous had it not led to so many melancholy consequences, was in the foundation of a garden for medicinal plants at Padua by the republic of Venice in 1533. This is the earliest indication of the existence of a suspicion that the hot, cold, and other imaginary qualities ascribed to plants, and the planetary influences said to control them, required re-examination; – or of a doubt of the truth of those statements which ascribed pulmonaria as a remedy for pulmonary complaints, because the white blotches on its leaves resemble an ulcerated lung; gromwell seeds for the gravel, because of their hard stony appearance;– or white dead nettle flowers for leucorrhœa, because of their whiteness. It must be confessed, however, that the establishment of the Paduan garden did little more than excite investigation, induce other governments to found similar institutions, and prove the opinion that was entertained of the importance of botany, notwithstanding the rubbish by which it was encumbered. Nor is it till comparatively recent times that the true method of applying botany to medical affairs, upon the fixed principles of science, has been generally recognised.

The adaptation of botany to medical pursuits is either direct or indirect,– either by way of illustration or by immediate application.

It is chiefly with regard to comparative anatomy and physiology that it is indirectly applicable. Embracing, as it does, the nature and the development of the lowest forms of organic tissue; affording excellent opportunities of studying the phenomena of life in beings whose structure is of the simplest kind, and whose want of locomotion prevents their escape from the eye of the observer; and presenting an admirable view of the motions of fluids in the ultimate cells of tissue, it is extremely well adapted to enlarge the views and to test the theories of the comparative anatomist and physiologist. It is naturally to be supposed, that as the two kingdoms of animals and plants start from one common point, where they are fused as it were into one, the first rays of divergence must be extremely similar, and all more remote rays must have a community of character which it cannot but be important for the physiologist to appreciate. For example, the singular mode of life of *filarias* is probably to be explained by that of the vegetable *monema*. Filaria is an animal belonging to the class entozoa, which burrows into the solid flesh of man, producing ulcers, and inflammation, and severe pain in the part affected. These creatures, which have occasionally been extracted from the human foot as much as an ell in length, and not more than half a line in diameter, consist of a simple tube, filled with inconceivable multitudes of excessively small, transparent worms, having a stiffish bristle-pointed tail, and a body marked by transverse lines, extremely like muscular striae. In plants, the monema, in like manner, consists of a simple tube, or tubes, containing myriads of young ones, which are evacuated when the tube is injured.

The mode of generation in plants, our knowledge of which has now been brought to a state of very considerable accuracy, has been asserted by one of the most cautious of botanists, himself a medical man, to be more likely to throw additional light upon the general problem of generation, than any inquiry into the phenomena of the animal kingdom.

You must, however, be careful that you are not misled by men of lively imaginations, who will see analogies between animals and plants where no analogies really exist, and who draw false arguments from the vegetable kingdom to support their theories of animal phenomena. And in this point of view botany is eminently useful, as enabling you to distinguish error from truth in a subject which it is most important you should rightly comprehend; for perhaps there is no department of human knowledge in which it is more easy to indulge in vain and fanciful speculations, than in drawing analogies between the animal and vegetable kingdoms.

Take, for instance, the very recent work of BRACHET, upon the ganglionary nervous system, a book which I am the more disposed to criticise, because it gained from the French Institute the Monthyon prize in physiology in 1826. It appears from the author's statement, that about two-thirds of his published work was what was submitted to examination for that purpose, which possibly explains how the errors I am about to notice, escaped the criticism of the French academicians.

He assumes, that a nervous system and vitality are two terms expressive of the same idea; and, consequently, he infers that plants must have nerves. Rejecting, however, the fanciful notions of his countryman DUTROCHET on this subject, he sets up a theory of his own. He thinks that the nodes of plants are their ganglia, that the pith is the grand nervous seat, the medullary processes nervous branches, and the bark a plexus of nerves which reach to the very surface of the leaves, where it is their business to remind the absorbents of the presence of circumambient substances. And he proves his theory by what? By a series of experiments, instituted with a full knowledge of at least the principal phenomena of vegetation? Upon evidence of which we were before ignorant? Upon some discovery which is tangible and appreciable? Not at all. He is satisfied with a few experiments, injudiciously conceived, because their results could not possibly prove anything, and conducted without any due precaution; he misunderstands his results where he has obtained them; he leaves out of consideration a multitude of important circumstances, of which a botanist would not have been ignorant; he admits that his experiments are extremely incomplete, although he adds, *"sufficient for him;"* and upon a heterogeneous mass of false reasoning, mixed up with misconceptions of the commonest and best understood phenomena, he builds his theory of the existence of a system of nervous ganglia in plants as well as animals! To show, even to those unacquainted with botany, the unsoundness of the speculations of this writer, it is sufficient to push his hypothesis to its genuine limits. If we do this, we shall find that plants, in which a nervous influence can scarcely be proved by the most careful experiments, are beings, the nervous system of which is, in fact, more highly developed than in any other part of the organic world; for they must, in reality, if we believe M. BRACHET's reasoning consist of *nothing but nerves enveloping capillary vessels.*

Again, with regard to RASPAIL's "New System of Organic Chemistry," I would strongly advise you to make yourselves well acquainted with botany before you form any opinion upon the speculations of that singular, but, in many respects, ingenious work. That it contains much matter exceedingly well worth attention I can scarcely doubt; but I must warn you, that your botany will show no inconsiderable part of what this extraordinary writer has advanced, to be purely hypothetical.

I have dwelt thus much upon the general considerations which connect botany with other sciences, because I was desirous of impressing upon your minds the fact that it bears upon many subjects of importance as well as upon those which *directly* concern the medical student. It is now time that I should explain to you what this part also is.

At one time, the world was contented with assigning certain medical properties to plants without inquiring whether some principle was not discoverable, by which the existence of such properties might be judged of *a priori.* In the absence of this principle, botany, as applied to medicine, was wholly empirical; it consisted in nothing more than a knowledge of certain supposed facts, which there were no means of generalising. It was impossible for any individual to put every supposed remedy to the test of experience, and equally beyond his power, in the absence of a safe and recognised principle of guidance, to judge of what was active or inert. The books of medical botany long remained encumbered with the chimerical fancies of the dark ages, and filled with the names of plants, the properties of which were purely imaginary. Thus alisma plantago, so much vaunted as a specific in hydrophobia, belongs to a group of plants destitute of sensible properties, and is itself inert. The water lily, which has been reckoned a narcotic, belongs to a natural order in which no such principles can be found, and does not itself possess them; and the Saponaria officinalis, once so much talked of in syphilis, would be at once pronounced, by a botanist, inactive, as it is now admitted to be.

Nor was this the only way in which the want of a guiding principle led to uncertainty and confusion. Well-known drugs were referred upon the reports of travellers to plants which did not produce them, and which botany, rightly applied, should have prevented men from believing to produce them. Thus myrrh was suppose to be yielded by an Arabian acacia, which furnishes no substance more aromatic than gum; catechu by a palm, which has nothing more active than sago in its constitution; jalap by a mirabilis; benzoin by a terminalia and a croton; and storax by a styrax; identifications alike contrary to theory and act. Besides this, there are many other ways in which Botany connects itself directly with medical duties. Everybody knows of what importance it is for a stranger, in a foreign climate, to be able to form some opinion of the properties of the plants which he meets with, and, at all events, to be able to distinguish poisonous kinds at first sight, although he should never have seen any one of the species of the country before. It is usually to medical men that one looks for advice upon the subject; and I need not mention how many inconveniences have been experienced in consequence of medical officers not being able to give such information. It will be sufficient to mention one recent case.

When Captain Belcher was on his survey of the west coast of Africa, in 1832, a number of bulbs were collected on Pullam Island, of which one of the crew having a sore tongue, was unfortunate as to taste. This man was deprived of his speech for half an hour. From the account given of the plant, it was obviously one of the poisonous amaryllideæ, which are common in equinoctial Africa; but it does not appear that the medical officers warned the sailors against their use, although from the want of vegetables which they had long experienced it was naturally to be expected that bulbs so very much like onions would be eaten by the crew. The surgeon of that ship would, in my opinion, have been morally responsible for any lives that might have been lost. If that man's tongue had not accidentally been sore, no warning would have been given, and a boat's crew might have miserably perished.

If, then, Botany will enable you to distinguish between error and truth, in judging of the sensible properties of plants, and if it will really enable you to determine, with considerable precision, the nature of the active principles contained in a species you have never before beheld; it is obviously a point of great interest to know in what way the science can be so applied. Given the external characters of a plant, to find its sensible properties, is a grand problem to solve; and one which it will be my business to demonstrate in future lectures.

At what time the suspicion first arose that the sensible properties of plants are indicated by their external form, and that botanical affinities are identical with medicinal analogies, is perhaps not now to be ascertained. Whether it originated in actual observation, or was the result of a theoretical view of the properties of organised matter, is equally uncertain. It is generally said to have originated with CAMERARIUS, a monk of Tubingen, in 1699. But the opinion is, doubtless, of much higher antiquity, and it may be, even, after all, nothing more than an emanation from that barbarous school which judged of the virtues of plants by their mere form, colour, or texture. I find it clearly enunciated in BAPTISTA PORTA's Phytognomica, published in 1588. "Ex partium similitudine compares virtutes cognoscuntur," says this old botanist, who seems thus to have distinctly expressed the scientific application of botany to materia medica. He was followed from time to time by several German and other physicians, and among them by LINNÆUS, who, in his dissertation upon the properties of plants, expressly declares, "that species of the same genus possess similar virtues; that those of the same natural order are near each other in properties; and that those which belong to the same natural class have also some relation to each other in their sensible qualities." It must be confessed that this was giving the theory a wider application than facts will justify; but, still, the principle, though narrowed in its application, remains undisputed. As the opinions of writers of great names must necessarily be the guide of those who are only entering upon the study of a science, and who consequently can have no opinion of their own, I may add that the same view has been adopted by JUSSIEU, DECANDOLLE, and the younger RICHARD, in France; by VROLIK, CASSEL, and others in Germany; by BARTON in the United States; and especially by M. FEE, whom we must regard as one of the most distinguished of the continental writers on medicinal plants.

There has, in fact, been no opposition to it which deserves to be mentioned, since the middle of the last century. It is true that our own times have witnessed the singular instance of a man unacquainted with the first principles of botany, boldly arraigning the conclusions at which the most learned men of the two last centuries have unanimously arrived, asserting that the laws they have deduced from a laborious and skilful examination of all the facts which bear upon the subject, are a mere tissue of folly and absurdity and bringing again before the public the exploded notions of writers like PLATZ and GLEDITSCH. With such a person I do not feel called upon to enter into a discussion; in fact, there is no common ground between us on which an argument could be constructed. Before a botanist could condescend to reason with such men they must first learn botany. To apply to this case the language of a celebrated Cambridge professor when recently speaking upon another subject,–"it would, indeed, be a vain and idle task to engage in such a controversy, to waste one's breath in the forms of exact reasoning unfitted to the comprehension of our antagonist, to draw our weapons in a combat where victory could gain no honour. It is too much to call upon us to scatter our seed on a soil at once both barren and unreclaimed; it is folly to think that we can in the same hour be stubbing up the thorns and reaping the harvest. The position of such opponents is impregnable, while they remain within the fences of their ignorance, which is to them as a wall of brass; for (as was well said, if I remember right, by Bishop Warburton, of some bustling fanatics of his day), there is no weak side of common sense whereat we may attack them."

The arguments by which the coincidence of botanical affinity and medical properties is supported, have been admirably set forth by Prof. DECANDOLLE.

If we attempt to discover theoretically the origin of the various substances employed in the healing art, we shall mostly find their true source in chemical combinations. When the inquiry relates to medicaments the nature of which is well known, such as salts or acids, the influence of their chemical combination cannot be questioned, since the least change in the proportion of their constituent parts alters the nature of their effects. The same law is to be applied to medicaments of a more compound character, such as those we procure from the vegetable or animal kingdoms. All organic matter is ultimately reducible to a certain number of substances, the chemical composition of which is but little variable, and which, if obtained in a state of purity, uniformly retain their respective properties; thus starch is always nutritive, gum or mucilage always emollient, fixed oil always lubricating, and volatile oil stimulating and aromatic; and so on. Now it is evident that these different elements, mixed in different proportions, will form compounds having new properties, intermediate, perhaps, between those of the substances that form them. We may conceive, moreover, that if, in a great number of cases, we cannot clearly explain the effects of compound medicaments, the impossibility is far less connected with the nature of things than with our own ignorance. But, independently of chemical action, all substances placed in contact with the human body, operate by simple mechanical effects, such as weight, bulk, the asperities or smoothness of the surface, the readiness with which they absorb or part with water, conduct or retain caloric, and so on. Hence, all the effects produced by medicines upon the human body must be referred either to their physical structure or to their chemical composition.

But does not the physical structure, or the chemical composition of a medicine, depend directly upon the organisation of the plant which produces it? and especially of that class of organs which regulate nutrition? Everybody knows that plants growing in exactly the same soil, produce substances entirely different, while, on the contrary, plants of analogous character yield the very same substance, let the soil in which they grow be what it may. Without calling in question the powerful influence exercised by soil on vegetation, it is impossible to suppose that any thing short of inherent special power, in each species, of furnishing its own peculiar products, is the true cause of the diversity of vegetable substances, when we see that if, in the same pot, and the same soil, under a receiver which contains a due quantity of air, we sow side by side two seeds, the one of a yarron, the other of a nettle, the first will after a few days produce a couple of leaves riddled with glands containing essential oil, while the other will bear a number of tubercles filled with a caustic liquid. Is it possible to doubt the powerful influence of the structure of the organs of nutrition, when we see the different parts of a vegetable or an animal contain totally different products, all elaborated from the same sap, or the same chyle?

But it may be objected that if the different substances found in plants are owing to the peculiar action of the organs of nutrition, botanical classifications must also be founded upon the organs of nutrition, if structure and properties are to coincide; and that classifications founded, like those of botanists, upon the organs of fructification cannot harmonise with medicinal virtues. This objection is more specious than sound. In all departments of natural history our systems are of necessity founded upon those parts which present the greatest variety between species and species, and the greatest constancy between individual and individual. Now it matters not what function you take as the basis of a natural classification, for one will lead as well as another to a natural result, provided we thoroughly understand it; functions are never isolated, but always modified and affected by other functions; and in truth no classification can be natural in which every system of organs or of functions is not in harmony. The study of natural affinities is nothing but the observation of the constancy, more or less great, of certain combinations of organs; and, following out that principle, the naturalist places side by side all those beings which possess the greatest number of identical or similar organs, and he separates those which have a smaller number in common; whence it results, that while the perfection of an artificial system consists in reducing the characters of classes to the smallest possible number of ideas, a natural arrangement is, on the other hand, the more perfect, the greater the number of ideas connected with the characters of the classes.

Now, if it be demonstrated that a natural group of plants is an assemblage of species having the greatest number of relations in their organs of reproduction, does not sound theory lead us to infer that such a group would also have the greatest number of relations in their organs of nutrition? Look at animals– their classes are established upon the organs of nutrition, taking that term in its most general sense. Do not these classes correspond with the organs of generation? And in plants facts are equally in harmony with theory. The divisions of mono-cotyledons, dicotyledons, and acotyledons, characterized by the organs of reproduction, are the same as those of endogens, exogens, and acrogens, characterized by the organs of nutrition; and so to so great an extent in the natural orders into which the classes themselves are subdivided, that I doubt very much whether we shall not some day use the organs of nutrition, when they are better understood, in preference to those of reproduction.

But to set theory aside, let us see whether facts do not completely bear me out in the statement that the properties and organisation of plants coincide. The beasts of the field acknowledge the truth of this axiom, in constantly rejecting certain classes of plants, and selecting others. Cattle never touch labiate plants, or those of the digitalis tribe; horses refuse cruciferous plants; cattle, horses, sheep, swine, and goats, avoid everything belonging to the nightshade tribe, while they devour with avidity grasses, leguminous and compound flowered plants. Insects furnish still better examples, for these creatures, although they do not always extend their predilection to all the genera of a natural order, by no means confine themselves to a single species of plant; on the contrary, they always select kindred species, in which an identity, or at least a great analogy, of properties is found. The turnip-fly, for instance, will eat radishes as well as turnips; the *cynips rosæ,* any kind of rose, but nothing of any neighbouring genus; and in the south of Europe, the cantharides, when the ash is defoliated by their attack, transfer their ravages to the lilacs and the olives, all of which are plants of the same natural order. Examples of this sort might be given without end. Let us transfer our consideration to medical plants. It was once thought that Jesuit's bark was furnished by some one species of cinchona; it is now known to be the produce of many species, and that bark of analogous properties is yielded by many plants of the same natural order. Rhubarb was believed to be furnished by some one rheum; no one can now doubt hat it is the produce of many distinct species; and our very docks, botanically allied to rhubarb in a close degree, are found to participate in its properties. It was ascertained that one of the kinds of ipecacuanha was furnished by a Brazilian violet; upon experimenting upon the violets of Europe, these roots were found to be emetic likewise. All malvaceous plants are emollient, all cruciferous plants antiscorbutic, all of the poppy tribe narcotic, all the gentian tribe febrifugal, all the euphorbia tribe acrid and purgative, all the ranunculus tribe caustic and dangerous.

Upon evidence of this kind, then, it would be useless to dwell at greater length. We will next consider what the value is of some plausible objection that may be made to the principle I have been endeavouring to explain. It is said that the *potato,* one of the most common articles of our own diet, and *cassava* an equally common food in South America, are produced by plants belonging to what are called poisonous families; but it is to be recollected that we only consume the amylaceous part of those plants, and there is no such thing known as poisonous fecula. The stems and the leaves of both the potato and cassava are unwholesome; the latter, in fact, dangerous. It may also happen that a poisonous principle is so concentrated in some species as to be strongly marked, and that in others it is so diluted as to produce no appreciable action; this is the case in the cow tree of South America, as contrasted with the poisonous artocarpeæ of the East Indies; or a peculiar secretion, common to all the species of a natural order, may have certain properties which will be absent from all those parts in which the secretion is not formed; as in the poppy, the milky juice of which becomes opium, but whose seeds, in which no milky juice exists, are perfectly inert; or, as in the fig, the fruit of which when ripe is destitute of a juice which is highly poisonous in many species, and very perceptibly acrid in its own leaves.

The peculiar mode of action of particular medicines, when applied to different parts of the body, or, when taken in different doses, is another source of apparent exception to general rules; but this question belongs to materia medica.

To conclude this discussion, I need only add that in 150 natural orders examined by DECANDOLLE in 1816, three orders only were found at variance with these principles; that is to say, containing exceptions which could not then be satisfactorily accounted for, so that the probabilities were 147 to 3 in favour of these exceptions being one day removed.

Having thus explained in what way botany is most directly connected with medicine, my next object will be to initiate you into the manner of understanding what botanical affinities are, and of putting in practice that of which I have thus explained the theory. For this purpose I find it necessary to reject the system of classification once most popular in this country, for it leads to no result, is inapplicable to medical purposes, except empirically, has not event the merit of facility in practice to recommend it, and is wholly unworthy the present state of botanical knowledge.

In its room I shall explain to you the systematic principles which were first distinctly laid down by the immortal RAY, and which his countrymen have not only had the folly to neglect, but the ingratitude to forget so completely, that to this very hour they have not found out that the honour of founding the school of philosophical botany belongs to England, and not to France.

1730.

Miss Drake. del.   Pub. by J. Ridgway 169 Piccadilly, Jan. 1. 1835.   J. Watts. sc.

Part IV

Lindley's Life-Long Love Affair with Orchids

Phillip Cribb

"If we are requested to select the most interesting from the multitude of vegetable tribes, we should, on the whole, perhaps, be willing to give the preference to the natural order of Orchideae. Whether we consider general elegance of individuals, durability of blossoms, splendid colours, delicious perfume, or extraordinary structure, it would be difficult to select any order superior to Orchideae in these respects, and few even equal to them."

John Lindley, *Collectanea Botanica* (1821)

COLOUR PLATE 18 (Opposite). *Acanthephippium bicolor* Lindley. Coloured engraving by S.A. Drake in *Botanical Register* 20: pl. 1730 (1835)

COLOUR PLATE 19 (Above). *Anneliesia candida* (Lindley) Brieger & Lueckel *(Miltonia candida* Lindley). Coloured lithograph by S.A. Drake in Lindley, *Sertum orchidaceum*, pl. 21 (1838)

This fulsome paeon of praise, from the pen of John Lindley at the tender age of twenty-two, is as clear a declaration of love at first sight as any given by any botanist. Appropriately it was the introductory statement to Lindley's first published account on a group to which he devoted much of the rest of his working life. Lindley's declaration accompanied the illustration of *Trizeuxis falcata*, ironically perhaps one of the dullest of all tropical orchids.

Orchids are the largest family of flowering plants (some argue that Compositae are as large or larger), one in ten plant species being an orchid. This is not necessarily obvious to Europeans or North Americans where orchids are relatively few in number and often considered to be rarities. Orchids are predominantly tropical or subtropical in distribution, the temperate regions of Europe and North America being comparatively poor in orchid diversity. For example, there are nearly three times as many orchids recorded from Hong Kong as from the British Isles, and the island of Borneo has as many orchids as the British Isles have vascular plants. The expansion of the British Empire occurred mainly in the tropics and subtropics, in India, South-east Asia, the West Indies and Guyana, and in Africa, opening these orchid-rich areas to the enquiring minds of explorers, administrators, missionaries, and traders. They sent back these strange and beautiful plants to England in increasing numbers, especially from 1820 onwards.

Back in England, increasing wealth, generated by expanding foreign markets and the Industrial Revolution, allowed the landed gentry to indulge in hobbies, growing rare plants being one of the most popular and prestigious. Orchids found immediate favour for their exotic origins and startlingly beautiful flowers. Growing and flowering them successfully was a challenge taken up throughout the land. Even some members of the Royal Family grew orchids; as early as 1783 we find that thirteen exotic species were being grown at the Royal Botanic Gardens, Kew (Aiton, 1789), no doubt delighting Princess Augusta and her son King George III. Royal patronage further stimulated interest in growing orchids, creating a demand for them that only the opening up of the tropics and subtropics to plant collectors could satisfy.

Lindley's interest in orchids was timely. It lasted a lifetime and started when tropical orchids were a rarity in the collections of a few rich men but extended to the period when they became established as one of the most desirable of all groups in cultivation, indeed a mania that all but rivalled tulipomania of the previous century in the Netherlands.

His orchid interests covered primarily their taxonomy and classification but also other aspects such as their cultivation and uses. The early influence of his father and his position as Assistant Secretary at the Horticultural Society of London no doubt stimulated his interest in orchid cultivation but as a taxonomist he needed to see the flowers of orchids that were being imported as non-flowering living plants. Far too many perished in their first few days in cultivation in the stove greenhouses then favoured for their cultivation. Lindley, through his official positions and more importantly because of his immense written output, was the dominant figure in the orchid world for over forty years until his death, the acknowledged expert on the subject to whom all others deferred. He knew and corresponded with all of the leading botanists of the day, and received orchids, both living and preserved, from a legion of correspondents.

Early influences

Lindley received patronage in his early botanical endeavours from three pivotal figures, William Hooker, Joseph Banks, and William Cattley. As a boy in Norwich he made friends with William Hooker, later to become Professor of Botany at Glasgow and subsequently the first official Director of the Royal Botanic Gardens, Kew. Hooker was a plantsman and botanist of wide interests, orchids being one of his favourite groups. He wrote accounts of a number of species when editor of *Curtis's Botanical Magazine*.

In 1821 Sir Joseph Banks employed John Lindley to assist Robert Brown in the curation of Banks's herbarium and library, remaining there for eighteen months until Sir Joseph's death. Banks and his wife grew orchids at Spring Grove, their home in Isleworth across the River Thames from Kew, experimenting with different methods of growing them to improve the survival of plants that often rapidly died in cultivation. More significant perhaps was Lindley's contact with Robert Brown, a meticulous and brilliant botanist. Brown and the botanical artist Ferdinand Bauer had accompanied Matthew Flinders on his circumnavigation of Australia from 1801 to 1803, collecting herbarium specimens of hundreds of the peculiar orchids of that continent and describing them in his seminal *Prodromus Florae Novae Hollandiae* (1810); here he established twenty new genera. We can imagine the impact on Lindley of Bauer's beautiful drawings of the weird and wonderful Australian orchids. Viewing these today in their folders at the Natural History Museum in London, one can easily relive Lindley's wonder at Nature's exuberance and intricacy.

The third influence on Lindley provided much needed money and access to living orchids in one of the finest living collections of plants in the country. This was owned by William Cattley of High Barnet, just north of London, a merchant with many business contacts, particularly with Russia through his cousin John Prescott in St Petersburg. Cattley employed the young Lindley in 1822 to illustrate and describe choice plants in his collection. *Collectanea Botanica*, which began to appear in 1821, marks the start of Lindley's publications on orchids.

From 1826 onwards Lindley was in an ideal position as Assistant Secretary at the Horticultural Society's garden to be the first to see many of the increasing

COLOUR PLATE 20. *Bollea violacea* (Lindley) Rchb.f. *(Huntleya violacea* Lindley). Type sheet in Lindley Herbarium, Kew, with drawing by S.A. Drake for Lindley, *Sertum orchidaceum*, pl. 26 (1830)

110

COLOUR PLATE 21a. *Brassavola nodosa* (L.) Lindley. Coloured engraving by S.A. Drake in
Botanical Register 18: pl. 1465 (1832)

number of new orchids coming into the country. In part these resulted from the efforts of the Horticultural Society's own collectors, notably Carl Theodor Hartweg in Mexico, a country rich in spectacular orchids of horticultural merit. It also put him into contact with most of the orchid growers in the British Isles, and it soon became natural for them to send flowers and plants to Lindley for identification.

An impressive debut

The *Collectanea Botanica*, Lindley's debut as a botanist, was published in fascicles between 1821 and 1825. It contains the descriptions and illustrations of seventeen tropical orchids. Lindley described four new orchid genera *Trizeuxis, Eria, Coelogyne* and *Cattleya* here for the first time, the last a worthy and lasting dedication to his patron William Cattley. *Cattleya labiata* (t.33, Colour Plates 7 and 24), the type species and one of the finest of all orchids, is a native of the coastal forests of Brazil. Swainson had sent it from Brazil to William Hooker and Cattley flowered it in his stove in November 1820. Its description marks perhaps the start of the mania for collecting and growing orchids that swept nineteenth century England, with growers eager to secure other novelties that might match or even surpass this magnificent plant. A second Brazilian species, *Cattleya loddigesii* (t.37), commemorated the nursery of Conrad Loddiges at Hackney in London which was pre-eminent in orchid cultivation during the first forty years of the century

The orchids in *Collectanea Botanica* came from many countries: *Vanda (Acampe) multiflora* (t.38) and *Vanda (Cleisostoma) teretifolia* (t.6) from China; *Goodyera pubescens* (t.25) from North America; *Dendrobium polystachyum (Polystachya concreta)* (t.20) and *Ionopsis utricularioides* (t.39A) from the West Indies; *Cypripedium (Paphiopedilum) insigne* from India; *Oncidium barbatum* (t.27) from Brazil: and *Tribrachia (Bulbophyllum) reptans* (t.41A) and *Eria stricta* (t.41B) from Nepal.

Equally as diverse were the nurseries and growers that supplied Lindley with flowering orchids. Apart from Cattley, we find acknowledgement of plants from William Hooker, the Horticultural Society at Chiswick, Mr Brookes' nursery at Newington Green, Robert Barclay, and Messrs Loddiges.

Lindley's Orchid Herbarium

Lindley's work on orchids was underpinned by his herbarium collection amassed over a period of some forty years. Mounted on herbarium sheets that are slightly larger than the standard Kew ones, the 7,000 or so specimens of this herbarium were the foundation of Lindley's impressive knowledge of the family and remain pivotal for modern taxonomic research on orchids, akin to Linnaeus's *Species Plantarum* as the starting point for the orchid specialist's studies. Lindley's orchids were separated from the rest of his herbarium after his death in 1865, and came to Kew where they remain to the present day: the rest of his herbarium is at the Botany School in Cambridge. The cupboards containing the blue folders of herbarium specimens (Colour Plates 20, 22 and 24) of John Lindley's orchids are one of the most frequently visited parts of Kew's renowned Herbarium. That Kew acquired this collection can be traced to the fascination for orchids of both the elder and the younger Hooker. On Lindley's death in 1865 Joseph Hooker urged his father to purchase Lindley's orchid specimens and his father speedily took his advice.

The reason why Joseph Hooker coveted Lindley's orchids lies in the wealth of specimens that Lindley accumulated from around the world, particularly the many type specimens in the collection. Over a forty year period Lindley managed to 'corner the market' in orchids. At the critical period, when knowledge of tropical orchids was expanding exponentially, Lindley was in his prime and was virtually unchallenged as the authority on orchids. Botanists following in his wake had to heed what Lindley had achieved and, therefore, access to his collection was critical.

Lindley's orchid herbarium formed the basis for his prodigious publications on the family. It contains many significant collections: orchids collected by Cuming in the Philippines; Nathaniel Wallich in India and Nepal; Thomas Lobb in Java and Borneo; Hugh Low in Borneo; Joseph Hooker in Sikkim; Jean Linden, Funck and Schlim in the Andes; and Allan Cunningham, Ferdinand von Mueller, Gunn and Drummond in Australia. Lindley's many horticultural contacts are also mirrored in his herbarium where there are the flowers sent to him for identification by the Duke of Devonshire, James Bateman, Rucker, Clowes, The Horticultural Society at Chiswick, and many others. The majority of these specimens are types, mostly of Lindley's own new species.

Something of Lindley's method can be seen from an examination of the contents of the blue folders. First of all he collected the pertinent literature on the genus and arranged it by species on herbarium sheets at the start of each genus. The herbarium sheets were subsequently arranged in numbered sequence, reflecting his treatment of that genus in *The Genera and Species of Orchidaceous Plants* or in *Folia Orchidacea*. Many specimens are accompanied by his own clear black and white ink drawings of a flower and floral dissections. Often where the material came from a cultivated source these are coloured. Coloured lithographs, or in a few cases original watercolours of Miss Drake's illustrations from the *Botanical Register,* also accompany many specimens. Lindley appears to have given generous access to his collection. H.G. Reichenbach, who eventually succeeded Lindley as the world's leading orchid expert, for one recorded a six week visit to Lindley, and his subsequent ability 'to work with great security, knowing pretty well the Lindleyan materials' (Gardener, 1965). He attended Lindley's funeral.

COLOUR PLATE 21b. *Bulbophyllum weberi* Ames *(Cirrhopetalum thouarsii* Lindley, 1838). Coloured engraving by S.A. Drake in *Botanical Register* 24: pl. 11 (1838)

COLOUR PLATE 22. *Catasetum barbatum* (Lindley) Lindley *(Myanthus barbatus* Lindley), male flowers. Type sheet in Lindley Herbarium, Kew

Describing the orchids

Lindley's prodigious energy allowed him to keep abreast of orchid introductions for nearly half a century, publishing accounts of new species and genera, often within months of their introduction and first flowering. There were both scientific and commercial imperatives for this. The novelties provided Lindley with a better understanding of orchid morphology and diversity leading to better and more detailed classifications. On the commercial side, the nurseries such as Loddiges and latterly Veitch and Linden needed names for the plants they were collecting and selling. The nurseries employed collectors, often merchants such as George Ure Skinner in Guatemala or diplomats such as Hugh Low in Borneo, to send them plants. They also started to send out their own professional collectors such as Thomas Lobb to Java and Borneo and Hugh Cuming to the Philippines, a trend that grew through the Victorian era, until by the 1890s Frederick Sander could boast that he had twenty-three active collectors in the field at one time. Novelties, especially attractive ones, fetched high prices in the auction rooms. Lindley was an important part of this network identifying newly imported plants merely for the price of a dried specimen in his own collection.

Perhaps the most important collection examined by Lindley was that of the East India Company, usually called the Wallich Herbarium after Nathaniel Wallich who collected much of it and organized it in Calcutta where he was Superintendant of the East India Company's Botanic Garden from 1815 until 1828. It was shipped to England in 1832, and lodged at the Linnean Society until transferred to Kew in 1913. Duplicates of Wallich's collections had, however, begun to be distributed in London from about 1825 onwards by the East India Company. Although David Don was the first botanist to look at the orchids, describing a number of them, by far the majority were described by Lindley, and a complete set of Wallich's orchid specimens can be found in his herbarium. Lindley often took up Wallich's manuscript names and his descriptions of them appear in his *Genera and Species of Orchidaceous Plants* (1830–1840). Wallich's Herbarium was, at the time, the largest and most complete tropical herbarium seen in Europe. It included not only plants from India, but also from Nepal, Burma, Singapore, and Java. Significant elements included those of Wallich from Nepal (1820), Singapore (1821), and Uttar Pradesh and Garwhal (1825); J.G. Koenig from Madras; Thomas Horsfield from Java; John Forbes Royle from Saharanpur and the Himalayas; J. Prince from Singapore; John Reeves from Canton, and many others. It provided the basis for our knowledge of the flora of the subcontinent.

Another important collection examined by Lindley was that made by the Belgian collectors Jean Linden, Funck and Louis Schlim in Venezuela and Colombia. Linden later founded in Ghent a famous nursery specialising in tropical orchids. Amongst the 143 species listed in Lindley's *Orchidaceae Lindenianae* (846) were many of supreme horticultural merit such as *Odontoglossum luteo-purpureum, Oncidium falcipetalum, Masdevallia coccinea,* and *Uropedium (=Phragmipedium) lindenii.* Lindley gave an account of sixty species of orchid from Western Australia in his *A Sketch of the Vegetation of the Swan River Colony* (1839), published as an Appendix to the *Botanical Register.* An additional forty-seven Australian orchids were listed in his *Plantae Muellerianae* (1853), and eighty, of which twenty-one were new, in his *A List of Orchidaceous Plants collected in the East of Cuba by Mr. C. Wright* (1858).

Lindley's last significant contribution to orchid taxonomy was his *Folia Orchidacea* (1852-1858), an attempt to monograph the family, a genus at a time. I doubt if any taxonomist would even consider such a task today, the sheer number of genera and species is too great. Lindley published accounts of forty-two genera and 1343 species over a five-year period. He mono-graphed several large and complex genera including *Oncidium* (209 species), *Epidendrum* (310 species) and *Pleurothallis* (280 species). As he pointed out some of these were ten times the size they were when he started working on *The Genera and Species of Orchidaceous Plants* in 1830. Completing the task, even then, was beyond the capabilities of any one man. Fritz Kraenzlin, another who attempted the task, published only the first volume of his *Orchidearum Genera et Species* (1897-1901), completing only the slipper orchids and Orchidoideae, before giving up.

Classifying the orchids

The classification of a large family such as orchids is difficult at the best of times, a result not only of the size of the family but also their complexity and diversity. Few botanists have had the time and access to a broad enough spectrum of orchid specimens to be able to make sense of them. Our understanding of the family is still evolving as we learn more about them. Recently, for example, analysis of molecular data has led to fresh insights on the delimitation of subfamilies, tribes and genera in the orchids. When Lindley first became interested in orchids, only the European orchids were at all well known. However, these are peripheral to the understanding of the family which is predominantly tropical in its distribution. The rapid influx of orchids from around the world, especially after 1820, gave Lindley unprecedented access to new species and genera that enabled him to assess carefully the work of previous authors. What were his primary sources?

In his *Species Plantarum*, Linnaeus (1753) had classified the orchids in his Class XX Gynandria (stamens adnate to the pistil) Diandrae (with two stamens). Olof Swartz (1800), who had greatly increased our knowledge of West Indian orchids by providing detailed descriptions of both plants and flowers, distinguished

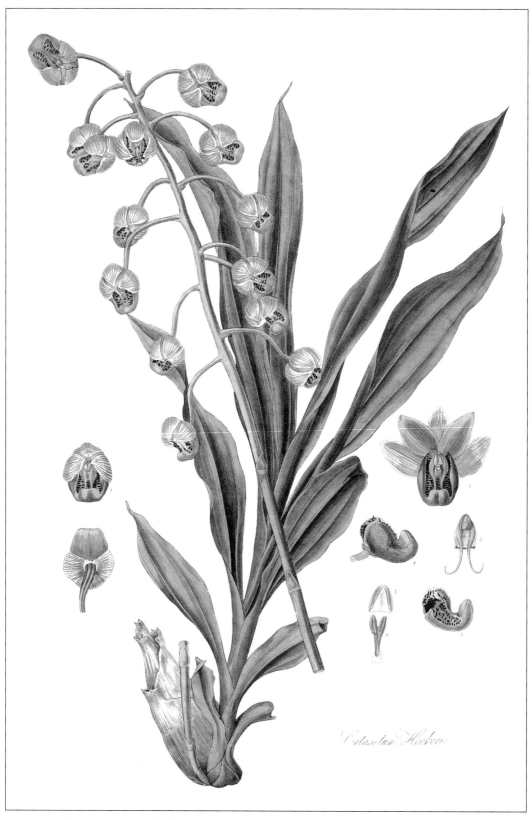

COLOUR PLATE 23. *Catasetum hookeri* Lindley, male flowers. Coloured engraving by W.J. Hooker in Lindley, *Collectanea botanica*, pl. 40 (1825)

COLOUR PLATE 24. *Cattleya labiata* Lindley. Type sheet in Lindley Herbarium, Kew

those orchids with a single anther (twenty-four genera) from those with two anthers (*Cypripedium*). Robert Brown (1810), Lindley's early mentor and later protagonist, coined the term *Monandrae* for the first group. He described twenty-six genera and 113 species of Australian orchids in his account of the plants he had discovered on Flinders' circumnavigation of the continent. The French botanist L.C. Richard (1818) provided a new terminology for the morphology of the orchid flower, emphasising the importance of the pollen in classification. Finally Carl Blume (1825) described many Javanese orchids and provided a classification of them based on pollen type: granular, powdery, or waxy.

In the Appendix of *Collectanea Botanica* we find Lindley's first published classification of the orchids (Lindley, 1825 reprinted as *Orchidearum Sceletos* in 1826). He recognised there four subfamilies and eight tribes:

Subfamily	Tribe
Neottieae	Neottieae
	Arethuseae
Orchideae	Gastrodieae
	Ophrydeae
Epidendreae	Vandeae
	Epidendreae
	Malaxideae
Cypripedieae	Cypripedieae

He listed 157 genera all but ten 'incerta vel tribis incertae' placed in the eight tribes above.

His *Illustrations of Orchidaceous Plants* (1830-1838), which was illustrated by Francis Bauer, and *The Genera and Species of Orchidaceous Plants* (1830-1840) are arguably his most significant and influential contributions to the study of orchids. The former comprises twenty fine lithographs based on Francis Bauer's illustrations and supplemented by five of Lindley's own drawings. They were made to 'determine both the distinctive characters of the genera, and the anatomy and physiology of the organs of fructification of the singular plants they represent'. Lindley developed his ideas on the floral organs and their homologies in his Prefatory Remarks, and it is possible to follow the development of his ideas through the *Genera and Species* and the three editions of the *Vegetable Kingdom*.

COLOUR PLATE 25. *Cattleya laminatum* Lindley, male flowers. Coloured drawing by S.A. Drake in Lindley Herbarium, Kew. Original of *Sertum orchidaceum*, pl. 38 (1838)

Catasetum laminatum.

COLOUR PLATE 26. *Catasetum macrocarpum* Richard *(Monachanthus viridis* Lindley). Type sheet in Lindley Herbarium, Kew. Female flowers top left and right; female and male flowers bottom left

COLOUR PLATE 27. *Catasetum purum* Nees. Coloured engraving by S.A. Drake in *Botanical Register* 20: pl. 1708 (1834)

Tab. 37

Cattleya Loddigesii.

COLOUR PLATE 28. *Cattleya loddigesii* Lindley. Coloured engraving by Barbara Lawrence in Lindley, *Collectanea botanica,* pl. 37 (1821)

Pl. 22

Cattleya superba

Miss Drake. del.
M. Gauci. lith.
Pub.d by J. Ridgway & Sons, 169, Piccadilly, June 1.st 1838

COLOUR PLATE 29. *Cattleya superba* Lindley. Coloured lithograph by S.A. Drake in Lindley, *Sertum orchidaceum*, pl. 22 (1838)

Tab 6

J. Lindley del.   *Vanda teretifolia*   *W.C. Edwards sc.*

COLOUR PLATE 30. *Cleisostoma simondii* (Gagnepain) Seidenf. *(Vanda teretifolia* Lindley). Coloured engraving by Lindley in Lindley, *Collectanea botanica,* pl. 6 (1821)

COLOUR PLATE 31. *Comparettia coccinea* Lindley. Coloured engraving by S.A. Drake in *Botanical Register* 24: pl. 68 (1838)

Cycnoches chlorochilon.

Alfd Drake del.
M. Gauci lith.

Pub.d by J. Ridgway & Sons 169 Piccadilly Nov.r 1 1838.

Printed by P. Simon

The Genera and Species of Orchidaceous Plants contains descriptions of all the then known orchids numbering some 1980 species in 301 genera, many newly described by Lindley, and a description of the family and classification that remained influential until superseded by that of Bentham & Hooker (1883). Many elements of his classification can still be recognised in present-day classifications of the family.

His introduction details his labours in completing this monumental account which 'proved a most laborious task to examine with the necessary care so large a number of plants of a very intricate structure, in a dried state'. He received orchids from many sources: European from Jacquin, Tineo, Tenore, Bentham, Hornschuch, Talbot and Strangeways; Siberian and northern Asiatic from Prescott, Fischer, Ledebour and Bunge; North American from Menzies, Torrey, Gray, Booth, Douglas, Drummond and William Hooker; Mexican from Karwinski, Deppe, Schiede and Hartweg; Andean species from Mathews, Jameson and Hall; Guyanan from Schomburgk and Martin; Brazilian from Martius, Salzmann, Forbes, Douglas, George Don, Macrae and Gardner; Chilean from Douglas, Cuming, Mathews, Cruckshanks, Bridges, Tweedie and Gillies; North African from Salzmann, Bové and Webb; South African from Drège, Burchell, Harvey and Ecklon; tropical African from George Don; Madagascan from Lyall; tropical Asian from Macrae, Walker, Royle, Wallich, Wight and Griffith; Chinese from Vachell and Reeves; Australian from Brown, Mueller, Allan Cunningham, Drummond and Gunn; and cultivated specimens from many growers but principally Messrs. Loddiges, James Bateman and George Barker.

Based on his extensive examination of orchids from every corner of the world, Lindley was able to describe the family in detail, placing it between the Apostasiaceae (which he considered a distinct family) and the Burmanniaceae, and these in turn between Iridaceae and Zingiberaceae. He recognised seven tribes in the family Orchidaceae (a term coined by him to replace the older Orchideae). These are the Malaxeae, Epidendreae, Vandeae, Ophreae (or Ophrydeae), Arethuseae, Neotteae, and Cypripedeae. In classifying orchids he maintained that 'the most important characters appear to reside in the pollen, which in many is consolidated into *firm waxy masses* of a definite number, and in others is either in its usual *loose powdery* condition, or is collected in *granules* or *small wedges* the number of which is far too great to be counted'.

He discounted the *Apostasia* and its relatives as orchids; although most contemporary authors include them it remains a matter of disagreement to the present day. He thought that 'their relation [to orchids] does not appear to be greater than to either of the two [Iridaceae and Zingiberaceae] now mentioned;... It may, however, be observed that Apostasia has apparently as

COLOUR PLATE 32. *Cycnorchis chlorochilon* Lindley. Coloured lithograph by S.A. Drake in Lindley, *Sertum orchidaceum,* pl. 16 (1838)

Mrs. Drake delt.   Pub. by J. Ridgway 169 Piccadilly May 1. 1840   G. Barclay sc

COLOUR PLATE 33. *Cymbidium finlaysonianum* Lindley. Coloured engraving by S.A. Drake in *Botanical Register* 30: pl. 24 (1844)

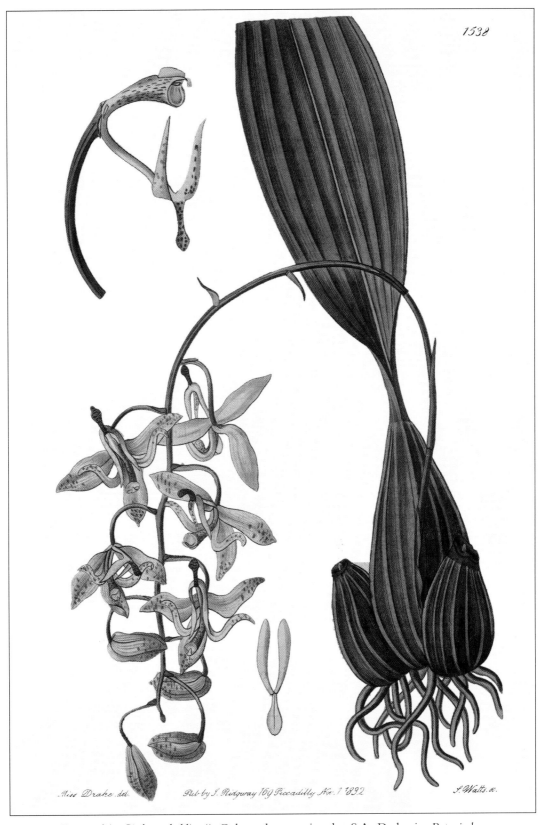

COLOUR PLATE 34. *Cirrhaea loddigesii*. Coloured engraving by S.A. Drake in *Botanical Register* 18: pl. 1538 (1832)

much claim to be regarded as a diandrous monadelphous Amaryllidaceous plant allied to Hypoxideae and standing, perhaps, in the same relation to that order as Gillesia to Liliaceae, as it has to be regarded as a trilocular Orchidaceous plant with the gynandrous organisation lost.'

Swartz 1800 Orchider med en anthera	Brown 1810 Monandrae sect.II	Blume 1825 Tribe II Granulosae	Lindley 1825 Neottieae	Lindley 1853 Neotteae
			Arethuseae	Arethuseae (incl. Gastrodieae)
	Monandrae sect.IV		Gastrodieae	
	Monandrae sects.I,II,III	Tribe III Pulvereae	Ophrydeae	Ophrydeae
	Monandrae sect.IV		Vandeae	Vandeae
		Tribe I Cereaceae	Epidendreae	Epidendreae
			Malaxideae	Malaxeae
Orchider med tuå anthere	Diandrae	Diantherae (include. Apostasia)	Cypripedieae	Cypripedeae

Lindley often changed his mind about the relationships of flowering plants in his natural classifications and this is reflected in his various publications on the Natural System of Classification. This is scarcely true of his treatment of orchids. His classification of 1853 at the tribal level scarcely differs from his earlier ones of the family. However, his treatment of the Cypripedieae (slipper orchids), as a separate family alongside Apostasieae and Orchideae in his Cohors II: Gynandreae his *Nixus Plantarum* (1833), and of Vanillaceae as a separate family in the second edition of his *Natural System of Botany* in 1836, are exceptions. By the time his *Genera and Species of Orchidaceous Plants* was completed they had resumed their place amongst the orchids.

Orchid illustrations

Lindley was a competent botanical artist as his early publications and the many sketches in his herbarium attest. He provided several of the plates for *Collectanea Botanica*, including those of *Trizeuxis falcata* (t.2), flowered by Cattley in 1820, and *Vanda (Aerides) multiflora* (t.38), flowered by Cattley in 1822.

Lindley was fortunate to work with two of the finest botanical artists of his generation: Francis (Franz) Bauer and Miss Sarah Drake. Bauer's detailed work provided the inspiration for Lindley and Bauer's *Illustrations of Orchidaceous Plants*, Lindley's contribution being the text and seven drawings based upon Bauer's sketches. One of the most striking is the colourful rendering of the transverse section of the ovary of *Bletia (Phaius) tancarvilleae* (Fructification t.IX).

On taking over the editorship of *Edwards' Botanical Register* he contributed, between 1824 and 1832, a number of orchid illustrations. Notable amongst these are *Catasetum macrocarpum* (t.840) in 1824, *Oncidium divaricatum* (t.1050) in 1827, and *Sophronia (Sophronitis) cernua* (t.1129) in 1828. However, he could not possibly have continued to illustrate orchids and write the text for the *Botanical Register* unaided. Fortunately, he obtained the services of a Norfolk artist, Miss Sarah Drake, who became the main artist for the *Botanical Register* from the late 1820s until its demise in 1847. Miss Drake also contributed about half of the plates for James Bateman's monumental *Orchidaceae of Mexico and Guatemala* (1837-1843), perhaps the most renowned and sought-after of all orchid books.

Few of Miss Drake's original watercolour paintings of orchids survive, the notable exception being the originals for Lindley's *Sertum Orchidaceum* (1837-1842). These are at Kew, and were formerly part of the Lindley Herbarium but have now been included in Kew's collection of botanical illustrations. They were drawn in sepia ink but few are fully coloured, having been prepared as templates for lithography, but the sheer quality of her artistry shines through (see Colour Plate 20). The *Sertum Orchidaceum*, subtitled 'a wreath of the most beautiful orchidaceous flowers', is Lindley's finest illustrated work on orchids, bringing together forty-nine plates of the highest quality and a splendid frontispiece in which eight orchid species are depicted. This and all but ten of the plates are the work of Miss Drake. The other plates were the work of seven botanists, collectors and artists. William Griffith drew plate 8, a composite of the Indian species *Oberonia griffithiana*, *O. rufilabris* and *Drymoda picta*. Descourtilz supplied three plates: *Cyrtochilum stellatum* (= *Miltonia flavescens*) (t.5), *Cattleya bicolor* and *Sophronitis grandiflora* (= *S. cernua*) (t.7), and *Leptotes serulata* (t.11); Richard Schomburgk supplied sketches for four plates; *Schomburgkia undulata* (t.10), *S. marginata* (t.13), *Sobralia liliastrum* (t.29), and *Diothonea* (= *Maxillaria*) *imbricata* (t.40). Miss Mearns drew *Miltonia clowesii* (t.34), and Mrs Powell drew *Houlletia brocklehurstiana* (t.43).

Sertum Orchidaceum does not compare with some of Lindley's other publications for its scientific merit although a number of new species are described in it. However, it does contain an important and often overlooked account of the 101 species then known of the tropical American genus *Oncidium*.

COLOUR PLATE 35. *Dendrobium chrysanthum* Wallich ex Lindley. Coloured engraving by Lindley in *Botanical Register* 15: pl. 1299 (1830)

Pl. 45.

Epidendrum vitellinum.

COLOUR PLATE 36. *Encyclia vitellina* (Lindley) Dressler *(Epidendrum vitellinum* Lindley). Coloured lithograph by S.A. Drake in Lindley, *Sertum orchidaceum,* pl. 45 (1841)

The cultivation of orchids

'To the cultivator who esteems plants for their beauty only; to the botanist, who rejecting outward attractions, is chiefly captivated by anomalous structure, or intricate organisation; or to the amateur, who wisely prefers these requisites combined; to all, or any of these, we conceive that accurate figures of foreign Orchidaceous plants cannot fail to be acceptable.'

John Lindley in *Illustrations of Orchidaceous Plants* (1830)

Lindley had inherited from his father a knowledge of horticulture but his recommendations on the cultivation of tropical orchids have long been considered to have led to the death of countless orchids. He was a great advocate of the stove house cultivation of orchids: in the B*otanical Register* (sub t. 1699) of 1835 he wrote: 'It is well known that the most considerable part of the Epiphytal Orchideae is found in the greatest vigour in damp sultry woods of tropical countries; and accordingly we endeavour in our artificial cultivation, to form an atmosphere for them as nearly as possible that which they would naturally breathe in such stations.'

However, he did admit that some orchids, 'a considerable minority', did not thrive in such conditions, citing amongst others *Oncidium nubigenum* found 'only on the cool mountains of Peru at 14,000 feet', *Dendrobium moniliforme* from Japan, and *Dendrobium aemulum* and *Cymbidium canaliculatum* from open dry forests near Port Jackson (Sydney) in Australia. He concluded with the sagacious comment that: 'These remarks will we trust suffice to cause a greater degree of attention being paid to the differences of constitution of particular species of Orchideous Epiphytes: for although we have only cited extreme cases, we may be assured that minor peculiarities, which it is not less important to study, exist in abundance.' Later he praised the success of his friend Joseph Paxton in growing orchids at lower temperatures.

Lindley's accounts of orchids in the *Botanical Register* nearly always contain notes on their provenance and cultivation, an invaluable guide to the many growers who subscribed to the journal.

Lindley officiated at the birth of one of the most far-reaching events in orchid horticulture in 1858 when he described *Calanthe* x *Dominyi*, the first artificial orchid hybrid. The cross between *Calanthe furcata (= C. triplicata)* and *C. masuca* had been raised and flowered in October 1856 by John Dominy, the 'indefatigable and very excellent' foreman for Messrs. James Veitch & Sons of Chelsea. Realising the implications for generic delimitation and nomenclature in orchids, Lindley is reported to have exclaimed to Veitch 'Why, you will drive the botanists mad'.

Lindley and Darwin

Charles Darwin was intrigued by orchids: 'You cannot conceive how the Orchids have delighted me' (letter to Joseph Hooker, 27 July 1861). His study of their pollination occupied much of his time in the two years following the publication of his *Origin of Species* in 1860. It seems strange that Darwin and Lindley corresponded so little on orchids, particularly as Darwin held Lindley's work in high esteem. Only two letters from Darwin to Lindley concern orchids. The first on 18 October 1861 is worth quoting:

> I have been extremely interested with Catasetum [a tropical American orchid], and indeed with many exotic Orchids, which I have been looking at in aid of an opusculus, on the fertilisation of British Orchids. I very much fear that in publishing I am doing a rash act; but Orchids have interested me more than almost anything in my life. Your work shows that you carefully understand that feeling!

The second letter of 1 November 1861, concerns the origins of the labellum and whether it is compound or not. Lindley had originally considered the petals and lip of orchids to be modified stamens, Brown thought the lip to be a fused petal and anther. Lindley (1853) later modified his views to conform more closely with those of Brown.

I am convinced that the slight correspondence resulted from Darwin's close contact with Joseph Hooker who not only encouraged Darwin's investigations of native orchid pollination but sent him living flowers of many exotic orchids from the Kew collection for his studies. Darwin, therefore, had little reason to bother Lindley who was well known to be exceedingly busy with his duties at the Horticultural Society, his lecturing duties at London University, and his editorial and authorial commitments.

Darwin had asked Joseph Hooker, on 11 August 1861, if he might borrow Francis Bauer and Lindley's *Illustrations of Orchidaceous Plants* (1830-1838). In this fine publication Lindley used Bauer's detailed illustrations of orchids made between 1791 and 1832 to determine the 'distinctive characters of genera, and the anatomy and physiology of the organs of fructification'.

Lindley had fallen out with Robert Brown, his sometime mentor, in 1830 following the publication of Lindley's *An Introduction to the Natural System of Botany*. The acrimonious split between Lindley and Robert Brown lasted until the latter's death. A reviewer suggested that the wording of the Introduction cast doubt on Brown's integrity by implying that his insights into orchid morphology and classification were the result of Bauer's detailed illustrations which had not been acknowledged. The offending passage is as follows: 'Should the reader take an interest in such investigations [of the chronology of

COLOUR PLATE 37. *Galeandra batemannii* Rolfe *(G. baueri* Lindley). Coloured engraving by S.A. Drake in *Botanical Register* 26: pl. 49 (1840)

COLOUR PLATE 38. *Galeandra devoniana* Lindley. Coloured lithograph by S.A. Drake in Lindley, *Sertum orchidaceum*, pl. 37 (1840)

COLOUR PLATE 39. *Paphiopedilum insigne* (Lindley) Pfitzer. *(Cypripedium insigne* Wallich ex Lindley). Coloured engraving by J. Curtis in Lindley, *Collectanea botanica*, pl. 32 (1821)

COLOUR PLATE 40. *Renanthera coccinea* Loueiro. Coloured engraving by A. Hart in *Botanical Register* 14: pl. 1131 (1828)

Pl. 20

Stanhopea Wardii

COLOUR PLATE 41. *Stanhopea wardii* Lindley. Coloured lithograph by S.A. Drake in Lindley, *Sertum orchidaceum*, pl. 20 (1838)

discoveries of orchid structure, physiology and anatomy] I refer him to the dates of Mr Bauer's drawings, and by comparing them with the dates of other publications he can judge for himself to what amount of credit this most admirable and original observer is entitled.'

Reading this I think most would regard it as a comment on Bauer's abilities and original observations rather than as a criticism directed at anyone in particular, but it was so taken by Brown who demanded a written apology from Lindley. Lindley thought that as he had intended no slight, no apology was necessary and indeed none was forthcoming. From that time onwards his relations with Brown deteriorated.

Darwin was intrigued by the tropical American orchids with unisexual flowers. Lindley had originally described three distinct genera: *Catasetum, Myanthus* and *Monachanthus* based on specimens collected in the tropical Americas. In the *Botanical Register* (under t.1951) of 1837, he described a plant sent to him by The Duke of Devonshire in November of the previous year which was a *Myanthus cristatus* changing into *Monachanthus viridis* and combining the features of both those genera and *Catasetum*. He reminded readers that he had written about a similar plant in the notes on *Catasetum cristatum* (t.966) in 1826. Both Richard Schomburgk and Mr Hillhouse had reported the same from Demarara (Guyana). In conclusion Lindley admitted being mistaken and reunited the three genera in *Catasetum*, considering the other two forms freaks or monstrous forms. It was left to Darwin to elucidate the nature of the three forms of *Catasetum*. By careful examination and experimentation on flowers sent to him by Joseph Hooker he affirmed that *Myanthus* was the male flower, *Catasetum* the female, and *Monachanthus* the hermaphrodite form. According to Oakes Ames, Darwin's hermaphrodite form was really the normal form of *Catasetum barbatum*.

The Botanical Register and Gardeners' Chronicle

Lindley's editorship of these two influential journals provided him with vehicles for the rapid publication of new species and genera of orchids and for his views on other orchid matters such as cultivation.

Genera such as *Aeranthes* (t.817), *Pholidota* (t.1206), and *Chysis* (t.1937) were first described in the *Botanical Register*. From 1836 onwards Lindley occasionally added short synopses of orchid genera of interest, for example, *Ionopsis* (after t.1904), *Oncidium* (after t.1920), and *Burlingtonia* (after t.1927).

Control of these journals must have satisfied his driving demon to publish knowledge quickly. His scathing attacks on Robert Brown in later life were fuelled by his opinion that Brown failed to publish information on important collections, such as the Horsfield material from Java, thereby seriously impeding advancement of scientific knowledge.

Conclusion

Lindley certainly dominated orchid science for over forty years from 1820. Because of his influential position at the Horticultural Society, he effectively cornered the market in access to the new orchidaceous discoveries that poured into Britain in increasing numbers during this period. This coupled with his prolific writing and publication on the subject ensured that others naturally deferred to his opinion on orchids during his lifetime. His taxonomic work on orchids has survived well the test of time. It is still possible to see the skeleton of Lindley's classification in modern classifications of the family. Many of the new genera he established survive enlarged but essentially unchanged today. Many of his new species are now well-known greenhouse favourites or the parents of modern orchid hybrids. His carefully assembled and well-curated herbarium, and its types, which is probably the most frequently consulted of all Kew's many collections, has been freely available to *bona fide* researchers ever since his death in 1865. This contrasts dramatically with the fate of the herbarium of his successor H.G. Reichenbach who placed a covenant on his own herbarium that barred access for twenty-five years following his death in 1889. In fact, because of the First World War, Reichenbach's Herbarium remained unopened in Vienna until 1921. The resulting chaos by this spiteful act is still being unravelled today.

Lindley holds an honoured place in the pantheon of early orchid scientists, and I would venture to say that the claim made by his successors that he was the 'founding father' of orchid taxonomy is fully justified.

Ribes sanguineum?

Part V

John Lindley as a Horticulturist
Christopher D. Brickell

Whilst the botanical achievements of John Lindley, particularly his work on Orchidaceae and his detailed survey of the vegetable kingdom, are well known, his great horticultural competence and knowledge, as well as his far-reaching influence in the horticultural world, are seldom recognised or appreciated nowadays. He combined a practical experience of horticultural methods with a sound understanding of the underlying theoretical principles, which he expounded in his widely esteemed *The Theory and Practice of Horticulture* (1855).

Lindley grew up among plants. His father, George Lindley, was a nurseryman at Catton near Norwich and the author of a *Plan of an Orchard* in 1796 and, with son John as editor, *The Guide to the Orchard and Kitchen Garden* in 1831. The area around Norwich abounded in wildflowers and here he early came to know the East Anglian flora.

At the age of sixteen John Lindley, fresh from the celebrated Norwich Grammar School and set on a horticultural career, spent some time in Belgium obtaining plants and seeds for a nurseryman and seed merchant at Camberwell, but in the next few years devoted himself to studying botany, horticulture and entomology and becoming a skilled botanical artist. He came to the notice of Sir Joseph Banks and in 1819 was appointed as an assistant in Banks' library when only twenty years of age. Two important results of this early endeavour included *Rosarum Monographia* (1820) and *Digitalium Monographia* (1821). The Horticultural Society of London commissioned him to paint roses and larches. Under the patronage of William Cattley he drew and described various plants in cultivation, mostly grown by Cattley, for his *Collectanea botanica* (1821-1925).

Lindley's long official association with the Horticultural Society (later the Royal Horticultural Society) began in 1822 when he was appointed Assistant

Colour Plate 42 (Opposite). *Ribes sanguineum* Pursh. Coloured engraving by Augusta Withers in *Transactions of Horticultural Society of London* 7: pl. 13 (1830)

Secretary of the Society's recently established garden at Chiswick, Middlesex, 'to have superintendence over the collection of plants and all other matters in the Garden and to keep all Accounts, Minutes of Report etc., under the direction of the President and Secretary'. His capacity for hard work and productive enterprise soon became evident. During his forty-one years of service with the Horticultural Society, as Assistant Secretary, Vice-Secretary and eventually Secretary, Lindley was undoubtedly the driving force behind most of the fruitful innovations adopted by successive Councils and very effectively put into practice by him.

Lindley and plant introductions

Early in its history the Council of the Horticultural Society resolved to send collectors abroad to find and introduce plants of garden value following the example of Sir Joseph Banks, a founder of the Society, who as Director of the Royal Garden, Kew sent plant collectors to various parts of the world.

Banks also maintained close links with John Reeves, an ardent gardener and amateur botanist, who as an agent in China of the Hon. East India Company was able to send Chinese plants to England on East India Company ships, an arrangement that began in 1817. These included not only many Chinese azalea, camellia, chrysanthemum and peony cultivars but plants such as *Primula sinensis*, *Wistaria sinensis* and *Prunus serrulata*, which was first described by Lindley in 1830.

In his boyhood Lindley had aspired to become a plant collector himself. His career, however, took a very different path, to the benefit of botany, horticulture and particularly the Horticultural Society. This early ambition he was able to satisfy through his encouragement of others to collect plants on behalf of the Society.

During the first few years after Lindley's appointment the Society sent a number of collectors overseas largely at the suggestion of Joseph Sabine, the Secretary of the Society. These included John Potts who went to Bengal and on to China in 1821 but died of fever a year later, as did John Forbes who was sent to Brazil in January 1822 and then to West Africa where he perished in August 1823. Both collectors had sent back plants of value to gardeners, Potts' contribution including large quantities of seed of *Primula sinensis*, *Callicarpa rubella* and the pale yellow *Hoya pottsii* named in his memory in view of 'the esteem in which he was held by his employers…'.

Lindley was undoubtedly much involved in receiving the collections and ensuring that these valuable introductions were properly cared for and later distributed. He was also very well aware of the hardships suffered by these collectors in search of plants for the Society. In the Society's *Transactions* 6:82 (1824) Lindley commented on Forbes' collections thus: 'The collection… is a good example of what skill and industry can effect. It is notorious that importations of seeds or plants from Rio have of late had so bad a reputation that collectors here universally consider them of little importance. The excellent, but unfortunate young man, however, from whom this was received, succeeded, during a very short residence, in getting together, and safely transmitting an assemblage of living plants, small indeed, but consisting entirely of either novel or extremely rare subjects, and, for its size, certainly one of the best collections ever sent to this country.'

Among many fine plants introduced by Forbes were two orchids described by Lindley, *Aeranthes grandiflora* and *Cattleya forbesii*.

Between 1821 and 1824 the Society employed four other collectors. One of Lindley's early assignments following his appointment was to travel to Liverpool to obtain a consignment of West African bulbs, seeds, plants and herbarium material collected by George Don, who had travelled with Joseph Sabine's brother Edward Sabine on a voyage of investigation to West Africa, the West Indies and Brazil for the Society. Much of his seed germinated well and the resulting plants were grown at the Chiswick garden, many being described as new species by Lindley and Sabine in the Society's *Transactions* for 1823 and 1826.

John Damper Parks, sent by the Society to China in 1823, introduced, together with numerous new chrysanthemum and camellia cultivars, the yellow Banksian rose, whilst James McRae was employed by the Society between 1824 and 1826 to visit Brazil, Chile, Peru and Hawaii. His collections, sent back from various parts during these years, were described as 'very large and of the greatest value to science'.

But for gardeners the most important collector of this period was David Douglas who during the 1820s introduced well over 200 species from his two expeditions to western North America in 1824 and 1829, both outstandingly successful. Previously he had travelled to New York in 1823 to obtain fruit trees and other interesting seed and plants for Chiswick where already some 3,000 fruit trees were grown. He brought back *Mahonia aquifolium* which was cultivated in the Philadelphia area from the Lewis and Clarke expedition of 1804-6 to the Pacific coast. Douglas was then chosen to explore the northwest of America and Canada. One can only imagine Lindley's excitement at the plethora of species, many new to science, that Douglas collected in western North America. Their value for gardens and forestry has been immense. They ranged from magnificent conifers – *Abies grandis, A. procera, Pinus coulteri, P. lambertiana, P. radiata, P. sabiniana* and *Pseudotsuga douglasii* (now *P. menziesii*), to *Garrya elliptica, Ribes sanguineum, Lupinus polyphyllus, Penstemon scouleri* and many familiar annuals, *Eschscholzia californica, Clarkia elegans, Mentzelia lindleyi* and *Limnanthes douglasii* as well as the alpine *Douglasia nivalis* (by some authors now placed in the genus *Androsace*).

Lindley's admiration for David Douglas and his work was well expressed in the *Botanical Register* for 1830 where, in reference to the introduction of *Ribes sanguineum*, he wrote: 'of such importance do we consider it to the embellishment of our gardens, that if the expense incurred by the Horticultural Society in Mr Douglas's voyage had been attended with no other result than the introduction of this species, there would have been no ground for dissatisfaction.' Lindley further praised Douglas by stating: 'It is not the number of objects that a public body or an individual accomplishes, that creates a claim to the public gratitude, so much as their utility; and in this view the gentleman who brought the first live plant of the now common China Rose to England deserves his country's gratitude in a greater degree than all the collectors who sent plants to Kew for the next twenty years. But if we consider that it is not *R. sanguineum* alone that the Horticultural Society has introduced through the same active traveller, but that the gigantic Pines of North-West America, one of which yields timber superior to the finest larch; *Acer macrophyllum*, the wood of which is as much better than our Sycamore as the species is superior in the beauty and amplitude of its foliage; *Gaultheria shallon*, an evergreen shrub of great merit; have all been secured to this country, and distributed in every direction – to say nothing of the beautiful Lupines, Penstemons, Barberries, Oenotheras, and other plants of less moment – when all this, we say, is considered, it is not too much to assert, that this result alone has justified all the expenditure of the Society's Garden from the commencement, and has stamped it with a character of great national utility which nothing but future mismanagement can shake.'

Douglas' final expedition for the Society in 1829 to California, although very productive in plants sent to Chiswick, sadly ended in his tragic death in Honolulu.

Thereafter the Society placed less emphasis on plant introductions for some years, although Theodor Hartweg's collections in Mexico, Guatemala and California in 1837 and from 1846-8 were of considerable importance. These and many fine Californian plants, among them the now ubiquitous *Cupressus macrocarpa, Ceanothus dentatus* and *Zauschneria californica*, were all raised at and then distributed from the Chiswick garden under Lindley's watchful eye. Among his herbarium specimens Lindley found sixty-three new species of Orchidaceae.

1842 was also a very important year for plant introduction as the Treaty of Nanking (Nanjing) was then signed between Britain and China after a long period of unrest. Lindley believed that the time had come to send a further collector to China and as a result the Council on 25 November 1842 'Resolved that the recent Treaty with China having rendered several of its ports accessible to British enterprise under regular protection, it is advisable that the Horticultural Society immediately avail itself of the opportunity thus offered for the introduction to Great Britain of the useful and ornamental plants of that immense Empire'.

Early in 1843 Robert Fortune, another remarkable Scotsman, then super-intendent of the hothouses at Chiswick garden, was chosen to go to China by a committee including Lindley, by now Professor of Botany at University College, London but still employed by the Horticultural Society. John Reeves, who after more than twenty years in China had retired as Inspector of Tea in Canton, was also a member of the selection committee. His unrivalled knowledge of the Chinese and the area near Canton proved invaluable to the almost self-effacing Fortune. He showed himself to be an outstanding collector as well as a man of persistence, integrity and courage with an unsuspected ability to maintain good relations with the Chinese. His opinion of them was, however, far from flattering and his suspicions that he might need firearms (at first not provided for him) were amply justified.

From this first expedition, his only one for the Horticultural Society, Fortune introduced a fine range of ornamental plants, successful in selecting those likely to thrive in Britain as may be judged from his introductions that grace our gardens today. His original remit from Lindley stated that 'in all cases you will bear in mind that hardy plants are of the first importance to the Society and that the value of the plants diminishes as the heat to cultivate them is increased. Aquatics, Orchidaceae, or plants with very handsome flowers are the only exceptions to this rule'. Clearly the cost of heating the glasshouses at Chiswick was as great a drain on finances then as it is in botanic gardens today!

One hundred and fifty years after Fortune sent his collections to Chiswick we still prize as garden plants numerous species that we owe to him and the staff at Chiswick. Who today would be without *Jasminium nudiflorum* in winter or herbaceous plants like *Dicentra spectabilis*, *Platycodon grandiflorus* and the hybrids descended from *Anemone hupehensis* var. *japonica* known as Japanese anemones? We also owe to Robert Fortune such outstanding garden plants as *Viburnum plicatum* f. *plicatum* (var. *sterile*) the Japanese Snowball tree, *V. macrocephalum*, the winter honeysuckle *Lonicera fragrantissima* as well as the Japanese Cedar *Cryptomeria japonica* and numerous cultivars of chrysanthemum and peony.

Lindley deserves to be recognised as an important enabler of plant collectors as it was he who encouraged their efforts, ensured that their plant introductions were grown and distributed after propagation, and described many that proved new to science – and gardens. Certainly had the staff at the Chiswick garden under his direction been less successful in establishing all those introductions, our gardens and those of many other countries around the world would be much the poorer today.

Lindley and horticultural education

In its *Transactions* for 1820 the Horticultural Society made clear its aims included horticultural education. The Society stated that it 'looked forward with confidence to that period when, either by their own increased efforts, or by an aid superior to their own, they may effect an establishment, which shall at once become a National School for the propagation of Horticultural knowledge, and a standard reference for the authenticity of every species of garden produce'. Naturally such a venture had to be based at the Society's garden at Chiswick on thirty-three acres of land leased from the Duke of Devonshire in 1821.

The responsibility for the development of the Chiswick garden inevitably fell on Lindley's shoulders although the real authority lay in the hands of the Secretary, the authoritarian Joseph Sabine. Gradually the facilities at Chiswick increased with extensive collections of ornamentals, fruits and vegetables being acquired from many parts of the world and glasshouses of the latest design being constructed to accommodate tender plants. At that time there was no better place available in the world for the training and education of professional gardeners.

The two-year course quickly established at Chiswick was based on practical work, initially with instruction in each department from what were then termed 'under-gardeners', really foremen. A small library was provided for the thirty-six young men on the course who were officially known as 'labourers' but they were not required to attend lectures.

This course found great favour with enthusiastic young gardeners wishing to progress in the profession and there were many applications from abroad as well as Britain. So much so that in 1826, by which time more than ninety young gardeners had gained admission, Council ruled that 'henceforth there should not be more than three foreigners at one time among the labourers in the Garden without special permission'.

It can be claimed justly that this far-sighted development by the Horticultural Society provided the basis for the whole of future horticultural education in many parts of the world. Obviously Lindley was very much involved in the horticultural education of these young gardeners and under-gardeners who, it appears at his instigation, formed a Mutual Improvement Society in 1828. Council at the time much favoured this development and the Council minutes for December 1828 state that the term 'Labourer' should be replaced by 'Student'. At the same time Council agreed to expend £50 – a large sum then – on books to improve the garden library to benefit the students. The direct descendant of this Mutual Improvement Society is the Lindley Society at Wisley that provides lectures and visits for the students today.

The early success of the course and the calibre of the students trained under Lindley's aegis may be judged by the quality and future careers of many of the students and staff at Chiswick, including Joseph Paxton, Robert Fortune and many others noteworthy in nineteenth-century horticulture.

The standards of the course were improved further when, in 1836, Council decided that no student gardener at Chiswick should be recommended for employment unless he had passed an examination which not only showed he could write and spell well but was also competent at arithmetic and in geography, botany and plant physiology.

This first formal horticultural examination was stated in the *Gardeners' Magazine t*o be 'A grand step' for the London Horticultural Society to have taken. The hope was also expressed that a national system of horticultural education might be established as a result. Loudon, the editor, attributed the idea to 'Dr Lindley who has thus rendered a most important service to the gardening world'.

It is perhaps not surprising that Lindley gave so much attention to improving educational opportunities for professional gardeners as he had been appointed as the first Professor of Botany at the recently founded University of London in 1828 (at the young age of twenty-nine!), Council having agreed that he should attend the University in this post for an hour each day during May, June and July. Lindley also started a series of three afternoon lectures on horticultural botany for Fellows of the Society at fortnightly meetings during 1831 at their meeting room in Regent Street. The popularity of this innovation resulted in an increase in the series to six lectures per annum and they may be seen as a forerunner of the lectures held at Vincent Square today by the Royal Horticultural Society on show days, no longer, alas, fortnightly as the number of RHS shows has been diminished in recent years.

A further boost to the student gardener course at Chiswick occurred when, in 1846, Lindley persuaded the Gardens Committee and Council to provide a reading room to supplement considerably the small library established some twenty-five years previously. Lindley, by this time Vice-Secretary of the Society, opened the new reading room by giving a lecture to the student gardeners in November that year, followed by a further ten lectures that winter and the following spring. Thereafter the Society offered prizes, as an encouragement to serious study, to those who achieved the best results in the August examinations held for student gardeners each year – a practice still continued at Wisley for the students to this day.

The annual report to the Fellows following this initiative shows the esteem in which Lindley was held for his innovative educational ideas. This stated 'The Council are strongly impressed with the value of the exertions made by the Vice-Secretary to promote this highly important object, as evidenced by the very interesting lectures delivered by him at the Garden, and by his valuable donations to the Garden Library'. Sadly the scheme more or less fell into disuse in later years due in part to a fall in numbers of students. Fortunately the discussion on the need for horticultural education was revived in the *Gardeners' Chronicle* in 1864 by an article from 'A very Old F.H.S.' published on February 13th that year. He wrote: 'Gardeners at present are educated in the gardens of the nobility and gentry – the head gardener, in some instances, receiving a premium with every youth he receives. This arrangement need not be changed. It is beneficial as far as it goes, but we all know that in such gardens only one routine is followed, so that a youth on leaving a garden perfect in all its appliances, becomes as it were at sea on leaving it; he requires finishing by learning the horticulture of the world, to be taught at Chiswick, which should be the University of Horticulture. Every youth on the termination of his apprenticeship in the provinces, should serve one year at least at Chiswick, and at the end of that term receive a certificate of ability – he should in fact take his degree. As far as I can see, no great expense would attend the opening of the doors of our school. Two or three professors, i.e. good gardeners, would be required to attend to the pupils, who should do the work of the garden, be instructed in pruning and training and general culture, and hear lectures in the different branches of horticulture, as is now the practice in the public gardens of France. No premium need be paid, but the pupils should give their work for one year's finishing.'

The *Gardeners' Chronicle* followed this up two weeks later with a leader which stated 'Chiswick, A school of Horticulture! The very idea is refreshing and the sound of the exclamation musical'. As a result, a Council member, Sir Wentworth Dilke, raised the matter of Chiswick becoming 'a school of horticulture for the whole empire'. In December that year Council requested the Society of Arts to nominate members to serve on a joint committee for the purpose of carrying out a system of examination of gardeners.

A Committee on the Improved Education of Gardeners provided a comprehensive report in 1865 recommending not only the establishment of an efficient school of horticulture for the training of gardeners at Chiswick but specifying the staff organisation and the collections of plants needed to achieve the results required. The final examinations were to include both the theory and practice of horticulture with examiners to be appointed by the Society. Most of the recommendations accepted by Council were simply refinements of the original school of horticulture established and developed under Lindley's jurisdiction. In 1863 he had resigned as the Secretary of the Society due to failing health and apparently took no part in the discussions but it is perhaps no coincidence that Lindley was the horticultural editor of the *Gardeners' Chronicle,* which revived the issue of horticultural education, from its inception in 1841 until 1865, the year in which he died.

The *Gardeners' Chronicle*, founded in 1841 by Lindley, Joseph Paxton, Charles

Wentworth Dilke and William Bradbury, was effectively a replacement for the *Gardener's Magazine* which had been the main outlet for gardening information in Britain and overseas since 1826 but ceased publication after the death of the redoubtable J.C. Loudon, its editor, in 1843.

Lindley was the first horticultural editor of this new weekly publication which, from its start, provided a remarkable record of all aspects of horticulture and gardening including regular reports on matters relating to the Horticultural Society, and later the Royal Horticultural Society, for more than a century and a quarter.

Lindley very clearly shaped the way in which the *Gardeners' Chronicle* developed into an informative, educational journal. His aim, very successfully achieved, was to make the *Gardeners' Chronicle* 'a weekly record of everything that bears upon Horticulture or Garden Botany and to introduce such Natural History as has a relation to Gardening...'. The aims, not surprisingly, were closely akin to those of the Society as may be gauged from the prospectus to the first issue of 2 January 1841 which states: 'Gardening is in many respects the art of creating an Artificial Climate, similar to that in which plants are naturally found: evidence, however, regarding the real nature of climate, as concerns vegetation, is greatly wanting. Physiological inquiries, and all those interesting topics which elucidate the harmony of nature, and the dependence of the various parts of the creation each on the other, will also form a subject of discussion. Another peculiar feature will be the introduction of information relating to Forestry or Arboriculture. This is one of the most important horticultural subjects to which the attention of the public can be directed; for it is often little understood by those who have occasion to practise it, although the amount of property affected by the management of timber stands second only to that of land. The natural laws which govern the production of timber and regulate its growth, the value of it, the extent to which it is influenced by soil, and consequently to what circumstances are to be ascribed the great inferiority in quality of the same species grown in different places, are all points to which attention will be given. We shall endeavour to collect information upon that very important but much neglected subject, the diseases of trees, and the cause of their decay, whether natural or accidental, as well as to convey the earliest notices of the introduction of new species, which promises to increase either the beauty or value of woodland property. When to plant, to prune, and to fell, will be stated weekly in the Calendar, together with the weekly garden operations... To the Florist our Miscellany will have much interest, not only because everything relating to those rare and beautiful productions which are his particular care will be constantly treated of in such a manner as to make him thoroughly acquainted with the merits or demerits of new varieties, and with their best modes of cultivation, but also because we shall take care that such opinions as may be given are the results of an honest examination by competent judges unbiased by personal interest.'

The success of Lindley's objectives was assured by the range of contributors and correspondents attracted to the new journal, ranging from gardeners in private service to curators of botanic gardens and erudite professors of botany as well as Fellows of the Horticultural Society. The value of the *Gardeners' Chronicle* to horticulturists and botanists in both educational and scientific terms was immense and much of the credit for maintaining the standard, quality and coverage must again go to Lindley. And undoubtedly when the Horticultural Society fell on hard times during the 1850s and might have had to give up the Chiswick garden, the *Gardeners' Chronicle* strongly supported the Society and its aims.

Among Lindley's many educative publications his *Theory and Practice of Horticulture*, first published in 1840 and then in a second, much enlarged edition in 1855 (Figure 17), had the most influence on gardeners. It provided a unique source of information on 'horticultural physiology' (to use Lindley's wording) as applied to the practices of horticulture, so that the reasons why plants developed in a particular way or reacted to certain conditions or plant practices could be readily understood by 'the intelligent gardener and scientific amateur'. He rejected strongly the speculative, unsupported statements of many writers and, as may be seen in the preface to the first edition of this book, was scathing of those with little sound knowledge of their subject. In particular he berated an author on the history of gardening (unnamed) who was of the opinion 'that the weak drawn state of forced Asparagus in London is occasioned by the action of the dung immediately upon its roots'! Equally fairly he praised 'the admirable papers of Mr Knight' (Thomas Andrew Knight, a founder member of the Horticultural Society) on the horticultural application of vegetable physiology. Lindley aimed in this book to bring together soundly based information on physiology and methods and to disabuse gardeners of unsupported and often misleading theories. In this he succeeded admirably; indeed the information he provided remains very relevant to this day.

Lindley defined horticulture as 'that branch of knowledge which relates to the cultivation, multiplication and amelioration of the Vegetable Kingdom' and divided it into two parts, the art and the science, which he considered essentially distinct although mutually dependent. These principles are those on which the Royal Horticultural Society bases its work today. The art of horticulture he considered involved the operations connected with cultivation, multiplication and amelioration of plants whilst the science was held to explain the reasons upon which the operations were founded. Today we would, no doubt, include under the 'art' of horticulture the uses and placement of plants in the garden and landscape although this might be considered part of 'amelioration' - using better the plants available.

THE

THEORY AND PRACTICE OF HORTICULTURE;

OR,

AN ATTEMPT TO EXPLAIN THE CHIEF OPERATIONS OF GARDENING UPON PHYSIOLOGICAL GROUNDS.

BEING THE SECOND EDITION OF THE

THEORY OF HORTICULTURE,

MUCH ENLARGED.

BY JOHN LINDLEY, PH.D. F.R.S.

Corresponding Member of the Institute,
Vice-Secretary of the Horticultural Society, Professor of Botany in University College, London,
&c. &c. &c.

"Though I am very sensible that it is from long experience chiefly that we are to expect the most certain rules of practice, yet it is withal to be remembered that the likeliest method to enable us to make the most judicious observations, and to put us upon the most probable means of improving any art, is to get the best insight we can into the nature and properties of those things which we are desirous to cultivate and improve."

HALES'S *Vegetable Staticks*, i. 376.

LONDON:
LONGMAN, BROWN, GREEN, AND LONGMANS.
1855.

FIGURE 17. Title-page of Lindley, *Theory and Practice of Horticulture* (1855)

Two distinct sections cover the science behind horticultural practices. He intended throughout to provide simple, proven explanations for the methods used and to avoid the inclusion of speculative or doubtful hypotheses likely to confuse gardeners. He states clearly that he aimed to teach 'those acquainted with the art of gardening what the great principles are upon which their practice is based'. In his first eight chapters he described the principal facts of plant physiology as then known to botanists; and in a further twenty-one chapters he demonstrated how these facts applied to traditional gardening. The

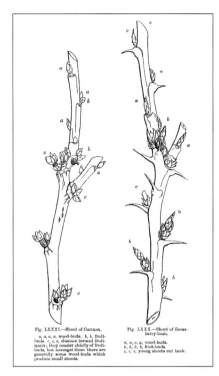

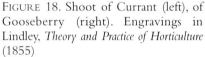

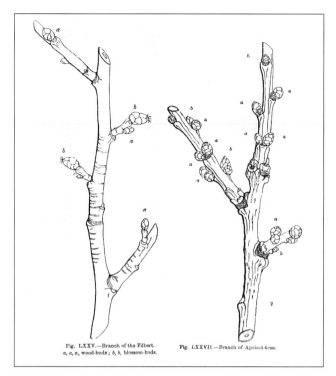

FIGURE 18. Shoot of Currant (left), of Gooseberry (right). Engravings in Lindley, *Theory and Practice of Horticulture* (1855)

FIGURE 19. Branch of Filbert (left), of Apricot (right). Engravings in Lindley, *Theory and Practice of Horticulture* (1855)

text is very readable, even today, with numerous specific examples to illustrate the physiological factors involved in seed and plant growth. It remains a fascinating book (Figures 18 to 20).

Lindley was very emphatic in acceptance or rejection of horticultural practices, praising warmly those which related clearly to known physiological factors and trenchant in condemning those shown to be incorrect.

As an example he gives advice on the application of manure to trees on the basis that the feeding roots, which he calls 'young fibres and spongioles', occur on a circumference just outside that formed by the branches. He continues by saying 'as the circle formed by the roots is generally greater than that of the branches, the proper manner of applying manure is, to introduce it into the ground at a distance from the stem about equal to the radius formed by the branches. And yet though this is so evidently right, I have seen a gardener, who ought to have known much better, sedulously administering liquid manure, by pouring it into the soil at the base of the stem; which is much the same thing as if an attempt were made to feed a man through the soles of his feet'.

The influence of this and other of Lindley's books on horticultural practice was undoubtedly very great, both during his lifetime and long thereafter. Appreciation abroad of his *The Theory of Horticulture* led to a Dutch translation and a German translation in 1842 and a Russian one in 1845, and if we look in textbooks today there are very few areas where he would be found wanting as a result of modern science applied to horticultural practice. There are, of course scientific developments of which he knew nothing, such as the debilitating effects of viruses on plants, and the arguments he put forward in his chapter 'Of the preservation of races by seed' would be questionable today, not surprisingly in view of the later enormous input into genetics and horticultural science.

The respect with which the horticultural fraternity regarded Lindley can be illustrated by a passage in the *Gardeners' Chronicle* of 5 June 1875, ten years after his death, by a head gardener Alexander Cramb. An illustration there shows Lindley as a heavily bewhiskered gentleman of very stern aspect who must have seemed a tartar to the young gardeners attending his weekly instructive evenings. Cramb comments on these aspirant head gardeners that for most 'the sight of a book, particularly if requiring the exercise of any mental effort, was about as palatable as a dose of bitter aloes'. Commenting on his own training, however, he says 'Dr Lindley's *Theory of Horticulture*, which was published at this time raised horticulture almost to an exact science, providing us with a knowledge of the natural action of plant life and its requirements, and so demolishing that huge monster – empiricism.'

Exhibitions and flower shows – and the development of plant trials

A further area of horticultural innovation with which Lindley was much involved was in the development of exhibitions and flower shows.

Exhibits during the early years of the Horticultural Society were few although some Fellows brought samples of vegetables, fruits and ornamental plants to meetings for the interest of those attending. The Society was, however, cautious about commenting favourably or unfavourably about such exhibits to

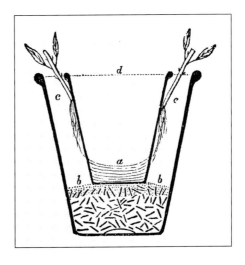

FIGURE 20. Forsyth's propagating pot; the outer earthenware pot with crock at bottom and sides filled with propagating compost into which cuttings are inserted; the inner earthenware pot closed at bottom with clay and kept filled with water. Engraving in Lindley, *Theory and Practice of Horticulture* (1855)

avoid the possibility of 'misapprehension, of jealousy, or jar, among a numerous and diversified Association'. A similar policy existed until the middle of the nineteenth century but Fellows still continued to bring or send exhibits to meetings; sometimes from the continent and occasionally in quantity. A Mr Joseph Kirke showed seventy-two apple cultivars at one meeting whilst in 1818 Messrs Whitby, Brame and Milne exhibited over two hundred dahlia cultivars.

This practice continued for many years to the great benefit of Fellows, as they often received propagating material of new introductions, but it was not until 1831 that Lindley arranged for a series of competitions to be held which proved very popular. Eventually there was insufficient space to accommodate the competitions at the Regent Street meeting rooms of the Society and they were transferred to the Chiswick garden.

Competitions for pineapples in February, camellias in April, rhododendrons in May, azaleas, roses and grapes in June, pineapples again and melons in July and dahlias, roses and grapes in September were held in that first year. To this series of competitions were soon added shows under canvas at the Chiswick garden and in 1833 shows were held in May, June and July with a September show added the following year. By 1836 they had replaced entirely the competitions Lindley had arranged five years earlier. They continued to be held for more than twenty years but gradually lost support and, equally importantly for the Society, income by the early 1850s, which financially became a very difficult period.

By 1859, however, Lindley was urging the need to develop a show garden to include a site for flower shows as he considered the Chiswick garden should be devoted entirely to horticultural work, particularly experimentation and the testing of fruit, vegetables and ornamentals. This latter development was the forerunner of the important and valuable trials held now at Wisley by the Royal Horticultural Society.

An astonishing array of plants had already been gathered together at Chiswick; 600 apple cultivars, 170 different grapes, 130 cherries, 137 different cucumber cultivars, 300 kinds of annuals and 150 cultivars of pelargonium were a small sample of the diversity of plants grown in the Chiswick trial grounds by 1860. In addition demonstrations on many aspects of gardening such as the pruning of fruit were held for Fellows. To Lindley and the excellent staff at Chiswick who so ably and fully supported him, it must have been a great pleasure to see the garden returned to its main purpose of growing plants rather than used for the fashionable Fêtes and other events that had become popular, but were now financially burdensome.

Following the death of Lindley in 1865 and the advent of the Kensington garden, the demise of the Chiswick garden came under consideration, partly for financial reasons but also because of the difficulty of growing plants within 'the smoke of London'. A reduction in the size of the garden from thirty-three acres to about eleven acres was agreed with the Duke of Devonshire's agents from whom the land was leased. In its curtailed form it continued until 1881 in tandem with the Kensington garden which received much criticism from Fellows.

Many Fellows considered that Chiswick was still the real home of the Society and Lindley would have agreed wholeheartedly with an article in the *Gardeners' Chronicle* for 1878 (p.529) which praised the work at Chiswick; 'Well done Chiswick! There at least is real loyalty to the fundamental aim of the Royal Horticultural Society, and most satisfactory efforts are found in force to promote its true work. 1st the Fellows of the Society show their interest in this work by visiting the Garden, and by their countenance strengthen the hands and encourage the heart of their superintendent. Then shall practical horticulture be once more the leading feature in the operations of the Society, and gardeners everywhere will have much cause to rejoice and be glad.' Words, perhaps, that might have been those of Lindley had he still been Secretary.

Lindley's part in saving the Kew botanic garden

The influence of Lindley cannot be properly assessed without reference to his involvement in the saving of Kew as a botanic garden. After the death of William IV in 1837 the Government contemplated the abolition of the gardens, then the property of the Royal Family which, largely due to the efforts of Sir Joseph Banks, contained a fine collection of plants of great scientific value and rarity as well as beauty, even though the garden had suffered neglect after the death of Banks in 1820.

Hoping to get rid of this encumbrance the Treasury appointed a committee consisting of John Lindley, Joseph Paxton (once a gardener at Chiswick) and John Wilson, a head gardener, to report on the management of the Royal Gardens at Kew. Within a few weeks of its appointment in 1838 the Committee submitted a report, obviously drafted by Lindley, which was critical of the state of Kew as a public botanic garden. It had little educational and no scientific purpose then.

The Lindley report concluded; 'The importance of public Botanical Gardens has for centuries been recognised by the governments of civilised states, and at this time there is no European nation without such an establishment except England'. It also stressed the educational and scientific value of such gardens and recommended the garden and pleasure grounds at Kew should be under the management of the Commissioner for Woods and Forests rather than the Lord Steward's department. This the report considered would allow Kew to become a scientific establishment and it was felt that cooperation should be sought with public gardens in the colonies and dependencies to introduce and distribute new plants.

Following the presentation of this report, the Council of the Horticultural Society sent a petition to the House of Commons strongly supporting the establishment of a public botanic garden at Kew.

As is the way of bureaucracy, however, almost two years went by before the Secretary to the Treasury in February 1840 asked Lindley to find out what the reaction of Council might be if the garden at Kew was abolished and the plants in the conservatories given to the Horticultural Society on the condition the public had free access to the Chiswick garden one or two days a week. The Treasury made it clear that no grant would be made towards the cost of maintaining the plants if the offer was accepted. One hundred and fifty years later the general attitude of the Treasury seems to be little changed!

Politely, but perhaps predictably, in view of the Society's precarious financial position, the Council refused the offer on a cost basis for housing and maintaining the plants and the impracticality and undesirability of admitting large numbers of the public to the relatively small Chiswick garden. Additionally, and most importantly, the Society made clear how unfortunate would be the abolition of the Kew garden.

Undoubtedly, behind the scenes, discussions and lobbying took place among supporters of the garden. In March 1840 Lord Aberdeen spoke in the House of Lords about Kew saying that the Horticultural Society 'which was well known to be anxious to forward horticultural pursuits refused to become parties to a transaction which had for its object the destruction of those Gardens'. The Government spokesman indicated, no doubt sensing considerable difficulties ahead, that there was not, and never had been, any intention to abolish the Gardens. Such were the ways of Government then as now!

Shortly thereafter the recommendations of the Committee were adopted and the gardens at Kew were transferred to the care of the Commissioner for Woods and Forests, a result for which Lindley and his Committee and the Horticultural Society Council of the day deserve much praise from all gardeners and botanists.

There were two candidates for the directorship of the now nationalised botanic garden, Lindley and his good friend Sir William Jackson Hooker, who ardently wanted the post. Lindley's stand had put him out of favour. He wrote to Hooker, then in Glasgow: 'It is rumoured that you are appointed to Kew. If so I shall have still more reason to rejoice at the determination I took to oppose the barbarous Treasury scheme to destroying the place; for I, of course, was aware that the stand I made and the opposition I created would destroy all possibility of my receiving any appointment'. One can only wonder what might have happened to Kew had there not been a man of Lindley's calibre to do battle with the Treasury and Government.

The Chiswick garden under threat

By 1855 it was evident that the Chiswick garden, which cost much of the Society's annual income, could not continue its activities on a large scale, important though they were. Income from the exhibitions organised at Chiswick had diminished markedly and the numbers of visitors had also dropped, to some extent due to the close proximity of Kew which under its new management was developing very rapidly and attracting many who would previously have come to Chiswick instead. Initially drastic economies were made including the loss of some positions at Chiswick. Lindley offered to renounce his salary, not for the first time, to assist the necessary reductions in costs and, although fortunately Council did not accept his offer, it indicated his devotion to the Society and the garden he had done so much to foster. Reorganisation had become necessary and many of the plant collections were disposed of or much reduced to make Chiswick less of a showplace and to concentrate on experimental work and trials of vegetables and fruit.

The Society was, however, still in debt although the overspend had gradually been reduced by economies such as the discontinuation in 1848 of the very costly, if extremely informative, *Transactions* and the curtailment of numerous other activities.

A Special General Meeting of Fellows was held in 1856 to consider the future and Lindley read a statement on the status of the Chiswick garden that included the conclusion that, in spite of the world-wide reputation and quality of the garden, it might well have to be abolished. 'That such a place should be relinquished was a conclusion to which nothing but the most imperious necessity could have conducted the Council; but the necessity seems to exist, and it is in part for the purpose of obtaining the authority of the Society to make so great a sacrifice, or of hearing what other course the Fellows may have to propose, that this meeting is convened'.

After much discussion, further proposals, and another meeting on 11 March the Council was authorised 'to terminate the tenancy of the garden at Chiswick as soon as the lease will permit, and that the property therein be sold, unless such a sum as the Council may require for maintaining the Garden shall have been subscribed before May 1'. Although the required sum was not achieved by this date, sufficient funds had been received through an appeal to Fellows to allow the retention of Chiswick but even so for a further period of more than ten years the Society's financial stability left much to be desired.

It would have been a sad day indeed had the garden at Chiswick been discontinued during Lindley's tenure of office. He had not only seen the garden develop from infancy to a great show garden with outstanding collections but had played a very large part in its development and success.

The *Gardener's Magazine* described him in 1830 as 'unquestionably a man of extraordinary talent and not less extraordinary industry', a tribute that could be amplified many times when full consideration of the significance of his work and beneficial influence on matters horticultural, both directly and as an enabler, is assessed for any horticultural hall of fame in the future.

Part VI

LINDLEY AND HUTTON'S 'FOSSIL FLORA OF GREAT BRITAIN'

William Gilbert Chaloner

Introduction

The Fossil Flora of Great Britain (1831–1837) was John Lindley's only serious excursion into palaeobotany (Figure 21). Although he clearly embarked on the venture with great enthusiasm, this seems to have worn thin by the end of the third volume. Lindley conceived the work as a service to the geological community, aimed at educating them in an area of their subject which they had neglected. It was a sort of botanical *noblesse oblige*. At the time that he embarked on the work, jointly with William Hutton (1797–1860), Lindley had not long been appointed to the Chair of Botany at the new University of London (later University College, London), in 1828. The writing of the text of the *Fossil Flora* was going to have to be fitted in to the numerous other activities with which he was over-filling his life.

The Fossil Flora of Great Britain which was subtitled *Figures and Descriptions of the fossil vegetable Remains found in a fossil State in this Country* was dedicated to Roderick Murchison, then President of the Geological Society, and later to become Director of the Geological Survey. Lindley and Hutton go on to record that the work 'owes it origin to his suggestion and its existence to his support'. It was intended that, rather like a modern flora, it would be an illustrated catalogue of the fossil plants then known to occur in Britain. As Lindley wrote to William Hutton in 1829, 'when I consider how new the study of fossil botany is, how small the number of subjects is known, and how imperfect our knowledge of every one of these subjects is, I feel confident that we shall succeed in producing something which will be both instructive to readers and useful to science'. In the introduction to volume I, the authors claim rather optimistically that for geologists 'overcoming the difficulties that offer themselves to a strict examination of fossil vegetable remains has come to be an object of indispensable necessity'. It was to be the objective of the *Fossil Flora* to meet that need.

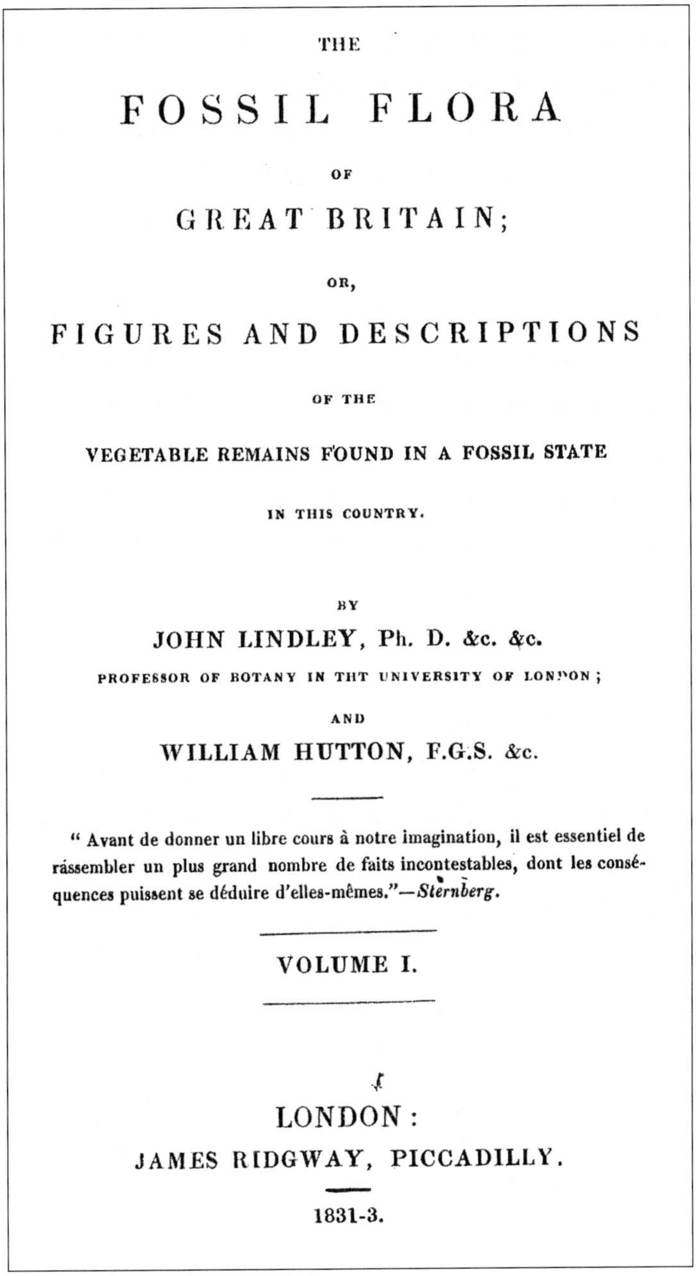

FOSSIL FLORA

OF

GREAT BRITAIN;

OR,

FIGURES AND DESCRIPTIONS

OF THE

VEGETABLE REMAINS FOUND IN A FOSSIL STATE

IN THIS COUNTRY.

BY

JOHN LINDLEY, Ph. D. &c. &c.

PROFESSOR OF BOTANY IN THT UNIVERSITY OF LONDON ;

AND

WILLIAM HUTTON, F.G.S. &c.

" Avant de donner un libre cours à notre imagination, il est essentiel de rássembler un plus grand nombre de faits incontestables, dont les conséquences puissent se déduire d'elles-mêmes."—*Sternberg.*

VOLUME I.

LONDON :

JAMES RIDGWAY, PICCADILLY.

1831-3.

FIGURE 21. Title-page of Lindley & Hutton, *Fossil Flora,* vol. 1 (1831-1833)

The production of the Fossil Flora

In order to persuade the publishers that the book would have adequate sales, it was necessary to obtain support from potential purchasers ahead of publication. John Hutton's role was evidently to include collecting sponsors as well as fossil plants, for by April 1831 Lindley was able to write to Hutton, in Newcastle, that 'the first part of the *Fossil Flora* will appear on the 1st of July. The assurance that … you have an hundred names upon your list has overcome the scruples of the Booksellers'.

It seems that in broad terms Hutton, as the geologist of the team, was to obtain the fossils, while Lindley as the botanist would be responsible for describing, interpreting and identifying them. According to Richard Howse (1890), Hutton had been collecting Carboniferous plant fossils since about 1829; he was at that time Secretary of the recently formed Northumberland, Durham and Newcastle-on-Tyne Natural History Society. Jarrow Colliery (and particularly the shale above the Bensham coal) was remarkably productive of fossil plant compressions. It seems from Howse's account (1890) that an important role in obtaining plant fossils was played by one Robert Fairley, the Master Wasteman at Jarrow Colliery, who must have had access to all the waste rock material coming out of the colliery at that time. Howse describes him as 'one of the most successful fossil collectors in the North of England'. Clearly the growth of Hutton's collection owed much to Fairley as well as to the miners at Jarrow.

Howse also records that 'it seems to have been agreed that Mr Hutton should collect the specimens and have drawings made from them; and that these drawings should be sent to London, with the specimens occasionally, and any remarks Mr Hutton wished to make along with them'. From Howse's account, it seems that the labels and specimens sometimes became separated between Newcastle and their reaching Lindley's attention, resulting in some errors in the locality citations. Lindley, for his part, seems to have been keen to keep himself distanced from any geological responsibility. He remarks in reply to a question from Hutton about the rate of subsidence involved in coal seam burial (correspondence July 1835) 'You know I am no geologist; but merely an auxiliary brought into the field to look after matters of a special kind'.

None the less, Lindley was prepared to defer to Hutton's views on the identity of the Carboniferous fossils at least. In August 1831 he wrote to Hutton 'tell me to which of Brongniart's species you think this [*Calamites*] belongs and in short give me all the information you can about the subject…'. In the Preface to the second volume, the authors discuss the evidence for the nature of the 'Carboniferous formation' and particularly the origin of coal. (From Lindley's correspondence, it appears that this preface was written by Hutton alone.) At that time there was a lively controversy concerning the question of whether the plant material destined to become coal had been transported a long distance, eventually sinking and becoming buried by overlying sediment, or whether it had formed, like peat, *in situ*. That is, in present-day terminology, whether coal was an autochthonous *(in situ)* accumulation or as some had argued, allochthonous. After a careful review of the evidence, Lindley and Hutton were 'compelled to the conclusion that beds of coal chiefly originated in vegetable matter which lived, died and was decomposed upon the spots where we now find it'. This was an important contribution from William Hutton to a controversy that was to run on for many years.

As had been planned, the *Fossil Flora* became a series of drawings principally of Carboniferous and Middle Jurassic plants from Britain, with accompanying descriptions and notes on the affinity of the plants prepared by Lindley. Andrews (1980) correctly states that the *Fossil Flora* 'appeared in several instalments between 1831 and 1837, and these are usually found bound into three volumes'. There is separate pagination within each of the three volumes and the contents of each instalment can be ascertained from the dates of publication engraved at the base of the plates.[1] There is no conspicuous systematic or stratigraphic sequence to the plants dealt with, although plants perceived to be related were often grouped together within a volume. The Carboniferous plants were mainly from the Coal Measures (Upper Carboniferous), especially from the Newcastle coalfield where Hutton was based, but with a number from other coalfields within Britain. There were also a number of Lower Carboniferous plants from Scotland, from the Oil Shales and the Burdiehouse Limestone. Finally, a few Triassic, Cretaceous and Tertiary plants are dealt with, more or less haphazardly, in the sequence of the work, as they happened to come into Lindley's or Hutton's hands from various sources.

By November 1833 Lindley was writing to Hutton 'I am now in want of materials for the next number of the F.F. and shall be glad of any you may have to send'. Other production problems worried Lindley too; he writes to Hutton on 5 November 1834 'I have this morning got notice from the engraver that the plates for the next number of the fossil flora must be put in hand immediately because of the vicinity of Xmas, when the workmen fall behind, are lazy and feasting'.

By December 1835 Lindley seems to be having serious misgivings about the whole enterprise. He wrote to Hutton: 'I am sorry to say that I find it becoming so much more difficult than ever for me to pay the necessary attention to the work [of the *Fossil Flora*] that I shall be compelled to give up my share of it after the next number which will complete the second volume'. Fortunately, Lindley held on to see the three volumes completed. But by 1837, he had evidently had enough of palaeobotany. He wrote in June of that year to Hutton 'I have at last put an end to *Fossil Flora* by completing Vol. III… I am drudging at the index just now.' By July, he wrote of the *Fossil Flora* 'I have fairly washed my hands of it: and so resolved am I to keep to my resolution of discontinuing the subject that I have sent away everything that I possessed in illustration… I shall sell my books relating to the subject and you may have them if you like at your own price'.

There seems to be no record of whether Hutton took up this offer. However, he evidently abandoned collecting fossil plants soon after the completion of the

Fossil Flora, for he left England in November 1846 for 'a prolonged residence on the shores of the Mediterranean' (Howse, 1890). His collection accumulated 'a considerable covering of dust and dirt' before being cleaned and re-housed by the Natural History Society. Most of the Carboniferous type material cited in the *Fossil Flora* came eventually into the care of the Hancock Museum, Newcastle, where it is still housed, although some of his specimens passed to the Geological Survey (Cleevely, 1983).

Despite Lindley finally and so firmly turning his back on palaeobotany, a postscript to the *Fossil Flora* was yet to appear under the editorship of G.A. Lebour, some twelve years after Lindley's death (Lebour, 1877). This took the form of sixty-five plates of illustrations of fossil plants, 'prepared under the supervision of the late Dr Lindley and Mr W. Hutton between the years 1835 and 1840' and was published by the North of England Institute of Mining and Mechanical Engineers. The original illustrations had been found, according to Lebour, among 'a large collection of drawings and papers which had belonged to the late Mr William Hutton'. A number of the fossils illustrated have no known locality, but virtually all, bar one Yorkshire Jurassic plant, are Carboniferous. The plates are accompanied by a brief text written by Lebour, but based on notes prepared by Lindley.

The reason for the omission of at least some of these figures from the *Fossil Flora* is self-evident. Plate XLIV, for example, is headed '?' and the notes describe it as 'Another very vague specimen which Lindley declined to name, his memorandum respecting it being:– "too imperfect"' (Lebour, 1877). One of the few new species described in this work is *Asterophyllites huttonii* Lebour (named for William Hutton); this is probably a synonym of *Annularia radiata* (Brongniart) Sternberg. Perhaps the most important illustration in this volume is a very fine portrait of William Hutton (date not specified) which forms the frontispiece. Understandably, this work seems to have gone rather unnoticed in the palaeobotanical literature. Indeed, it gets no mention even in Andrews' very thorough history of palaeobotany (Andrews, 1980).

The illustrations and the link with W.C. Williamson

As indicated above, the strategy of the production of the *Fossil Flora* involved Hutton having drawings prepared of at least some of the fossil plants to be included, which were then to be sent to Lindley in London who would interpret them botanically, and prepare notes on them. Hutton also evidently sent some of the fossils themselves to Lindley, but in some cases Lindley saw only the drawings.

In the present-day context it is easy to express astonishment that Lindley would accept such a 'second-hand' access to the very material that he was to describe. The more so, as he was a talented botanical artist and could obviously

FIGURE 22. *Lindleycladus lanceolatus* (Lindley & Hutton) Harris *(Zamia lanceolata* Lindley & Hutton) from the Middle Jurassic of Haiburn Wyke, Yorkshire. Drawing by W.C. Williamson in Lindley & Hutton, *Fossil Flora* 3: pl. 194 (1836). Lindley assigned it as a species of the living cycad genus *Zamia*, under the name *Zamia lanceolata*, believing it to be a compound pinnate leaf. Harris reinterpreted it as a leafy shoot and made it the basis of a new genus named for 'the pioneer palaeobotanist Dr J. Lindley', citing the specimen on which this illustration was based as the type

have made the drawings himself. However, this procedure should in fairness be judged in the context in which he was working. I remember the late Professor Tom Harris defending Lindley, when I expressed some surprise at this arrangement. Harris (*pers. com.* c.1970) said that in Lindley's eyes the compression fossils with which he was dealing were in effect 'pictures' of the plant on the rock, anyway; so that it was not unreasonable to get a competent artist to re-draw the 'picture', and that Lindley would then interpret that drawing instead of the original.

Harris (1979) named one of the Yorkshire Jurassic plants for John Lindley, *Lindleycladus lanceolatus* (Lindley and Hutton) Harris (see Figure 22). The history of this species illustrates rather well how the procedure worked. The fossil in question came from the middle Jurassic at Haiburn Wyke, north of Scarborough (from the Haiburn Formation of the Ravenscar Group, of modern usage). The specimen was drawn by the young W.C. Williamson (1816-1895) in Scarborough, and the drawing and a description sent to Lindley in London; Williamson must then have been about nineteen years old. The only description of the plant in the *Fossil Flora* is that written by Williamson, which Lindley and Hutton quote in full, attributing it to him. It seems unlikely that Lindley ever saw the specimen itself; indeed, this seems to have been the case for most of the Middle Jurassic plant fossils from the Yorkshire Deltaic Series illustrated in the *Fossil Flora* by Williamson.

The specimen on which *Lindleycladus* was based consists of a narrow axis bearing helically arranged lanceolate leaves with a suggestion of parallel venation, as Harris interpreted it. Lindley followed Williamson's interpretation in seeing it as a pinnate cycad-like leaf; his only comment on the specimen was to say that 'this leaf has no doubt been produced by some one of the Cycadeoideous stems of the Oolitic rocks, but there seems no present probability of our ascertaining by which'. However, this uncertainty did not stop him from assigning it to a living genus of cycads, and he published it as a new species under the name *Zamia lanceolata*. Harris (1979) reinterpreted the compound leaf as a leafy shoot, and put his new genus in the Podozamitaceae, an enigmatic family of fossil conifers.

All of this brings us to a strange personal encounter between two leading British palaeobotanists, John Lindley and W.C. Williamson. Williamson was later to become a pioneer of coal-ball studies which revealed the anatomy of a range of British Upper Carboniferous plants (see Andrews, 1980). He was also to become Professor of Botany in Owens College, Manchester, the forerunner of Manchester University. His name was immortalised in one of the most memorable of Jurassic plants, *Williamsonia* Carruthers.

At the time of Williamson's first involvement with the *Fossil Flora,* he was a boy of sixteen working as an apprentice to Mr Wedell, an apothecary in Scarborough. He records in his autobiography (Williamson, 1896) that in 1832 Hutton had written to the then Secretary of the Literary and Philosophical Society of Scarborough 'to enquire if there was anyone in the town capable of figuring and describing the new plants from the Gristhorpe deposit' (the Middle Jurassic Deltaic Series, exposed in Cayton Bay south of Scarborough). Williamson continues that he was brought the letter, and was urged to undertake the task: 'I did so, and contributed to the pages of that work almost as long as its quarterly parts continued to be issued'. He notes with obvious delight: '...some of the palaeontologists familiar with ... [The Fossil Flora] ... may be amused to learn that most of my drawings were prepared at the end of

Mr Wedell's kitchen table, whilst the housekeeper was occupied at the other end with the several processes of providing the day's dinner'.

Some eight years later, Williamson enrolled as a medical student at University College London, where Lindley had been appointed as the first Professor of Botany. As was thought appropriate at that time, medical students took a basic course in botany. When Professor Lindley called the class roll (Williamson's wife recalls, in a footnote to his memoirs), the ensuing exchange took place: "'W.C. Williamson?" repeated Mr Lindley. He looked at the white faced delicate lad before him, and thought "Oh, son or grandson of our correspondent perhaps", but said "W.C. Williamson from where?" "Scarborough" answered the youth; a small conscious smile tucking itself away in his sleeve, meanwhile, "Scarborough" repeated Professor Lindley. "Are you then in any way related to one W.C. Williamson with whom we corresponded some time ago?" "I had the pleasure, sir, of corresponding with you myself some years ago". "You, yourself!" And the teacher in botany began to wonder whether student or professor would have the better time'.

Fossil cuticles

Nearly all the plants described and figured in the *Fossil Flora* are preserved in the state called a 'compression fossil'. This means that the plant part concerned was buried in mud with sufficient organic matter present for the sedimentary environment to become anaerobic, so that biodegradation was halted as the plant tissue became flattened. In Lindley's time, such fossils were seen as perhaps in some way comparable to a drawing of the plant in charcoal, showing its shape and detail of venation, but nothing of its internal structure. Later, such fossils came to be investigated by oxidative maceration, which involved removing the coaly material of the original tissue, leaving only the cuticular covering. Such a fossil cuticle preparation could then be examined under the microscope, and revealed detail of the epidermal cells and stomata. Bornemann (1856) has traditionally been credited with making and illustrating the first cuticle preparations from German Triassic plants (Andrews, 1980). He seems to have regarded them as an interesting feature of his fossils, but did not use cuticle characters as a basis for strengthening any systematic assignments. Indeed it was not until Nathorst, followed by H.H. Thomas, Florin, and others, came to apply cuticle preparations to systematic work that the full value of cuticle studies came to be appreciated (Andrews, 1980). Their work, and that of Harris on Triassic and Jurassic fossil cuticles, transformed the study of compression fossils. However, Lindley and Hutton must be acknowledged as the first to prepare a fossil cuticle, and to illustrate the cell outlines of the epidermis which it revealed. In volume II of the *Fossil Flora* (Lindley and Hutton, 1833-35) they illustrate a cuticle prepared from *Solenites murrayana* (Figure 23). This gymnosperm, now regarded as a member of an extinct order, the Czekanowskiales (Harris et al., 1974), was described by Lindley and Hutton as having very narrow linear leaves 'either adhering loosely to their matrix… or collected into firm flexible masses'. They go on to record 'it occurred to us that if it were possible to separate the tissue from the carbonaceous matter, by some powerful solvent, the transparency of the specimens might be restored and some insight obtained into their anatomical structure.' They treated the leaves with boiling nitric acid, washed the detached leaves and revealed the epidermal cell outlines (Figure 23, E). However, they were evidently interested in the tubular nature of the cuticle (hence the generic name) representing the combined upper and lower cuticles of the needle-like leaf. As bubbles appeared within the cuticular tube (Figure 23, C and D) Lindley compared the leaves with *Isoetes*, with its air chambers within the leaf tissue. Although he seems to have realised that the gas filling the fossil cuticular tube was somehow quite different from the four longitudinal chambers in *Isoetes*, he hung on to the *Isoetes* idea, and suggests that *Solenites* was at least close to that living genus. Strangely, Lindley and Hutton never seem to have attempted to macerate any other of the Yorkshire Jurassic plants; if they had, palaeobotany might have taken a leap forward of nearly a hundred years in the application of the cuticle technique!

Past climates and experiments with fossils

In volume III of the *Fossil Flora*, Lindley and Hutton quote at some length the views set out by Adolphe Brongniart in his *Prodrome* (1828) to the effect that the ratio of lycopods and ferns on the one hand to the phanerogams on the other was influenced by climate. Brongniart had suggested that the prevailing temperature and humidity were the principal two factors involved. This line of thought he attributes to R. Brown and d'Urville. Brongniart suggests that these two climatic factors (temperature, moisture) are the underlying cause for the ratio of ferns plus lycopods to the phanerogams (gymnosperms plus angiosperms) to be 1:40 in temperate Europe, whereas in the humid tropics the figure is 1:20. He goes on to remark that in island situations the ratio is even lower, citing 1:10 in the West Indies, and in St Helena and Tristan de Cuna, to 2:3. Brongniart suggested that the high proportion of cryptogams to phanerogams in the Coal (Carboniferous) floras of Europe was the result of the same climatic influence, suggesting that the isolated coal basins of Europe, perhaps separated by marine environments, were comparable to a series of island floras.

Our view of this line of thought must inevitably be coloured by the subsequent discovery that most of the 'ferns' of the Carboniferous were actually seed ferns (gymnosperms) and so 'phanerogams' of Lindley's usage. This did not emerge until Oliver and Scott recognised the Pteridosperms in 1904 (see

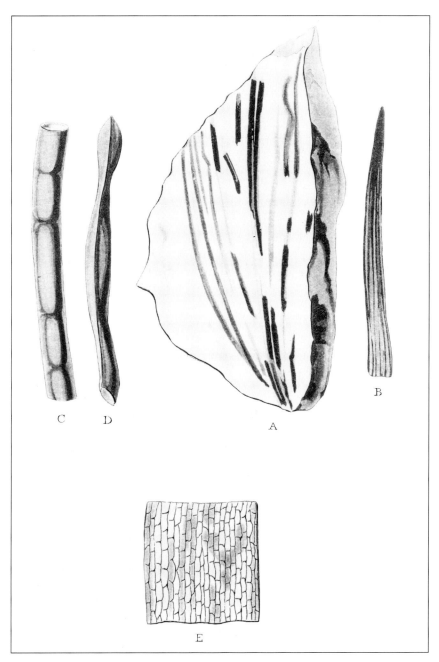

FIGURE 23 *Solenites murrayana* Lindley & Hutton, with detached cuticle (lower figure) from the Middle Jurassic of Gristhorpe Bay, Yorkshire. Drawing by W.C. Williamson in Lindley & Hutton, *Fossil Flora* 2: 123 (1834). The appearance of the leaves shown at A, seemingly arising from a common source, were seen by Lindley as 'conformable to the structure of *Isoetes*'. Leaves at C and D had been macerated in boiling nitric acid. The cuticular tube of the leaf had become reinflated by gases generated in that process. Lindley compared the bubbles of gas within the leaves to the air cavities within the *Isoetes* leaf, but acknowledged significant differences. The detail of the epidermal cells seen in E represents the earliest illustration of microscopic structure seen in a fossil cuticle. Lindley regarded *Solenites* as 'more nearly allied to *Isoetes* (a lycopod) and *Pilularia* (a fern) than to anything else now known'. Harris et al. (1974) assign it to an extinct order of gymnosperms, the Czekanowskiales

Andrews, 1980). However, it must be noted that Lindley also remarked (volume 3, p.3) with prophetic foresight: 'The remarkable fact that Ferns are scarcely ever met with in fructification in a fossil state is also a circumstance upon which no light is thrown by the theory of a high temperature and damp insular atmosphere'. (This perceptive observation was presumably based on the fact that most of the Carboniferous seed ferns, which are a prominent element in most coal measure floras, have indeed no sori of sporangia on their leaves, as do most modern ferns).

Lindley's interpretation of the proportion of cryptogams in the Carboniferous is further complicated by the fact that he regarded the spore-bearing (cryptogamic) trees of *Sigillaria* to be seed plants, phanerogams. However, as an early attempt to rationalise how one might interpret the environment of coal formation from the composition of the fossil flora, it strikes a familiar note. It is also interesting that the composition of the flora is being seen by both Brongniart and Lindley as governed largely by the contemporary climate, without reference (in the case of isolated island floras) to how the plants got there. The proportion of ferns in isolated island floras is certainly influenced by the capacity of fern spores for long-distance air transport, compared with seed plants with larger less mobile propagules.

Lindley's main concern in this controversy was not so much the validity of the plant taxonomy, as the differential preservation of different plant groups. He believed that the Carboniferous flora (and indeed all the ancient floras) was essentially comparable in its broad systematic composition to that of the present day. The differences observed were, he believed, the result of differential destruction of certain elements of the flora in the course of fossilisation; what would now be called 'taphonomic bias'. He writes (vol. 3, p.4) 'I was led to suspect that possibly the total absence of certain kinds of plants, the constant presence of others… might be accounted for by difference in the capability of one plant beyond another of resisting the action of water'. He accordingly set up an experiment to investigate the fossilisation potential of a wide range of plants by immersing 177 specimens in a 'large iron tank' and over a period of two years leaving them uncovered and in the open air, topping up the water as it evaporated. The plants were chosen from 'all the more remarkable natural orders, taking care in particular to include representatives of all those which are either constantly present in the Coal Measures, or as universally absent'. He carefully listed every specimen used, and its fate after the elapse of the two years. He concluded that 'Dicotyledonous plants in general are unable to remain for two years in water without being totally decomposed'. Conifers and cycads were singled out as being able to survive his experiment; and while among monocotyledons the palms and other fibrous plants survived, grasses and sedges did not. He concluded that 'the numerical proportion of different families of plants found in a fossil state throws no light whatever upon the ancient climate of the earth'.

The plant fossil record and evolution

Lindley and Hutton's belief that geologists would find fossil plants useful in correlating rocks is oddly at variance with Lindley's rejection of any evidence of evolutionary change presented by the fossil plant record, when he writes (*Fossil Flora*, Vol. 1, xvii) – 'of a still more questionable character is the theory of progressive development, as applied to the state of vegetation in successive ages'. The concept of progressive development was in effect what would now be called evolution, without particular reference to the mechanism of the process. (For a discussion of the changing usage of 'evolution' and 'development' through the last century, see Gould, 1977.) The 'theory of progressive development', which Lindley rejected, amounted to a belief, as he outlines it, that 'in the beginning, only the most simple forms of animals and plants were created, and that a gradual advance took place in their degree of organisation, till it was closed by the final creation of warm-blooded animals... and dicotyledonous trees.' For he goes on to say that 'in the vegetable kingdom, it cannot be conceded that any satisfactory evidence has yet been produced on the subject'. Lindley's rejection of evolutionary change through the course of time really impeded his disinterested interpretation of some plant fossils, and perhaps drove him into pushing some of his fossil plants into implausible modern genera (for example his assignments of *Solenites* and *Lindleycladus* discussed above).

None the less, Lindley seems to be quite content with the recognition of major changes in animal life through the course of geological time. In the preface to volume 1 the authors write 'That the face of the globe has successively undergone total changes, at different remote epochs, is now a fact beyond all dispute; as also, that long anterior to the creation of man, this world was inhabited by races of animals to which no parallels are now to be found'.

The general idea that there have been no significant changes in the broad composition of global vegetation through geological time is also evident in Lindley's preparedness to assign Carboniferous fossils to the angiosperms solely on the evidence of vegetative characters. For example, he writes of the arborescent lycopod *Sigillaria* (of which the spore-bearing cones were then unknown) that 'it is extremely probable, indeed almost certain that *Sigillaria* was a Dicotyledonous plant, for no others at the present day have a *true separable bark*'. His rejection of evolutionary change was indeed a serious impediment, since he sought to interpret all fossil plants in terms of groups now extant. As the distinguished palaeobotanist Albert Long has written (in Andrews, 1980) 'Unfortunately, Lindley only knew extant plants and his knowledge was almost an encumbrance impeding the correct interpretation of the fossils'.

As we have seen from his conclusions from his taphonomic experiments, Lindley was inclined to see the paucity of other angiosperms in the

Carboniferous flora as due to their poor capacity to survive fossilisation, rather than to their absence from the flora. The lack of fossil grasses, even in Tertiary rocks, presented a particular problem. In his introduction to vol. I, Lindley writes that 'no trace of any glumaceous plant [broadly, grasses and sedges] has been met with, even in the latest Tertiary rocks'. He goes on to make one of his most revealing observations illustrating his concept of the nature of successive creations.'It may, indeed, be conjectured, that before the creation of herbivorous animals, Grasses and Sedges were not required, and therefore are not to be expected in any beds before the [Jurassic] Forest Marble, and Stonesfield Slate; but it is difficult to conceive how the animals of the upper Tertiary beds could have been fed, if Grasses had not then been present'.

The Fossil Flora: the assessment of posterity

The context in which the *Fossil Flora* was written is so well reviewed by Andrews (1980) that little need be said of this here. A number of earlier works had been published dealing with British plant fossils, most notably Artis' *Antediluvian Phytology* (Artis, 1825) and Witham's *Fossil Vegetables* (Witham, 1831). The former contained some twenty-four plates of British Carboniferous plant fossils, while Witham's work concentrated on the internal structure of plants revealed by thin sections. The *Fossil Flora*, in contrast, dealt largely with compression and impression fossils, and includes few specimens showing internal anatomy. Its concept was also of course on a far grander scale than that of either of the earlier works.

Andrews (1980) records that the *Fossil Flora* 'has been variously maligned by later workers', but cites a generous comment on it made by the Cambridge palaeobotanist, Newell Arber. Kidston (1891) wrote a rather less kindly critique dealing only with the the Carboniferous plants. He wrote that 'the point where Lindley and Hutton's *Fossil Flora* breaks down under critical examination is the inaccuracy of the plates; and this charge cannot be brought, but in a slight degree, against their contemporary workers. It is a point difficult to excuse, and has led to much confusion'. Seward (1898), writing a historical sketch at the start of his four-volume work on fossil plants, brushes past the *Fossil Flora*, and extols the work of Witham for its importance in dealing with microscopic structure. He wrote 'If we look back… and peruse the pages of Lindley and Hutton's classic work… and finally take stock of our present knowledge of such [fossil] plants we realise what enormous progress has been made in palaeobotanical studies.' This rather withering assessment is a harsh judgement on the first, and only, attempt at a fossil flora of Britain!

I think in fairness that the *Fossil Flora* should be judged more for the authors' perception of what palaeobotany held for the future, than in the value of their catalogue itself. In the introduction to volume I they wrote: '…the probable condition of the atmosphere at the most remote periods – what gradual changes that climate may have undergone since living things first began to exist – whether there have been from the commencement, a progressive development of their organisation – all these are questions which it is the province of the Botanist to determine, or which his enquiries must at least tend very much to elucidate'. Changing climate, the composition of the atmosphere in the geological past and evolutionary change are all topics of lively interest now, a hundred and fifty years on. The preparation of fossil cuticles by oxidative maceration and the idea of experimenting with the process of fossilisation were both fundamental pioneering contributions; and yet those two important elements of palaeobotany had to wait nearly a century before they were exploited by others.

---

1. I am indebted to Professor W.T. Stearn for the following summary of publication of the *Fossil Flora*.
Volume 1 (1831-1833)
>   Plates 1-10, July 1831; 11-20, October 1831; 21-30, January 1831; 19bis, 31-39, April 1832; 40-49, July 1832; 50-59, October 1982; 60-69, January 1822; 70-79, April 1833.
Volume 2 (1833-1835)
>   Plates 80-89, July 1833; 90-99, October 1933; 100-109, January 1834; 110-118, April 1834; 119-127, July 1834; 128-137, October 1834; 138-146, January 1835; 147-156, April 1835.
Volume 3 (1835-1837)
>   Plates 157-165, July 1835; 155-176, October 1835; 177-184, January 1836; 185-194, April 1836; 195-203, January 1837; 204-230, July 1837.

References

Andrews, H.N. 1980. *The Fossil Hunters: in Search of ancient Plants*. Cornell University Press, Ithaca, New York. 421pp.

Bornemann, J.G. 1856. *Uber Organische Reste der Lettenkohlengruppe Thuringens*. Leipzig, 85pp.

Brongniart, A. 1828. *Prodrome d'une Histoire des Végétaux fossiles: Dictionnaire des Sciences Naturelles* 57; 16-212.

Cleevely, R.J. 1983. *World Palaeontological Collections*. British Museum (Natural History) and Mansell, London, 365 pp.

Gould, S.J. 1977. *Ever since Darwin*. Norton, New York. 285pp.

Harris, T.M., Millington, W. & Miller, J. 1974. *The Yorkshire Jurassic Flora* 4: 1, *Ginkgoales* 2, *Czekanowskiales*. London, British Museum (Natural History). 150 pp.

Harris, T.M. 1979. *The Yorkshire Jurassic Flora* 5: *Coniferales*. British Museum (Natural History). 166 pp.

Howse, R. 1890. Contributions towards a catalogue of the Flora of the Carboniferous System of Northumberland and Durham. Part I. Fossil Plants from the Hutton Collection. *Natural History Transactions of the Northumberland, Durham and Newcastle-on-Tyne Natural History Society* 10: 19–151.

Kidston, R. 1891. Notes on the Palaeozoic species mentioned in Lindley and Hutton's Fossil Flora. *Proceedings of the Royal Physical Society, Edinburgh* 10: 345–391.

Lebour, G.A. (Ed.) 1877. *Illustrations of Fossil Plants; an Autotype Reproduction of selected Drawings prepared under the Direction of Dr. Lindley and W. Hutton between 1835 and 1840.* Northern England Institute of Mining and Mechanical Engineers, Newcastle. pp. i–iv, 1–139, 65pl.

Lindley, J. & Hutton, W. 1831–37. *The Fossil Flora of Great Britain, or Figures and Descriptions of the vegetable Remains found in a fossil State in this Country.* Vol. 1, pp. 1–218, pls. 1–79 (1833). Vol. 2, pp. 1–206, pls. 80–156 (1835). Vol. 3, pp. 1–205, pls. 157–230, (1837). John Ridgway, Piccadilly, London.

Seward, A.C. 1898. *Fossil Plants for Students of Botany and Geology.* Vol. 1, 1–452. Cambridge University Press.

Williamson, W.C. 1896. *Reminiscences of a Yorkshire Naturalist.* George Redway, London. 228 pp.

Part VII

THE LINDLEY LIBRARY
AND JOHN LINDLEY'S LIBRARY

Brent Elliott

The Creation of the Lindley Library Trust

After thirty-one years as Assistant Secretary of the Horticultural Society of London, Lindley was appointed Secretary in 1858. It was not a time for celebration: the Society, after more than half a century of alternately flourishing and troubled circumstances, seemed finally on the point of collapse, due to loss of revenue. In 1854 the Society's *Journal* ceased publication; in 1856 the Society sold its herbarium, and began trying to sell its offices in Regent Street, in which venture it finally succeeded in 1859. And, using the not altogether convincing argument that without the offices, it had no accommodation, the Society put its Library up for sale at Sotheby's.[1]

The sale took place over four days, from 2 to 5 May 1859 and fetched a total of £1,112.1.6. Among the works sold, to list only those the auctioneers found it worth mentioning in their announcement, were Sibthorp and Smith's *Flora Graeca,* the *Flora Danica,* Tenore's *Flora Napoletana,* Vellozo's *Flora Fluminensis,* Gallesio's *Pomona italiana,* Bateman's *Orchidaceae of Mexico and Guatemala,* Lindley's *Sertum orchidaceum,* 'the splendid publications of Jacquin' and a wide range of original drawings. Neither the *Flora Napoletana* nor the *Flora Fluminensis* has ever been replaced in the Society's Library, and only an incomplete set of the *Flora Danica* has been acquired since.[2]

The sale of the Library did not take place unopposed. The leading gardening newspaper, the *Gardeners' Chronicle*, declined to comment on the matter, but then Lindley was its editor. Its leading rival, the *Cottage Gardener*, known for its occasional anti-Lindley stance, denounced the proposed sale months in advance: 'Why, the first thing every Society aims at is to obtain a library. Their libraries are the pride of our Mechanics' Institutes… Will it, then, have to be said, in this age of progress and diffusion of knowledge, that the Horticultural Society sold its library because it could not afford to keep it?'[3] Within two weeks of the Library's sale, the *Gardeners' Chronicle* reported that 'the Council have at last succeeded in placing the Society in a safe position'.[4] The implication, unstated in Lindley's periodical, is that the sale of the Library (nowhere mentioned in the article) was unnecessary and could have been prevented with little expenditure of effort.

Lindley appears to have purchased items at the sale of the Society's Library himself. One of the lots sold on the fourth day consisted of Suter's *Flora Helvetica* (1802), and two works of Swartz, *Nova Genera et Species Plantarum* (1788) and *Flora Indiae occidentalis* (1799-1800). All three formed part of the Lindley Library, the Suter volume still bearing the Horticultural Society's stamps, and an inscription from Charles Annesley, who had presented it to the Society in 1822. The purchase price for the three books was two shillings.

It is worth noting at this point that the smaller library established at the Society's Chiswick garden for the use of its students was not included in the sale; this library was transferred to the Society's new garden at Wisley in 1903 and has thus had an unbroken existence since the 1820s.

Lindley retired from his position as Secretary in February 1863 and died in November 1865. In January 1866 the Society learned that his personal library was available for sale and began to consider means of acquiring it. By May the Council had put £600 toward this purpose.[5] In that month also (22-25 May), the Society convened an International Horticultural Exhibition and International Botanical Congress, which netted an unforeseen surplus of nearly £3,000, and by September the thought was being voiced that the cost of purchasing Lindley's library could be debited to that surplus. George Fergusson Wilson, who had become a Council member the year before, wrote to the *Gardeners' Chronicle*, 'One mode already suggested, viz., the purchase by the Exhibition Committee of the Lindley Library, to be placed in bookcases, where Fellows of the Royal Horticultural Society could easily refer to it, would, I think, be a fair one.'[6]

At the next year's annual general meeting the acquisition of Lindley's library came under scrutiny, not only as to the purchase arrangements – could the Society use the Exhibition Committee's profits, and could it afford to buy the collection otherwise? – but as to its long-term welfare. Edgar Bowring argued that 'it would be better that it should not be held as the property of the Society, for fear of what might by any mischance occur, and they would do better to act in the position of trustees'.[7] In due course a compromise was reached between Council and the Exhibition Committee, whereby each party nominated Trustees, and a Trust Deed was drawn up. Among its provisions were the accommodation of the Library intact even if the Society moved or folded, and the obligation of the Society to pay for a Librarian if one was employed. At the first meeting of the Lindley Library Trust, on 24 March 1868, the selection of the Trustees was finalised: Thomas Moore (Curator of the Chelsea Physic Garden), Maxwell T. Masters (Lindley's successor as editor of the *Gardeners' Chronicle*), Robert Hogg (editor of the *Journal of Horticulture*, the successor to the *Cottage Gardener*), John Clutton (the Society's Treasurer), Henry Young

Darracott Scott (its incoming Secretary), William Wilson Saunders (its outgoing Secretary) and Sir Charles Wentworth Dilke. The Trust Deed was formally signed on 5 May 1868; the surplus from the Exhibition became the Trust's fund, and the Society was refunded its £600. There was now a new library, held as a trust and inalienable by the Society, partially administered by the Society, and accessible to its fellows.

   Public response was immediate and enthusiastic, to judge by the donations made in the early years. Lindley's collection amounted to 1,300 volumes, including several journals; by the time the Lindley Library Trust had been established, three years had elapsed since Lindley's death, and the Trust had to advertise for the issues for the intervening years to be donated.[8] In many cases the sets were completed. James Bateman responded to the plea by completing the Library's set of Reichenbach's *Xenia orchidacea*; Queen Victoria presented two works, splendidly bound with prominent donation labels worked on to the front boards: Roxburgh's *Plants of the Coast of Coromandel* (1795-1819), and Hooker's *Filices exoticae* (1859). Other early donors specified in the Trustees' minutes included Bentham, Hooker, and J. Russell Reeves, whose 1868 gift included the 1817-28 edition of Curtis' *Flora Londinensis,* Gaertner's *De Fructibus et Seminibus* (1788-1807), and Nees von Esenbeck's *Genera Plantarum Florae Germanicae* (1833-45). At a later (unspecified) date, Bateman also presented a magnificent copy of Hernandez' *Rerum medicarum Novae Hispaniae* (1651). The last major gift of the century was received in 1894, when the nurseryman James Douglas presented Jean-Jacques Rousseau's signed copy of Albrecht von Haller's *Historia Stirpium indigenarum Helvetiae* (1768). The greatest donation of all came in 1936, when the bequest of Reginald Cory brought an immense number of titles that had been sold in 1859 and not hitherto replaced, as well as some of the actual drawings then dispersed. And since Cory had bought different editions from those Lindley had, the Lindley Library has the probably unique advantage of holding both the original edition of Sibthorp and Smith's *Flora Graeca* and the Bohn re-issue, and the original edition of Rumphius' *Herbarium Amboinense* and the Uytwerf re-issue.

   As the original Trustees died, they were replaced by others: E.A. Bowles, John T. Bennett-Poë, William Carruthers, Sir John Bretland Farmer (the editor of *Annals of Botany*), George Maw (author of *The Genus Crocus*), and the nurseryman Harry Veitch, with William Wilks, the Society's Secretary, *ex officio*. The Trust's last years can be seen as a contest between Masters and Wilks over the control of the Library. The question of dual ownership had long been looming, since the Society had continued to buy books out of its own budget; these were entered in the Lindley Library's catalogue (see below), and in the early days such books were frequently stamped twice, once with the Trust's stamp and once with the Society's South Kensington stamp. In 1888, the Society abandoned its Kensington site and moved its offices into rented accommodation on Victoria Street; the Lindley Library's room doubled as the Council Room. The following year, Council placed the charge of any books belonging to the Society in the hands of the Trustees; twenty years later, Council set up a committee to meet the Trustees in order to distinguish the Society's books from the Trust's.

Masters was the last of the original Trustees to die, and at the very meeting at which his death was announced, in 1907, the possibility was discussed of handing the Trust over to the Society's Council. In 1910 the Charity Commissioners gave their approval for a new Trust Deed, which named Council as the sole Trustee. In the Annual Report, Wilks wrote that this move was necessary because there had been nothing to stop the Trust from removing the books from the Society's custody.

So on 22 November 1910, the Lindley Library came under the direct control of the Royal Horticultural Society, and for practical purposes, the Lindley Library Trust was succeeded by the Society's Library Committee. The remaining members of the Trust, Bennett-Poë, Bowles, Veitch, and Wilks, were retained as members of the Committee, with B. Daydon Jackson of the *Index Kewensis*, C. Harman Payne of the *Florist's Bibliography*, and the orchid grower J. Gurney Fowler as new members. So smooth was the transition that no formal statement of library policy was required; as Bowles was to say in 1920, 'every possible book of use to horticulturists should be included'. It was not until 1988-1989 that a Library Review Committee undertook an itemised list of core and selective subjects as an official guide to purchasing policy.

Since 1910, the legal status of the Lindley Library Trust has for practical purposes been a means of ensuring that the Library could not be disposed of. But a distinction still remained between the contents of the Lindley Library, which until the 1980s was financed by its Trust fund, topped up from time to time by the sale of duplicates, and those books which the Society purchased out of its own money. In 1925, H.D. McLaren (later the 2nd Lord Aberconway, and the Society's President from 1931-1953) proposed that a means be established of distinguishing from the Lindley Library's books those books owned by the R.H.S., which could in principle be sold; Sir William Lawrence, the Society's Treasurer, and E.A. Bunyard, the nurseryman and Chairman of the Library Committee, opposed the notion. In 1926 the Library's Trust Deed was revised to include an amendment that all books owned by the Society would be deemed to belong to the Lindley Library.

From 1904, when the Society's New Hall (now the Old Hall, or even, in commercial parlance, Hall 1) on Vincent Square was opened, the Library occupied an area on the upper (second) floor of its offices, with a large reading room and a librarian's office. By the 1920s it was rapidly outgrowing this space. In that decade the Society constructed a New Hall behind its original one, and the transfer of the Library into the new building was discussed and rejected. A grant from the Carnegie Trust enabled the Society to add a third floor to the Vincent Square building, specifically for the Library; the architect of the facilities was Binnie. Baron Henry Schröder had paid for the furnishings of the Library in 1904; these furnishings were transferred to the new floor, and his son Baron Bruno Schröder paid for them to be extended in the same style. There was now a reading room and a stack room of equal size but far greater density of shelving. After the Second World War, the Library took over a basement storage area; in the early 1960s the old kitchens in the basement were converted into a further storage area, to part of which mobile shelving was added in the 1980s. By the 1990s the Library, with a steadily increasing purchasing budget, was bursting at the seams, and a design was produced by Rick Mather for an entirely new library facility on the ground floor and basement.

The Carnegie Trust, in making its grant for the construction of the Library facilities, imposed the condition that it be open not only to members of the Society, but to students, and that it lend books through inter-library loan. Since then, the Library at Vincent Square has been effectively open to the public, or at least to anyone with a bona fide horticultural enquiry. The Wisley Library has remained dedicated to the students and staff of the garden, with other readers having to apply to the Director for permission to use it. In 1996, a small reading room was opened at Wisley for the use of members and the public and has proved a most successful venture.

From the original purchase of 1,300 volumes, the Lindley Library has grown enormously. In the collection at Vincent Square (accurate figures are not currently available for the Wisley Library, which holds roughly a fifth of the amount of the London holdings), there are, at the time of writing, over 50,000 volumes of books and pamphlets, some 1,500 periodical runs (400 of them current), 18,000 drawings (including a collection of 6,000 orchid portraits), trade catalogues representing some 3,200 firms, and the Society's archives.

Let me conclude the story of the Lindley Library with a list of its Librarians:

1872–75	W.T. Thiselton Dyer	
1875–78	William Botting Hemsley	
1878–80	Samuel Jennings	Assistant Secretary
1880–90	James West	R. Microscop. Soc.'s Librarian, seconded
1890–97	John Weathers	Assistant Secretary
1897–33	H.R. Hutchinson	
1933–52	William T. Stearn	
1953–56	Miss L.D. Whiteley	
1957–82	Peter F.M. Stageman	
1982–	Brent Elliott	

From 1931 to 1939 F.J. Chittenden was simultaneously R.H.S. Technical Adviser Editor of R.H.S. publications and Keeper of the Lindley Library as compensation for his removal from the directorship of the Wisley Garden, but the actual librarians were H.R. Hutchinson directly followed by W.T. Stearn during this period.

The Cataloguing of the Lindley Library

It would be helpful if a complete catalogue of Lindley's collection had been prepared and published immediately. Unfortunately, the policy of the Trustees on cataloguing was dutiful but unimaginative. Alfred W. Bennett, the lecturer on botany at Westminster Hospital, was commissioned to prepare a catalogue, and he did this by the simple expedient of annotating an interleaved copy of Pritzel's *Thesaurus Litteraturae botanicae* (1847-51), which was then bound up with the words 'Lindley Library Catalogue' on the front board, but with Pritzel's title on the spine. Works listed by Pritzel were simply ticked to show their presence in Lindley's collection; additional titles were written on the interleaved pages. Bennett made mistakes in the rendering of dates in Roman numerals, and was erratic in his treatment of names. However for his job of at least creating an entry for each item in the collection he certainly deserved the honorarium of 30 guineas.

The problem arose over subsequent additions to the collection. Exactly the same procedure was used by the first Librarians, Thiselton Dyer, Hemsley, and West, with the result that ticked entries in the Pritzel catalogue (as opposed to additional titles entered in handwriting, in which case one can at least distinguish Bennett's hand from his successors) cannot be used to distinguish Lindley's own copies from copies donated to or purchased by the Trustees up to the late 1890s. At least when books were added that had been purchased by the R.H.S., not the Lindley Library Trust, they were marked 'RHS' in the margin. The Trustees' minutes frequently record donations to the Library, and booksellers' invoices are pasted in, but the number of individual titles thus recorded is only a fraction of what the Trustees acquired. And even then the donations are not always itemised: Charles Wentworth Dilke, for example, donated forty-three volumes of Ray Society publications; but as Lindley already had some Ray Society publications in his collection, it would be rash to attempt to say whose were whose.

In 1897 John Weathers, the Society's Assistant Secretary and therefore acting Librarian, compiled a new catalogue, which was published under the Society's auspices in 1898. The marking-up of Pritzel's *Thesaurus* thereupon ceased, so at least post-1897 additions cannot be confused with Lindley's own stock. Weathers, incidentally, was not a great cataloguer either; errors in his catalogue were one of the reasons for his dismissal from the Society's service late in 1897.

In the wake of Weathers' catalogue, the new Librarian, H.R. Hutchinson (who had been a clerical assistant to B. Daydon Jackson at Kew in compilation of the *Index Kewensis)*, initiated a card catalogue, which has been carried through into the 1990s, with six different handwritings, typescript, and computer printing; and with varying standards of cataloguing, with British Museum and Cambridge University Library rules at different times, in addition to Hutchinson's minimalist entries. A new printed catalogue was published in 1927. During the 1930s, William T. Stearn's work on cataloguing the Cory Bequest became the basis for fifteen papers on the dates of botanical works which he published in the newly founded *Journal of the Society for the Bibliography of Natural History*. Today, a computerised catalogue is in progress which will make the contents of the collection accessible to scholars at a distance, while being searchable in a way that a printed catalogue cannot.

Disposal of works

The failure to differentiate new purchases from the original copies is not the only source of ambiguity in the Pritzel catalogue; another is the failure to record disposal and replacement.

On the completion of Bennett's catalogue in 1868, the Trustees disposed of a number of superfluous items to the bookseller J. Wheldon for £50.14.6. Most of these works were zoological. The journals and proceedings of the Geographical Society also went, and an incomplete set of *Curtis's Botanical Magazine*, as did a work by Chapman called *The American Rifle*, indicating an interest of Lindley's not otherwise apparent from the literature. By no means all duplicates in the collection were sold; some were transferred to the students' library at Chiswick.

This process of attrition has continued in some ways in the intervening century and more. The 1927 amendment to the Trust Deed allowed for the sale of duplicate copies in order to replenish the Library's finances, and over the ensuing sixty years sales of duplicates were held from time to time. The concept of 'duplicate' was not satisfactorily defined at the outset: coloured and un-coloured copies of the same work, for instance, have been treated as duplicates, and one of the two sold. As a result of this policy, Lindley's own copies, if unsigned, unannotated, and altogether lacking in distinguishing marks, have from time to time been disposed of as duplicates when superior copies of works have been donated or purchased.

This process may have begun as early as 1875. Lindley's collection held the first volume only of Siebold and Zuccarini's *Flora Japonica*. This was one of the titles listed in the *Gardeners' Chronicle* when the Trustees launched their appeal for donations of wanting parts; and obviously no one came forward with the second volume. In a memorandum written in the Trustees' minute book after the meeting of 2 December 1874, Maxwell T. Masters recorded that a complete set of the *Flora Japonica* had been purchased, and Lindley's own copy must thereafter have been sold.

The Contents of Lindley's Library

We can now discuss the contents of Lindley's collection of books but we cannot, unfortunately, document its growth.

Lindley did not, as a rule, annotate his books, and on the surviving evidence seldom even wrote his name in them. It may be that he signed his copies more often in the 1820s than later in life. In some cases, a later hand has written his name on the title pages or fly-leaves. In a few cases (Blume's *Collection des Orchidées*, Schleiden's *Grundzüge*), there are notes in Lindley's hand noting the date of receipt.

Possibly subsequent rebinding has removed Lindley's signature from some of the works in his collection. Indeed, a number of authors' signatures were deliberately removed at some point, by cutting off an upper portion of fly-leaf or title page, presumably to make a collection of famous names.[9] This was not done systematically or efficiently, for various signatures still remain. Presentation inscriptions that do not include a signature have been left, and in a few cases (Chavannes' *Monographie des Antirrhinées*), the author's letter of presentation has been tipped in.

Where Lindley did annotate works extensively, he preferred to have them bound interleaved, so that his comments could be written unconfined on facing pages, and the margins of the printed page reserved for ticks and crosses. Among the works he annotated were Jussieu's *Genera Plantarum*, Brongniart's *Prodrome d'une Histoire des Végétaux fossiles* (1828), Hedwig's *Theoria Generationis et Fructificationis Plantarum cryptogamicarum* (1784), and some of his own works. His early (1819) translation of Achille Richard's essay on fruits and seeds has a list of botanists to whom he presumably sent copies; his *Nixus Plantarum* (1833) is marked with corrections; and the third edition (1853) of his *Vegetable Kingdom* is annotated with amendments for a future but never achieved edition.

Lindley appears, so far as the visual evidence reveals, to have used the same firm of bookbinders throughout his career: Hering's of 9 Newman Street, whom he continued to use after the firm was taken over in 1844 by Clyde.[10] His practice in binding was frequently designed to frustrate attempts to arrange the contents of his library by subject. Raoul's *Choix des Plantes de la Nouvelle-Zélande* was bound with Bennett and Brown's *Plantae Javanicae*; La Billardière's *Icones Plantarum Syriae rariorum* and Hedwig on cryptogamic botany bound with

Schmidel's *Dissertationes botanici*; Lindley's own work on *Victoria regia* bound with Bateman's *Orchidaceae of Mexico and Guatemala*. The most extreme development of this principle of binding together works of similar size is to be found in his collection of pamphlets.

One major feature of Lindley's library was a series of 127 volumes, mostly labelled 'Botanical Tracts', containing pamphlets that ranged from common-or-garden copies of Linnean Society offprints to rare copies of seedlists from St Petersburg. Each volume contained an initial page with a list of contents in Lindley's handwriting. A few volumes were grouped according to a theme, but for the majority the only common factor shared by the works in a given volume was their comparative uniformity of size. These pamphlets, many of which are inscribed by their authors, provide our best record of the extensive network of international connections that Lindley built up. Among the authors represented in substantial quantity are John Hutton Balfour, George Bentham, Willibald Besser, Alexander Braun, Cambessèdes, De Candolle, Caspary, Choisy, F. Cohn, Colla, Decaisne, Alexander Dickson, Duchartre, Endlicher, Ettingshausen, Fenzl, Gasparrini, Gaudichaud-Beaupré, Asa Gray, Hasskarl, J.S. Haworth, Henslow, Kunth, Link, Miquel, Mohl, Morren, Ferdinand Mueller (at the beginning of his career), Nägeli, Parlatore, Planchon, C.B. Presl, Achille Richard, Schleiden, Séringe, Tenore, Vriese, and Wikström.

When did Lindley have the 'Tracts' bound up? The sequence includes four volumes with the subordinate title of 'Agricultural tracts', four of 'Horticultural', and three of 'French horticultural tracts', most of them late in the sequence, and there are individual volumes on *Rosa* and beetroot, and two on the potato blight. The first volume of all contains Lindley's manuscript report of 1852 on the use of chicory to adulterate coffee and related material, and the early volumes consist largely of works from the 1850s. On the basis of the distribution of dates, of the diversity of bindings (even where there is no evidence of subsequent rebinding), of inconsistent numbers inked on cloth spines, of labels pasted on and of evidence of other labels having been removed, I conclude that Lindley had long been binding groups of pamphlets together in this manner, but at some point after 1856 decided to unify his miscellaneous volumes in one common series. A further evidence that the arrangement was undertaken as a single act is the fact that the volumes are arranged in order of height: the first forty-six volumes are quartos, the remainder octavos.

A further eleven volumes of 'Botanical Tracts' were added during the Trust's time, but meanwhile Maxwell T. Masters had started to follow Lindley's example, and bind up his miscellanea in a separate series entitled 'Botanical Pamphlets'. The chronological range of these was ultimately from the 1850s to the beginning of the twentieth century; the series would have ended at Masters' death with volume 128 had not a further seven volumes of the late nineteenth century material been added afterwards. The purely chronological sequence in this pamphlet run can be seen from the indiscriminate mixture of volume sizes.

It is interesting evidence of Lindley's mental decline in his last years that his book purchasing effectively came to an end in 1863; the only new books added to his collection thereafter, as far as I can trace, are presentation copies. Periodical subscriptions also began to slide from that year, and only the Horticultural Society's publications and the *Gardeners' Chronicle* continued intact through 1865. The only foreign journal to be received in his last year was *Revue Horticole*, and some issues of that were wanting when it came into the Trustees' hands. Most of the periodicals were indeed made up by donors; more difficult to make up were wanting instalments of part-works. So, for instance, Lindley had acquired the first volume of Tulasne's *Selectorum Fungorum Carpologia* (1861), and the Trustees had to appeal for the donation of the subsequent two volumes (1863-65).

It is also worth remarking that Lindley's collection contained a set of his own works, including foreign translations and copies of some of his articles in the Horticultural Society's *Transactions* bound individually as pamphlets. There were some exceptions, however: his posthumous publications (the *Treasury of Botany* with Thomas Moore and the *Pinetum Britannicum* with Ravenscroft) were understandably not represented, he had only an incomplete set of his *Folia orchidacea*, and there was no copy at all of his *Pomological Magazine* (one was soon supplied by donation). And although Lindley had written the text of the last two and a half volumes of Sibthorp and Smith's *Flora Graeca*, the limited print run, and the formidable cost of the work made them beyond his reach, apart from a volume labelled 'pars Lindleyana', containing the text only, not the plates, of the volumes he produced. The Trustees advertised for a donation of the earlier part of the work, and at an unspecified date a set whose binding bears the arms of the Sutherland family was added to the Lindley Library; the 'pars Lindleya' was transferred to Chiswick and is now in the Wisley Library.

Subject breakdown of Lindley's library

Lindley's library differed from the libraries of certain other great botanists, like those of Sir Joseph Banks, whose catalogue was published by Dryander while Banks was still alive, and Aylmer Bourke Lambert, the sale catalogues of whose library and herbarium, annotated with the prices fetched, are contained in Lindley's 'Botanical Tracts'. These were intended as comprehensive self-sufficient libraries, the equivalent of the libraries later established at Kew and the British Museum (Natural History), accessible more or less freely to scholars. Lindley himself had been employed in Banks' library at the beginning of his career, and was obviously aware of the nature and social purposes of such collections, which formed a model of similar enterprises such as William Roscoe's in Liverpool.[11] But his own library was not intended to be self-sufficient and complete in the way the collections of these wealthy men had been.

Botany predominates over horticulture in Lindley's collection. A comparison of his library with that of the Horticultural Society as sold in 1859 makes it clear that he seldom purchased for himself books accessible to him at the Society's offices. There was a certain degree of duplication, but much of it consisted of Lindley's own works and the Horticultural Society's publications. Where major monographs and expensive illustrated works appeared in both collections, in some cases at least Lindley's copies came to him from the authors, and where there is no written evidence of presentation, the fact that the authors were his friends and colleagues, Hooker, Bateman, Brown, De Candolle, makes it at least possible that Lindley's copies were gifts. In 1850, for example, J.J. Bennett gave Lindley a copy of Robert Brown's *Prodromus Florae Novae Hollandiae*, but Lindley never opened the pages; presumably there was a copy in the Horticultural Society's library. In short, Lindley's personal collection was built up as a supplement to the Society's, and was devoted primarily to those subjects which the Society had not made it a policy to acquire.

Not surprisingly for the author of *The Vegetable Kingdom*, Lindley being an active taxonomist had a strong collection of works on systematic botany. He possessed the second (1783) edition of the *Philosophia botanica*, two editions of the *Species Plantarum* (Trattner's third edition, 1764, and Willdenow's fourth edition, 1797-1830), and the Römer and Schultes edition (1817-30) of the *Systema Vegetabilium*. Of greater interest is the number of works on natural classification and its competing systems, from Jussieu until Lindley's own time: Jussieu's *Genera Plantarum* (1789), one of the few books Lindley annotated; Lamarck's *Encyclopédie méthodique: Botanique* (1781-1817); Kunth's *Synopsis Plantarum* (1822-25) and *Enumeratio Plantarum* (1833-43); G. Don's *General History of dichlamydeous Plants* (1831-8); K.F. Meisner's *Plantarum vascularium Genera* (1836-43); Reichenbach's *Handbuch des natürlichen Pflanzensystems* (1837); and Walpers' *Repertorium* (1840-41), not to mention a handy reference work like Steudel's *Nomenclator botanicus* (1840-41). The climax of the collection was a set of De Candolle's *Prodromus* up to part xv (1862); many individual parts are inscribed to Lindley by De Candolle.

As for works on individual families and genera of flowering plants, Lindley's collection was replete with pamphlets but weak on major monographs. The following list is interesting from several points of view: Reichenbach on *Aconitum* (1823-27); Pallas on *Astragalus* (1800); Boott on *Carex* (1858-67); George Bentham's *Labiatarum* (1832-6); De Candolle on *Leguminosae* (1825-26); Naudin's *Melastomacearum* (1849-53); the 1842 edition of Lambert's *Genus*

Pinus; and De Candolle's *Plantarum historia succulentarum (*1799-1829). Some of these (De Candolle, Naudin) were presentation copies to Lindley; of the rest, Bentham and the original edition of Lambert were present in the Horticultural Society's library; and the subject matter was in some cases irrelevant to garden planting, other than for a botanical garden. In addition to his own, Lindley (unsurprisingly) had Allen's and Hooker's monographs on *Victoria regia*. The absence of much orchid literature apart from his own writings is easily explained by his pioneering role in the taxonomy of this family; but he did have a presentation copy of Blume's *Tabellen* (1825), Linden's *Pescatorea* (1860), and one of the last works he must have acquired was Darwin's *Fertilization of orchids* (1863).

Revealing of Lindley's pattern of acquisition is the high proportion of works on cryptogamic botany. Apart from such general works as Greville's *Scottish cryptogamic Flora* (1823-29), Kuetzing's *Phycologia* (1843), and Martius' *Icones Plantarum cryptogamarum* (1828-34), Lindley had important works on algae by Agardh and Hassall; Fries' *Lichenographia* (1834); works on fungi by Roques, Fries, Berkeley, and Nees von Esenbeck, as well as James Bolton's *History of Fungusses* (1788-91), Corda's *Icones Fungorum* (1837-42), and the works of the brothers Tulasne; on mosses by Berkeley, Hooker; on liverworts by Nees; and on ferns by G.W. Francis, Fée, Swartz, and Thomas Moore. Apart from some of the last category, these are works which the Horticultural Society had not had in its Library; it can readily be imagined that Lindley needed access to them for the cryptogamic sections of *The Vegetable Kingdom* and his other taxonomic works, as also for his university teaching.

As for floras, which are of immense taxonomic assistance, Lindley's collection became stronger the more it moved away from the temperate countries which provide the majority of hardy garden plants. For the continent of Europe, we find Bulliard's *Herbier de la France* (six volumes bound in three), De Candolle's edition of Lamarck's *Flore Française*, and Gouan's *Flora Monspeliaca* (1765); Suter's *Flora Helvetica* (1802); Viviani's *Florae Lybicae Specimen* and *Flora Corsicae Specimen* (both 1824), and Gussone's *Flora Siculae Prodromus* (1827-8); Cavanilles' *Icones et Descriptiones Plantarum … in Hispania* (1791-1801); a couple of works by Fries to represent Scandinavia; Grisebach's *Spicilegium Florae Rumelicae (*1843-5) for the Balkan regions; and Vaucher's *Histoire physiologique des Plantes de l'Europe* (1841). This is an odd scattering of works, but the principal floras were in the Horticultural Society's Library.

Asia was better represented: Bunge, Gmelin, Ledebour, Pallas, and Marschall von Bieberstein for Russia and the Caucasus; Hooker and Wallich for the Himalayas; Boissier's *Diagnoses* for southwest Asia. For the Indian peninsula, he had Roxburgh's *Flora Indica (*1832), Royle's *Illustrations of the Botany … of the Himalayan Mountains* (1839), and the works of Robert Wight. On Indonesia he was particularly well supplied: Blume's *Flora Javae, Rumphia,* and *Enumeratio Plantarum*; Bennett and Brown's *Plantae Javanicae* (1838-52); and a set of Rumphius. Loureiro's *Flora Cochinchinensis* (1790), Blanco's *Flora de Filipinas* (1837), and the first volume of Siebold's *Flora Japonica* complete this area. Of all these works, only Loureiro, Marschall von Bieberstein, Roxburgh, Royle, and Wallich were in the Horticultural Society's Library. Lindley can thus be seen as building up a collection of the major works on India and southeast Asia to fill for his own systematic purposes the gap in the Society's holdings.

On Africa he possessed little apart from Mungy's *Flore de l'Algérie* (1847) and Schultes' revision of Thunberg's *Flora Capensis* (1818-20). He did have an incomplete set of Webb and Berthelot's *Histoire naturelle des Iles Canaries*. For Australasia he had Guillemin's *Icones lithographicae Plantarum Australasicae* (1827); Ronald C. Gunn's manuscript notes on Van Diemen's Land (1838); Raoul on New Zealand; and Hooker's *Botany of the Antarctic Voyage*.

For North America he had works of John Torrey and Asa Gray, Pursh's *Flora Americae Septentrionalis* (1816), Beck's *Botany of the northern and midland States* (1833 – an autographed copy), Hooker's *Flora Boreali-americana* (1833-40), and Michaux' *Histoire des Arbres forestiers de l'Amérique* (1810-13), together with its English translation as *North American Sylva* (1817-19). On Central and South America he was better equipped: Achille Richard on Cuba (1838-42), Saint-Hilaire's *Flora Brasiliae meridionalis* (1825-33), Poeppig's *Nova Genera ac Species Plantarum* (1835-45), Martius' *Nova Genera et Species* (1824-32) and a few portions of the *Flora Brasiliensis*. He did not have Humboldt, Bonpland and Kunth; but both the *Plantes equinoxiales* and the *Nova Genera et Species Plantarum* were in the Society's Library.

As a general rule, then, Lindley's collections were strongest for those parts of the world in which the Horticultural Society's Library was deficient; and the motive of taxonomic sufficiency is an obvious reason for his acquisitions.

After taxonomy, plant morphology was a major strength of Lindley's collection. None of the following works was owned by the Society, but the author of the *Elements of Botany* had a clear need for such literature: De Candolle's *Organographie végétale* (1827), Gaudichaud-Beaupré's *Recherches générales sur l'Organographie* (1841), Goethe's *Metamorphose der Pflanzen* (1790), together with its French translation, Le Maout's *Atlas élémentaire* (1846) and *Flore élémentaire* (1855), Lestiboudois' *Phyllotaxie anatomique* (1848), Schleiden's *Die Pflanze* (1848 – bound together with Henfrey's translation), and Sprengel's *Entdeckte Geheimniss der Natur* (1793). Lindley kept abreast of the developing cell theory, with Mohl's *Anatomy and Physiology of the vegetable Cell* (1852), Schwann's *Mikroskopische Untersuchungen* (1839), and a presentation copy of Robert Brown's *Brief Account of microscopical Observations* (1828). Theis' *Glossaire de botanique* (1810) and Bischoff's *Handbuch der botanischen Terminologie* (1833-44) were of obvious utility to the man who tried to standardise botanical terminology.

The author of *Medical botany* also had an obvious need for works like Fée's *Cours d'Histoire naturelle pharmaceutique* (1828 – an incomplete set), Richard's *Elémens d'Histoire naturelle médicale* (1831), Guibourt's *Histoire abrégée des Drogues simples* (3rd edition, 1836), Geiger's *Pharmaceutische Botanik* (1839-40), Pereira's *Materia medica* (3rd edition, 1849), and Séringe's *Flore du Pharmacien* (1851). But neither he nor the Society possessed the major works on medicinal plants by Plenck, Churchill and Stephenson, Kerner, or Woodville; Lindley must have sought them out elsewhere.

Lindley did little antiquarian collecting. He owned a copy of the 1633 edition of Gerard's *Herball,* and a 1542 Fuchs, but otherwise the most interesting pre-Linnaean item in his collection was a copy of Piso's *De Medicina brasiliensi* (1648), with a label saying "BM Dupl. 1818". Of miscellaneous important works of botanical illustration, the following are worth singling out: De Candolle's *Plantes rares de Genève* (1824-45), Delessert's *Icones selectae Plantarum* (1820-46), several works by Jacquin, L'Heritier's *Sertum anglicum* (1788), Schnizlein's *Iconographia* (1843-47), and the works of Robert Sweet.

As for works of practical horticulture, these were of course well represented in the Society's Library, and we find that, apart from various works of Loudon, Rivers, Henry Phillips, Charles M'Intosh, and Lindley himself, his collection was unsystematic and scattered in its coverage, and strongest in the areas of fruit culture and forestry, works on forestry practice being the best sources for arboricultural technique in Lindley's day. The eighteenth century editions of Duhamel du Monceau, Poederlé's *Manual de l'Arboriste* (1788), Bechstein's *Forstinsectologie* (1829-35), the 1848 edition of Steuart's *Planter's Guide*, and Brown's *Forester* (1861); Thomas Andrew Knight's *Culture of the Apple and Pear* (1797), Noisette's *Jardin fruitier* (1821), and Odart's *Ampélographie universelle* (1849); Glendinning, Hamilton, and Mills on pineapple cultivation; M'Ewen on the peach and nectarine (1859), give the flavour of this aspect of the collection. When Miles J. Berkeley contributed a series of pioneering articles on vegetable pathology to the *Gardeners' Chronicle*, Lindley had them cut out and pasted in a volume.

Interestingly, Lindley owned a copy of Chevreul's *Cercles chromatiques*, but no copy of Chevreul's main work on simultaneous contrast of colours, either in French or in English, came to the Lindley Library Trust. Nor was there a copy of the work which had replaced Chevreul in Lindley's estimation as the authority on colour planning for the garden, Gardner Wilkinson's *On Colour* (1858). Nor did they appear in the Society's sale catalogue. Since Lindley had cited these works in his leaders in the *Gardeners' Chronicle*, it seems likely that they remained in the possession of the *Chronicle's* office, and therefore that

Lindley's collection was not built up from copies received for that journal.[12]

Lindley's private collection of periodicals was impressive and, at least as far as British titles were concerned, rivalled the Horticultural Society's own. Among botanical journals were: *Annals of Natural History*, *Annales des Sciences Naturelles*, *Botanische Zeitung*, *Linnaea*, *The Phytologist*, *Transactions of the Botanical Society of Edinburgh*, *Transactions* (and *Proceedings*) *of the Linnean Society*, and the *Zeitschrift für Wissenschaftliche Botanik*, as well as the various journals that Sir William Hooker had edited (*Botanical Miscellany*, *Journal of Botany*, *London Journal of Botany*, and *Icones Plantarum*). Among horticultural periodicals were Paxton and Main's *Horticultural Register*, *The Florist* (and its successor *The Florist and Pomologist*), *Revue Horticole*, *Illustration Horticole*, *L'Horticulteur Français*, and two specimen issues of *Le Bon Jardinier*. A complete set of Loddiges' *Botanical Cabinet* was supplemented by the *Botanical Register* and Paxton's *Flower Garden*, both of which Lindley himself had edited, and of course for the same reason there was a run of the *Gardeners' Chronicle*.

It should be apparent from this survey that, although the Lindley Library purchase was intended as a partial replacement of the Horticultural Society's lost library, it did not achieve that end. Lindley's collection duplicated the Society's significantly only in its range of periodicals and of some important illustrated books; the remaining duplication was of scattered titles. Lindley had never attempted to create a library that would rival the Society's; his private purchasing had been geared to filling the gaps, important for his work as a botanist, left by the Society's acquisitions policy. His books therefore gave the Society exactly what it had not had before: a botanical library strong in the fields of taxonomy, morphology, and certain categories of exotic floras. But the Lindley Library purchase also provided a stimulus to collecting books that the Society, in this troubled period, might otherwise have lacked; and although there are works sold in 1859 whose absence is still to be lamented, the Lindley Library today has largely recovered the ground lost in that sale, and built a great and flourishing collection from that basis.

---

1. The story of the sale of the original Library, and the foundation of the Lindley Library as its replacement, has been told skimpily in H.R. Fletcher, *The Story of the Royal Horticultural Society 1804-1968* (Oxford University Press, 1969), and more fully and polemically by W.L. Tjaden in two articles, 'The loss of a library', *The Garden (Journal of the Royal Horticultural Society)*, vol. 112 (1987), pp. 386-388, and 'The Lindley Library of the Royal Horticultural Society, 1866-1926', *Archives of Natural History*, vol. 20 (1993), pp. 93-128.

2. A photocopy of the 1859 sale catalogue, annotated with prices (but not, alas, with names of purchasers), is held in the Lindley Library..

3. *Cottage Gardener*, vol. 21 (1858-59), p. 241 (leader for the issue of 18 January).

4. *Gardeners' Chronicle,* 1859 (14 May), p.423.

5. Royal Horticultural Society, Minutes of Council, 23 January, 20 February, and 30 April 1866.

6. *Gardeners' Chronicle,* 1866 (20 September), p. 924.

7. *Gardeners' Chronicle,* 1867 (10 February), p. 154.

8. *Gardeners' Chronicle,* 1868 (5 December), pp. 1258-9.

9. An example of the end result of such a process may be seen in the Lindley Library, in the *carte de visite* album of Andrew Murray, Lindley's successor as Assistant Secretary of the Society. Instead of annotating the photographs himself, Murray inserted examples of the sitters' signatures clipped from letters − annoying to have to read for cataloguing purposes, and even more annoying when the absence of a convenient signature means that the portrait is unidentified.

10. See J.G. Marks, 'Bookbinding practices of the Hering family, 1794-1844', *British Library Journal,* vol. 6 (1980): pp.44-60. Binders' notices are too infrequent in Lindley's copies to give a useful sequence of his purchasing. His copy of Roxburgh's *Flora Indica* (1832) was bound by Clyde, therefore after 1844, but this fact alone does not date the purchase.

11. For the significance of these libraries, see Hortense S. Miller, 'The herbarium of Aylmer Bourke Lambert', *Taxon,* vol.19 (1970): pp. 489-553, esp. pp. 496-7; Blanche Henrey, *British botanical and horticultural literature before 1800* (Clarendon Press, 1975), vol. 2, pp. 33-36; E.F. Greenwood, 'A history of Liverpool natural history collections', *Journal of the Society for the Bibliography of Natural History,* vol. 9 (1980); 375-82, esp. pp.376-7.

12. For Lindley's advocacy of first Chevreul and then Wilkinson, see *Gardeners' Chronicle,* 1841; p. 291; 1849: pp. 787-8; 1850; pp. 4-5, 36, 116-117, 165, 181; 1857, p. 382; 1859, p. 216; and the discussion in Brent Elliott, *Victorian Gardens* (Batsford, 1986), pp. 123-8.

Postscript. During the Second World War, while William T. Stearn was serving in the Royal Air Force (1941-1946), Mrs Florence M.G. Cardew (neé Lorimer, 1883-1967) was Acting Librarian of the Lindley Library and began its cataloguing; see Helen Wang, 'Stein's Recording Angel, Miss F.M.G. Lorimer', *Journal of the Royal Asiatic Society,* Third Series, vol. 8 (1998), pp. 207-228. She began her varied career by cataloguing the Asiatic material of Sir Aurel Stein.

Part VIII

LINDLEY DOCUMENTS IN THE BRITISH COLUMBIA ARCHIVES

Kathryn Bridge

Within the British Columbia Archives in Victoria, B.C., Canada is an extensive archival collection documenting the family of Henry Pering Pellew Crease (1823-1905) and his wife, Sarah, née Lindley (1826-1922). It is the largest family archival collection in western Canada from the nineteenth century. The Crease Family Collection (as it is known) documents the family in England before emigration and, later, their lives in British Columbia. The Collection contains manuscripts, legal papers, diaries, correspondence, reminiscences, building plans, photographs, paintings and drawings created or collected by four generations of family members.

Sarah Crease, John Lindley's eldest daughter, known in the Lindley household as Totty, married in 1853 Henry Crease, a young English barrister, a friend of her brother Nathaniel. In 1858 Crease sought a livelihood in British Columbia. By 1861 he had become Attorney General of British Columbia and ultimately rose to be Supreme Court Justice. In 1859 Sarah with their three children set out on the five-month long voyage to British Columbia to join her husband, arriving there in February 1860; they never returned to England. At first the life of Sarah, like that of other colonial women, was very hard but she adapted herself gradually and successfully. After the death of her parents, John Lindley in 1865 and his wife Sarah in 1869, Sarah Crease requested that the immense quantity of family papers, correspondence, mementoes, sketches etc. stored at the family home should be sent to her in British Columbia. These now form part of the Crease Family Collection.

The Crease Family Collection contains several letters written by Lindley to his daughter, his son-in-law and other family members. Letters written by family members, in particular Lindley's wife Sarah (née Freestone), his son, Nathaniel, and daughter, Barbara, mention Lindley and thus record his activities. These letters and references have been painstakingly located and reproduced in Robert M. Hamilton's invaluable series: *John Lindley, A Gathering of his Correspondence: Part One – 117 letters 1818-1836* (1994), *John Lindley, A Gathering of his Correspondence: Part Two – 135 letters 1836-1850* (1996), *John Lindley, A Gathering of his Correspondence: Part Three – 173 letters by him 1819-1865* (1996), *A Gathering of his Correspondence: Part Four – 173 letters 1820-1860* (1998). Additionally, Hamilton's *Sarah Lindley, Family letters to Henry Crease* include full text transcriptions of the letters dated 1849-1959 excerpted by the *Gathering* series.

The Crease Family Collection contains approximately thirty-five linear metres of textual records dating from the mid-eighteenth century to the late 1960s. Almost half of this volume are the legal records and working papers of Henry Crease whose legal career in the colony of Vancouver Island and the mainland colony, later province of British Columbia, earned him a knighthood in 1895. Thereupon Sarah became Lady Crease. The collection also holds over 3,000 paintings and drawings, each created by a family member. Included are several small pencil and watercolour sketches by John Lindley; pencil, ink and watercolour sketches of the Lindley home and gardens by Sarah Lindley (Crease), Barbara Lindley, and Henry Crease. Many of these have been reproduced in Mr. Hamilton's volumes. Numerous photograph albums also document the family, although they only include a handful of photographs of John Lindley. These, again, have been reproduced in Hamilton's volumes. The plans and cartographic records are almost entirely related to British Columbia with the exception of some mining records from the Crease family's days in Cornwall.

The Crease Family Collection was deposited in the B.C. Archives over several decades as family circumstances and changes dictated a need to safeguard the material. Although significant items were acquired from the 1920s through the 1960s, three principal deposits were made. The first occurred in 1939 with the acquisition of some 300 letters and letterbooks. In 1948, when the family home, *Pentrelew,* was broken up and auctioned, the Archives purchased much of Crease's legal correspondence, many family letters, photographs and a large library collection, which included several Lindley botanical publications. Unfortunately, these latter were later dispersed or removed from the collection. In 1968, Arthur Crease, youngest son of Sarah and Henry Crease, and the only surviving one of their seven children, bequeathed to the Archives the diaries, journals, sketches, correspondence, photographs, and other family archival records then in his custody.

The Crease Family Collection was accessioned as four discrete manuscript groups, with the photographs, maps and plans and art works separately accessioned. Thus, there is no central index to simplify searches. The Collection is of principal importance for its documentation of the social fabric of nineteenth century British Columbia, and the Crease family, in particular. Because it includes records created by family members in Britain, a generation before emigration to British Columbia, which document life in England (especially the mining and business operations of the Crease and Smith families in Cornwall), the Collection has wide-reaching significance. The documentation of John Lindley, although minor in quantity, but great in interest, is important for Lindley scholars because it presents not only the family viewpoint, unavailable from other sources, but provides much information, hitherto unknown, about his career.

Sarah and Henry Crease were determined record keepers and creators, passing on their love of documenting and safekeeping to their children. For this reason, the Collection remained intact within the family until its transfer to the British Columbia Archives, where it remains now, preserved for examination by historians and other scholars.

Part IX

The Lindley Medal of the Royal Horticultural Society

William Louis Tjaden

John Lindley died on 1 November 1865, after an association with the Horticultural Society of London (later the Royal Horticultural Society) which had begun in 1822. In appreciation of his services to the Society and horticulture, on 19 December 1865 a member of the Society's Council, Henry Cole, proposed that a medal be established in his memory, to be called the Lindley Medal and to be awarded especially at the Floral and Fruit Meetings of the Society. The proposal was apparently readily agreed: Cole and another Council member, Lt. Colonel Henry Scott, were 'requested to settle the further conditions of this prize'. At the same meeting on the recommendation of the Floral Committee it was agreed that Mr Veitch should be 'awarded a Lindley Medal for his beautiful collection of orchids shown this day', fifty-three specimens of *Lycaste skinneri*, no two alike, according to *The Gardeners' Chronicle*. There was no discussion of the design of the medal recorded at this meeting: it could be inferred that it was left to Cole and Scott. Nor was there any further mention of the design until some years later.

On 23 January 1866 another nurseryman, William Bull, then becoming famous for stove house plants, was awarded the Lindley Medal, and in April Veitch was awarded another. The next mention of the medal was at a Council Meeting on 19 March 1867 when 'Authority was given to the Assistant Secretary to get the Lindley Medal struck'. Not only was another Lindley Medal awarded on the same day, but on 4 June 1867 it was 'resolved to present copies of the Lindley Medal to Mrs Lindley, Nathaniel Lindley and Miss Lindley'. In March 1868 two more awards were made for orchids, one to the Duke of Devonshire, the other to Veitch. In August 1869 a Mr Goode was awarded the medal 'for his magnificent specimen of *Lilium auratum*'. In 1870 no exhibit was deemed worthy of the medal.

The first record of dissatisfaction with the design of the medal to be found in the Council minutes is in May 1871, after two more awards for orchids were made in March and April. The minutes of 3 May record that 'Several suggestions were made for getting over the difficulty of obtaining a good likeness engraved on the Lindley Medal of the late Dr Lindley.' The Council was unaware that Lindley's artistically talented daughters Sarah and Barbara had drawn excellent profiles of their father. Ultimately 'Colonel Scott promised to put the matter in the hands of Mr Townroe of the South Kensington Museum who had been successful in producing a cast of the late Captain Fowke'. Further awards of the medal were made on 17 May 1871 and in November 1872, the latter for a plant of *Nepenthes rafflesiana* bearing forty-five pitchers. The design was mentioned again in March 1873: 'It proving hopeless to obtain a good likeness of the late Dr Lindley, it was resolved to ask Professor Dyer to furnish any names of species of plants identified with the late Dr Lindley so that a selection of the same might be made of an inscription to the medal'. Another award was made in May 1873, to Lord Londesborough 'for his *Utricularia montana*'. In November 'A design of the Lindley Medal as prepared was submitted and rejected by the Council. The subject was afterwards referred to a Sub-committee of Sir Coutts Lindsay and Mr Dobree'. By January 1874 a Lindley daughter had provided a profile drawing of Lindley; accordingly Lindsay and Dobree in January 1874 'submitted their design and report on the Lindley Medal which was adopted by the Council and Sir Coutts Lindsay was requested to obtain an estimate for the obverse, the Seal of the Society to be the reverse'. In June 1874 Sir Coutts Lindsay reported on the progress of the medal, and at last, on 19 October 1874, 'A specimen of the Lindley Medal cast in metal was laid on the table and (its consideration) ordered to be postponed'. At the next meeting, on 19 November 'The new dies of the Lindley Medal were laid on the table by Sir Coutts Lindsay and Mr Dobree and approved'.

The Lindley Medal, as made in 1874 and in use since then, is the same size as the Knightian Medal at 1¾ inches (45mm) in diameter (Figure 24). The obverse has Lindley's head, wearing spectacles and facing left, within a laurel wreath. Around this are the words 'Dr John Lindley F.R.S. Born Feb. 5 1799. Died Nov. 1 1865'. The reverse has the Society's name on the upper half around a central figure representing Flora bearing a wreath, and standing on a plinth. No space is left for the details of the award, which are engraved on the edge. Underneath the head on the obverse is the word HAKOWSKI, presumably the draughtsman and engraver of the die. The wording of the Council minutes quoted above does not show adequately what happened. It seems that in November 1873 a design with plants associated with Lindley was rejected, but was followed within two months by an acceptable drawing of Lindley's head from a daughter. None of the few medals made between 1867 and 1874 may now survive, and their design is unknown. The minutes, however, do not support the inference by Simmonds, quoted by Fletcher, *Story of the Royal Horticultural Society 1804-1968* (1969:200), that no Lindley Medal existed in those years. The dies made in 1874 were 'new dies'. An unresolved point is that, according to Fletcher (1969:54),

Figure 24. The Lindley Medal of the Royal Horticultural Society

the Society's seal until 1903 was the reverse, the 'god of the gardens' side of the original 1811 medal. The reverse of the Lindley Medal was ordered to bear the Society's seal, but it has a new design of Flora alone.

The last of the fifteen Lindley Medals awarded between 1865 and 1874 was the only one for fruit, agreed by Council on 15 July 1874 for a collection of apples and pears exhibited in the previous October by Francis Dancer. After the considerable trouble taken from May 1871 to November 1874 to obtain an improved medal, further awards could be expected, but apart from one in March 1878 in silver-gilt, there were no more until 1903. The reasons are not stated. Fletcher (1969: 206-208) shows that by 1873 the Society had become a body divided in its relationships with its landlord at South Kensington, the Commissioners of the 1851 Exhibition. Two of the Commissioners, Messrs Cole and Scott, were also Council members. It was they who had suggested the institution of the Lindley Medal in December 1865. They were ousted from Council in 1873 together with others. Whether the medal was subsequently unpopular in Council because of this association is conjecture. Another explanation is more likely.

When Council announced in 1865 that a Lindley Medal would be introduced, the *Gardeners' Chronicle* reported that it would be 'second in value to the Gold Banksian'. This implied that it would be in gold, but smaller: if in silver or silver-gilt, Flora medals in these metals would have surpassed it in value. The manufacturer's bill for the new dies submitted in July 1875 was £70, but included one gold medal. It is not recorded that this was a presentation medal: possibly it went to Mr Dancer for his fruit. The new Lindley Medal was, however, so much dearer in gold than its predecessor that Council, in the straitened financial circumstances of the time, would have been reluctant indeed to award it again. It was not forgotten, however, by the exhibitors.

In May 1877 John Wills wrote, hoping that his large group of plants shown in the Conservatory at South Kensington on 2 May, would be considered by

Council to be worthy of a Lindley Medal. Council resolved that he should be awarded a 'Large Gold Medal' only. This meant the larger 1½ inch Gold Banksian, obviously not the Society's Gold Medal, the Flora in gold. The reason for refusing the Lindley Medal was not stated: probably it was because it was more expensive. Wills persisted, writing again in late June and saying that he still considered that he was entitled to a Lindley Medal. He would not have done so if the medal were of silver or silver-gilt. He complained then also that the award he had received at the Great Summer Show on 19 June, a Gold Medal (a small Banksian), was not in accordance with the schedule, and he remarked that Messrs Veitch (a rival) had received the large Gold Banksian for a plant of N*epenthes sanguinea* in their group of stove-house plants. In May and June 1877, too, John Goode wrote several letters complaining that the Lindley Medal he had won nearly eight years earlier had been kept by his then employer, Lady Ashburton. He was told that she had been sent the medal in accordance with Society rules, and the matter could not be re-opened. He might not have protested so strongly if the medal had been silver.

The Silver Gilt Lindley Medal awarded in March 1878 went to Sir Trevor Lawrence for a group of orchids. It is the only reference to the metal recorded in Council minutes. Sir Trevor, President of the Society from 1885 to 1913, would not have minded that the award was in silver-gilt, even if the general expectation had been that it should be in gold. As a silver-gilt or even silver medal, however, there was no obvious need for it so long as large and small Gold Banksian Medals were awarded. Only after 1899, when the new small (Society) Gold Medal became the only gold medal awarded for exhibits at the time of their exhibition, could the Lindley Medal in silver-gilt and silver occupy a useful niche.

The Lindley Medal is now only awarded for an exhibit of special scientific or educational interest at a Society's flower show. Individual plants are not eligible for this medal.

[The above is a revised version of an account in 'The medals of the Royal Horticultural Society' in *Archives of Natural History* 21(1): 77-112 (1994).]

Part X

LIST OF THE PUBLISHED WORKS OF JOHN LINDLEY

J.M. Allford

[This list of John Lindley's publications was painstakingly compiled by Miss J.M. Allford in 1953 for the Diploma in Librarianship, University College, London and is printed here by gracious permission of University College. Copies of it were deposited in the library of University College, the Lindley Library and the herbarium library, Royal Botanic Gardens, Kew, but it has remained unpublished until now. Her numbering of entries and chronological sequence (sometimes irregular and inconsistent) together with her bibliographic format (not always in accordance with present day procedure) have been maintained. Subsequent editions and translations of Lindley's books are listed under the first edition. Miss Allford acknowledged the help of the librarians of the Bodleian, British Museum, British Museum (Natural History), Cambridge University, Royal Botanic Gardens, Kew, University of London and especially the Lindley Library of the Royal Horticultural Society.

I have amended the list by the insertion of dates of publications unknown to Miss Allford; these are taken from M.J. van Steenis-Kruseman and W.T. Stearn in *Flora Malesiana*, ser. I, vol. 4: clxii-ccxix (1954), F.A. Stafleu and R.S. Cowen, *Taxonomic Literature*, 2nd ed., 3: 49-60 (1981), and A.T. Gage and W.T. Stearn, *A Bicentenary History of the Linnean Society of London* (1988).

The dates of publication of the individual parts of *Transactions of the Horticultural Society* (10 volumes, 1807-1848), to which Lindley contributed many papers; are given in *Flora Malesiana*, ser. I, vol. 4: ccxiv-ccxv (1854).

The list below graphically demonstrates Lindley's astonishing industry – W.T.S.]

1819

1. Marrana zebrina. *in Botanical Register, 5* (1819), No. 385.
   Coloured engraving drawn by W. Hart.
   This is Lindley's first published work.

2. Calycanthus fertilis. *in Botanical Register, 5* (1819), No. 404.
   Coloured engraving drawn by Lindley.

3. RICHARD, Louis-Claude. *Observations on the structure of fruits and seeds*; translated from the *Analyse du Fruit* ... and illustrated with plates and original notes by John Lindley. London, John Harding; Norwich, Wilkin and Youngman. 1819.
   xx, 100 p. 6 plates, 8.5".
   The plates are engravings drawn by Lindley.

4. Rosa alpina. *in Botanical Register, 5* (1819), No. 424.
   Coloured engraving drawn by Lindley.

5. Rosa Banksiae. *in Botanical Register, 5* (1819), No. 397.
   Coloured engraving drawn by W. Hart.

6. Rosa ferox. *in Botanical Register, 5* (1819), No. 420.
   Coloured engraving drawn by Lindley.

7.   Rosa kamchatica. *in Botanical Register, 5* (1819), No. 419.
        Coloured engraving drawn by Lindley.

8.   Rosa multiflora. *in Botanical Register, 5,* (1819), No. 425.
        Coloured engraving drawn by Lindley.

9.   Rosa rubrifolia. *in Botanical Register, 5* (1819), No. 430.
        Coloured engraving drawn by Lindley.

10.   Rosa spinosissima; reversa. *in Botanical Register, 5* (1819), No. 431.
        Coloured engraving drawn by Lindley.

1820

11.   Begonia pauciflora. *in Botanical Register, 6* (1820), No. 471.
        Coloured engraving drawn by M. Hart.

12.   Calycanthus laevigatus. *in Botanical Register, 6* (1820), No. 481.
        Coloured engraving drawn by M. Hart.

13.   Hovenia acerba, *in Botanical Register, 6* (1820), No. 501.
        Coloured engraving drawn by M. Hart.

14-15. *Rosarum monographia;* or a botanical history of Roses. To which is added, an appendix for the use of cultivators in which the most remarkable garden varieties are systematically arranged. London. James Ridgway, 1820.
        xii, 156 p. 19 plates 9.7".
        Plates are engraving, all drawn by Lindley except No. 9, which was drawn by J. Curtis; and all are coloured except No. 19.

        Rosarum monographia … a new edition, London, James Ridgway 1830.
        xxxix, 156 p. 19 plates 9.8".
        The text is a page for page reprint of the first edition.

1821

16-17. HOOKER, William Jackson, *Flora Scotica;* or, a description of Scottish plants arranged both according to the artificial and natural methods. Edinburgh, Archibald Constable, and Co.; London, Hurst, Robinson, and Co. 1821.
        2 volumes.
        In his preface Hooker states that the natural arrangement of the Phanerogamia (vol. 2, p. 161-197) is the joint work of himself and Lindley.

18.   *Collectanea botanica;* or figures and botanical illustrations of rare and curious exotic plants. London, printed by Richard and Arthur Taylor, Shoe Lane. Sold by J. and A. Arch; T. and G. Underwood; W. Wood; Hatchard and Son; J. Harding; Nornaville and Fell; J.H. Bohte; W. Clarke. 1821-1825.
        48 leaves, 41 plates, 16.9".
        Issued in 8 approximately monthly parts from April 1821; parts 1-6 (plates 1-31), in 1821; part 7 (plates 32-36) probably 1832; part 8 (plates 37-41, A-B, Orch. scletos) Jan. 1826. The plates are coloured engravings drawn by:-

W. Hooker	7
W.J. Hooker	27, 40
I. Curtis	32, 33
Ferdinand Bauer	35, 36
Barbara Lawrence	37
John Lindley	The remainder.

        Plate 41 was originally numbered '42', and the number altered. A copy of the original plate '41' showing 'Rodriguezia secunda' is bound with copy 'A' of this book in the Lindley Library.

19. Cymbidium xiphiifolium, *in Botanical Register,* 7 (1821), No. 529.
    1 coloured engraving drawn by M. Hart.

20. *Digitalium monographia;* sistens historiam botanicam generis, tabulis omnium specierum hactenus cognitarum illustratum ut plurimum confectis ad icones Ferdinandi Bauer, penes Gulielmum Cattley. Cura Johanni Lindley. Londini: typis Ricardi et Arthuri Taylor: Prostant venales apud J.H. Bohte … 1821.
    32 leaves 28 plates. 19".
    Plates are coloured engravings by Ferdinand Bauer except Nos. 4, 8, 9, 16 and 25 which are drawn and engraved by Lindley.

21. Raphiolepis indica. *in Botanical Register,* 6 (1821), No. 468.
    1 coloured engraving drawn by M. Hart. Quoted from an 'unpublished tract on Pomaceae' no. 22.

22. Observations on the natural group of plants called Pomaceae. *in Transactions of the Linnean Society, 13* (1822), p. 88-106.
    4 plates drawn by Lindley. Read April 4 and 18 1820, published between 23 May and 21 June 1821.

23. SABINE, Joseph. Account of a newly produced hybrid passiflora *in Transactions of the Horticultural Society, 4* (1822), p. 258-268.
    1 plate and diagrams drawn by Lindley, who also assisted in the description of the plant.

1823

24. DONN, James, *Hortus Cantabrigiensis;* or an accented catalogue of indigenous and exotic plants cultivated in the Cambridge Botanic Garden … Improved and Augmented … by Frederick Pursh … Tenth edition with numerous additions and corrections, by John Lindley. London: C. & J. Rivington; Longman, Hurst, Rees, Orme and Brown; T. Cadell; John Richardson; J. Mawman; Baldwin, Cradock and Joy; T. Hamilton; and Sherwood, Jones and Co. 1823.
    viii, 398 p. 7.5".

25. DONN, James. *Hortus Cantabrigiensis;* … eleventh edition with numerous additions and corrections by John Lindley. London: printed for C. & J. Rivington; Longman, Rees, Orme, Brown and Green; T. Cadell; John Richardson; J. Newman; Baldwin, Craddock and Joy; Sherwood, Gilbert and Piper; Hamilton, Adams and Co; E. Edwards; and G.B. Whittaker. 1826.
    viii, 416 p. 7.4".
    Later editions were not edited by Lindley.

26. Allium Cowani, *in Botanical Register,* 9 (1823), No. 758.
    Coloured engraving drawn by Watts.

27. Amaryllis candida. *in Botanical Register,* 9 (1823), No. 724.
    Coloured engraving drawn by M. Hart.

28. Dendrobium squalens, *in Botanical Register,* 9 (1823), No. 732.
    Coloured engraving drawn by M. Hart.

29. Erinus Lychnidea, *in Botanical Register,* 9 (1823), No. 748.
    Coloured engraving drawn by Hart.

30. Erythrina speciosa, *in Botanical Register,* 9 (1823), No 750.
    Coloured engraving drawn by Hart.

31. Eulophobia gracilis, *in Botanical Register,* 9 (1823), No. 742.
    Coloured engraving drawn by Hart.

32. Gnidia denudata, *in Botanical Register,* 9 (1823), No. 757.
    Coloured engraving drawn by Hart.

33. A notice of certain seedling varieties of Amaryllis, presented to the Society by the Hon. and Rev. William Herbert, in 1820, which flowered in the Society's garden in February, 1823, *in Transaction of the Horticultural Society, 5 (*1824), 337-40.
   1 coloured engraving drawn by B. Cotton. Read, 4 March 1823, published October 1823.

34. Ocymum febrifugam, *in Botanical Register, 9* (1823), No. 753.
   Coloured engraving drawn by Hart.

35. Oenothera acaulis, *in Botanical Register, 9* (1823), No. 763.
   Coloured engraving drawn by Hart.

36. Oncidium euridum, *in Botanical Register, 9* (1823), No. 727.
   1 coloured engraving drawn by M. Hart.

37. Ponthieva petiolata, *in Botanical Register, 9* (1823), No. 762.
   Coloured engraving drawn by Hart.

38. Schizopetalon Walkeri, *in Botanical Register, 9* (1823), No. 752.
   Coloured engraving by Hart.

39. Stapelia hirsuta var. atra. *in Botanical Register, 9* (1823), No. 756.
   Coloured engraving drawn by Hart.

40. Stapella normalis, *in Botanical Register, 9* (1823), No. 755.
   Coloured engraving drawn by Hart.

41. Tillandsia flexuosa; & pallida, *in Botanical Register, 9* (1823), No. 749.
   Coloured engraving drawn by Hart.

1824

42. Instructions for packing living plants in foreign countries, especially within the tropics; and directions for their treatment during the voyage to Europe, *in Transactions of the Horticultural Society, 5* (1824), 192-200.
   1 engraved plate drawn by Lindley. Read 5 November 1822, published May 1823. A revised and enlarged version of the instructions appeared as:-

43 Instructions for collecting and packing seeds and plants in foreign countries … London, printed by William Nicol, for the Horticultural Society 1825, 32 p. 9.4".

44. A sketch of the principal tropical fruits which are likely to be worth cultivating in England for the dessert, *in Transactions of the Horticultural Society, 5* (1824), p. 79-126.
   Read 18 December 1821 and January 1822, published August 1822.

45. The theory of vegetable physiology of M. Aubert du Petit Thouars; or of the increase of plants by means of buds, or fixed embryos, *in Philosophical Magazine, 64* (1824), p. 81-3.

46. Upon the theory of vegetable physiology of M. Aubert du Petit Thouars; in reply to Sir Jas. Edw. Smith, *in Philosophical Magazine, 64* (1824), p. 456-7. The above and two letters by Sir J.E. Smith were reprinted with further comments and reply by Lindley as:-

47. A letter to the editors of the *Philosophical Magazine and Journal:* Upon the correspondence between Sir James Edward Smith and Mr. Lindley, which has lately appeared in that Journal. London, James Ridgway and Sons. 1825. 26 p. 7.5".

48. [LINDLEY, John, Editor.] *The Botanical Register,* consisting of coloured figures of exotic plants, cultivated in British gardens; with their history and mode of treatment. The designs by Sydenham Edwards, and others. London, James Ridgway, *10 (*1824) to *14 (*1828).

   Continued as:-

   [LINDLEY, John, Editor.] *Edwards' Botanical Register …* 15 (1829) to *33* (1847). Lindley's name does not appear on the title page until 1829, but from volume ten he wrote practically all the articles, and appears to have been responsible for any editorial notes which appeared. It was discontinued in 1847.

49. *Appendix* to the first twenty-three volumes of *Edwards's Botanical Register:* consisting of a complete alphabetical and systematical index of names, synonymes, and matter, adjusted to the present state of systematical botany; together with *A sketch of the vegetation of the Swan river colony.* With nine coloured plates, containing eighteen coloured figures of plants, and with four woodcuts. By John Lindley ... London (James Ridgway, ...) 1839-1840.

    Publ: in three parts, as below: p. [i]-iv, *Sketch:* [i]-lviii, [1, expl. pl.], *Index:* [i]-lxiv, *pl.* 1-9 (col).

Part	Appendix pages	Plates	Index	Dates
1	i-xvi	1-4	i-xxxii	1 Nov. 1839
2	xvii-xxxii	5-7	xxxiii-xlviii	1 Dec. 1839
3	xxxiii-lviii explanation of plates	8-9	xlix-lxiv	1 Jan. 1840

1825

50. Some account of the Prangos Hay Plant of Northern India, *in Quarterly Journal of Science, Literature and the Arts, 19* (1825), p. 1-7.

1826

51. An account of ten varieties of Persian Melons, *in Transactions of the Horticultural Society, 6* (1826), p. 553-562, published February 1827.

52. Observations upon the natural laws which govern the production of double flowers, arising out of a remarkable case of præternatural formation in the flowers of an Amaryllis, *in Transactions of the Horticultural Society, 6* (1826), 6, 309-316.
    Read 6 December 1825, published May 1826.

53. *Orchidearum sceletos.* Londini: Typis Ricardi Taylor, 1826.
    28 p. illus. 9.4".

54. Report upon the effect produced on certain plants in the garden of the Horticultural Society, by the frost which occurred during the night of April 29th, 1826, *in Transactions of the Horticultural Society, 6* (1826), p.493-500.
    Read 20 June 1826, published December 1826.

55. Report upon the new or rare plants which have flowered in the garden of the Horticultural Society at Chiswick from March 1824 to March 1825, *in Transactions of the Horticultural Society, 6* (1826), 261-299.
    Read 3 January 1826, published May 1826.

56. Report upon the new or rare plants which have flowered in the garden of the Horticultural Society at Chiswick, from its first formation to March 1824, *in Transactions of the Horticultural Society, 6* (1826), p. 62-100.
    1 hand coloured engraving drawn by Charles J. Robertson.
    Read 20 July and 3 August 1824, published May 1825.

57. Sur la nouvelle famille des Gilliésiées. *Annales des Sciences Naturelles* (Paris), *9* (1826), p. 266 - 273.

1827

58. An account of a new genus of plants called Reevesia, *in Quarterly Journal of Science, Literature and Art,* July-December (1826), p. 109-112.

59. De plantarum, praesertion cryptogamicarum, transita et analogia commentatio-Bischoff, *in Quarterly Journal of Science, Literature and Art,* January to June, 1827, p. 362-371.
    A book-review printed anonymously.

60. Notice of a new genus of plants [Douglasia] discovered in the Rocky Mountains of North America by Mr David Douglas *in Quarterly Journal of Science, Literature and Art,* July-December, 1827, p. 283-5.

1828

61.   An account of a new genus of plants, named Macraea, *in Quarterly Journal of Science, Literature and Art,* January-June, 1828, p. 104-6.

62.   *The promological magazine;* or, figures and descriptions of the most important varieties of fruit cultivated in Great Britain, 3 volumes, 1828-30.
>   Published in parts.
>   There is no pagination, but each article is numbered and occupies one leaf with one plate. Volume 1, 1828 contains articles 1-48, Volume 2, 1829, 49-96, and Volume 3, 97-152. The plates are coloured engravings by Mrs Withers (Nos 1-16, 19-22, 24-27, 29-31, 33-152), and by O.M. Curles (Nos. 17-18, 23, 28, 32).
>   Reissued as

63.   *Pomologia Brittanica;* or, figures and descriptions of the most important varieties of fruit cultivated in Great Britain. London, Henry G. Bohn, 1841.

1829

63.   An introductory lecture delivered in the University of London, on Thursday, April 30th, 1829. London, John Taylor, 1829. 26 p. 8.5".

64.   *A synopsis of the British flora;* arranged according to the natural orders containing vasculares, or flowering plants. London: Longman, Rees, Orme, Brown and Green, 1829.
>   xii, 360 p. 7.1".
>   This was intended to be volume 1 of a two volume work, but the promised volume on flowerless plants was never published, and is not mentioned in later editions.

65.   *A synopsis of the British flora* ... Second edition. London, Longman, Rees, Orme, Brown, Green, and Longman, 1835.
>   viii, 376 p. 7.1".

66.   *A synopsis of the British flora* ... Third edition. London, Longman, Orme, Brown, Green, and Longmans. 1841.
>   viii, 382. 7.1".
>   A new impression of the third edition was published in 1859 as:-

67.   *A synopsis of the British flora* ... Third edition. London, Longman, Brown, Green, Longmans, and Roberts, 1859.
>   viii, 382 p. 1859, 6.7".

68.   LOUDON, John Claudius, Editor. *An encyclopaedia of plants* ... the specific characters by an eminent botanist ... London; Longman, Rees, Orme, Brown, and Green, 1829.
>   Lindley, the eminent botanist of the title, was mainly responsible for this work. It was reprinted in 1840 with a supplement, but Lindley does not appear to have made any further contribution to it.

69.   *The genera and species of orchidaceous plants* ... London (Ridgways) April 1830 to October 1840.
>   In parts. The first four parts are entitled "The genera and species of orchideous plants". Each signature (of 8 pages) was dated at the bottom of the first page; these dates of the signatures may be taken as the actual dates of publication as follows:-

Pages	Dates	Pages	Dates	Pages	Dates
1-40	Apr 1830	207-214	Apr 1833	381-388	Jan 1840
41-80	May 1830	215-256	May 1833	389-412	Feb 1840
81-94	Jun 1830	257-264	Aug 1835	413-428	Mar 1840
95-110	Jul 1831	265-296	Sep 1835	429-440	Apr 1840
111-133	Aug 1831	297-334	Oct 1835	441-528	Sep 1840
134-158	Dec 1832	335-350	Nov 1838	529-553	Oct 1840
159-190	Jan 1833	351-366	Dec 1838	[i] xvii	Oct 1840
191-206	Mar 1833	367-380	Jan 1839		

A facsimile was published by A. Ascher & Co at Amsterdam in 1963.

AN
INTRODUCTION

TO THE

NATURAL SYSTEM OF BOTANY:

OR,

A SYSTEMATIC VIEW

OF

THE ORGANISATION, NATURAL AFFINITIES AND
GEOGRAPHICAL DISTRIBUTION

OF THE WHOLE

VEGETABLE KINGDOM;

TOGETHER WITH THE USES OF THE MOST IMPORTANT SPECIES IN MEDICINE,
THE ARTS, AND RURAL OR DOMESTIC ECONOMY.

By JOHN LINDLEY, F.R.S. L.S. G.S.

MEMBER OF THE IMPERIAL ACADEMY NATURÆ CURIOSORUM;
OF THE BOTANICAL SOCIETY OF RATISBON; OF THE PHYSIOGRAPHICAL SOCIETY OF LUND;
OF THE HORTICULTURAL SOCIETY OF BERLIN;
HONORARY MEMBER OF THE LYCEUM OF NATURAL HISTORY OF NEW YORK, &c. &c.
AND PROFESSOR OF BOTANY IN THE UNIVERSITY OF LONDON.

"C'est ainsi que sont formées les familles très naturelles et généralement avouées. On extrait de
tous les genres qui composent chacune d'elles les caractères communs à tous, sans excepter ceux qui
n'appartiennent pas à la fructification, et la réunion de ces caractères communs constitue celui de la
famille. Plus les ressemblances sont nombreuses, plus les familles sont naturelles, et par suite le
caractère général est plus chargé. En procédant ainsi, on parvient plus sûrement au but principal de
la Science, qui est, non de nommer une plante, mais de connoître sa nature et son organisation
entière." — JUSSIEU.

LONDON:

LONGMAN, REES, ORME, BROWN, AND GREEN,
PATERNOSTER ROW.

M.DCCC.XXX.

Figure 25. Title-page of Lindley, *Introduction to the Natural System*
(1830)

70.   *Illustrations of orchidaceous plants;* by Francis Bauer. With notes and prefatory remarks by John
Lindley. London. James Ridgway and Sons. 1830-38.
   iv, xiv, p. 37 leaves 35 plates. 14 ½".
   Plates are hand-coloured lithographs in two series viz:- tab 1-tab 15 'fructification', and
   tab 1-tab 20 'genera'. Published in 4 parts.

Part	Plates	Date
1	Fruct 1-3, 6, 8-10; Genera 1-3	Nov – Dec 1830
2	Fruct 5, 12-15; Genera 4, 6-9	August 1832
3	Fruct. 4, 7, 11; Genera 5, 10-13	Dec 1834
4	Genera 16-20	Oct – Dec 1838

   Illustrations from this are reproduced in J. Stewart & W.T. Stearn, *The Orchid Paintings of
   Francis Bauer*, London 1993, *Orchideen. Zeichnungen von Franz Bauer*, Hanau 1994.

71.   *An introduction to the natural system of botany;* or, of systematic view of the organisation, natural
affinities, and geographical distribution of the whole vegetable kingdom ... London:
Longman, Rees, Orme, Brown, and Green, 1830
   x/viii, 374, 2, p. 8.5".
   A second edition was published as:-

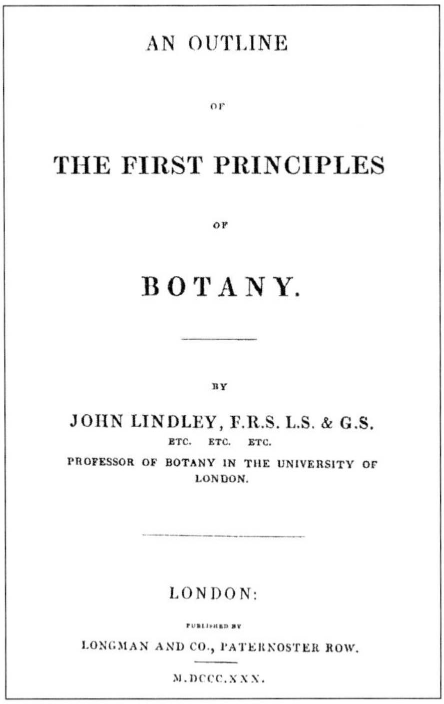

AN OUTLINE

OF

THE FIRST PRINCIPLES

OF

BOTANY.

BY

JOHN LINDLEY, F.R.S. L.S. & G.S.
ETC.   ETC.   ETC.
PROFESSOR OF BOTANY IN THE UNIVERSITY OF
LONDON.

LONDON:
PUBLISHED BY
LONGMAN AND CO., PATERNOSTER ROW.
M.DCCC.XXX.

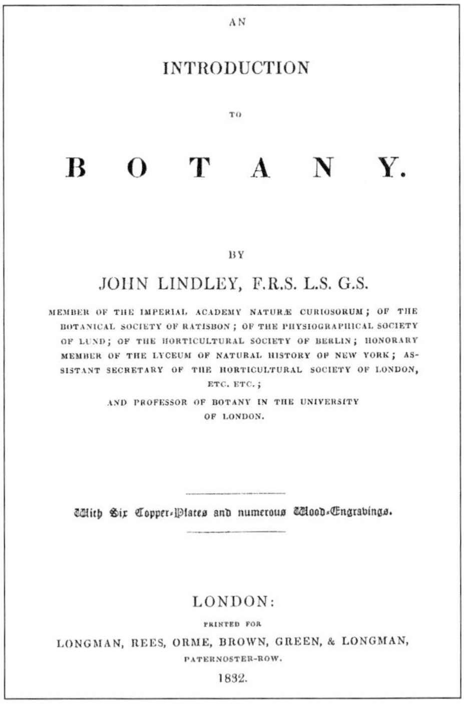

AN

INTRODUCTION

TO

B O T A N Y.

BY

JOHN LINDLEY, F.R.S. L.S. G.S.
MEMBER OF THE IMPERIAL ACADEMY NATURÆ CURIOSORUM; OF THE
BOTANICAL SOCIETY OF RATISBON; OF THE PHYSIOGRAPHICAL SOCIETY
OF LUND; OF THE HORTICULTURAL SOCIETY OF BERLIN; HONORARY
MEMBER OF THE LYCEUM OF NATURAL HISTORY OF NEW YORK; AS-
SISTANT SECRETARY OF THE HORTICULTURAL SOCIETY OF LONDON,
ETC. ETC.;
AND PROFESSOR OF BOTANY IN THE UNIVERSITY
OF LONDON.

With Six Copper-Plates and numerous Wood-Engravings.

LONDON:
PRINTED FOR
LONGMAN, REES, ORME, BROWN, GREEN, & LONGMAN,
PATERNOSTER-ROW.
1832.

Figure 26. Title-page of Lindley, *Outline of first Principles of Botany* (1830)

Figure 27. Title-page of Lindley, *Introduction to Botany* (1832)

72.   *A natural system of botany* … second edition … London: Longman, Rees, Orme, Brown, Green, and Longman, 1836.
xxvi, 426 p. 8.6".
See also 119.

73.   *Einleitung in das naturliche System der Botanik* … Weimar, Landes-Industrie - Comptoirs, 1833.
4, viii, 524 p. 8.5".
A German translation of 71.

74.   Notice of five varieties of pears, received in the year 1826, *in Transactions of the Horticultural Society,* 7 (1830), p. 175-179.
2 hand-coloured engravings drawn by Mrs Withers. Read 19 December 1826, published May 1830.

75.   *An outline of the first principles of Botany.* London, Longman & Co. 1830.
x, 106 p. 4 plates, 5.6".
The four copper plates carry diagrams drawn by Lindley. The book was first issued without plates and the four plates issued towards the end of the year.

76.   *An outline of the first principles of Botany.* Second edition with corrections. London, Longman and Co.
1831. x, 106 p. 4 plates.

77.   *Grundzüge der Anfangsgründe der Botanik,* Weimar, Verlag des Landes-Industrie-Comptoirs, 1831. viii, 116, 4 plates of diagrams 6.7".
No. 71 anonymously translated into German without preface, or comments by translator.

78.   *Principi fondamentali di botanica* … traduzione del Giardiniere Giuseppi Manetti … con note del medasimo. Monza, Tipografia Corbetta, 1834.
96 p. T1-T4 - 4 leaves of diagrams 7".
Italian translation of No. 71.

79. Report upon the new or rare plants which flowered in the garden of the Horticultural Society at Chiswick between March, 1825 and March 1826, *in Transactions of the Horticultural Society,* 7 (1830), p. 46-75, and p. 224-232.

> Part 1, Tender plants, read 17 October 1826, published May 1827.
> Part 2, Hardy plants, read 4 and 18 September 1827, published April 1828.

80. Some account of the Mela Carla, Malcarle, or Charles Apple, *in Transactions of the Horticultural Society,* 7 (1830), p. 259-62.

> With 1 hand-coloured engraving drawn by Mrs Withers.
> Read on 19 February 1828, published April 1828.

81. WALLICH, Nathaniel. *Plantae asiaticae rariores.* London, Paris, Strasbourg, Treuttel & Würtz, 1830-32, 3 vols.

> Descriptions by Lindley are contained in:-
> Vol 1 pages 25, 31-2, 33, 34 (1830)
> Vol 2 pages 4-5, 5-6, 7, 41, 46, 85 (1831)
> Vol 3 pages 4, 50, 282 (1832)
> Drawings by Lindley are reproduced on plates 211 and 283.

1831

82. LINDLEY, George. *A guide to the orchard and kitchen garden* ... edited by John Lindley. London, Longman, Reese, Orme, Brown, and Green 1831.

> xxxii, 602 p. 5".
> John Lindley states that his own contribution to his father's book consisted of little more than the preface and of seeing it through the press.

83. An account of a remarkable instance of anomalous structure in the trunk of an exogenous tree, *in Journal of the Royal Institution, 1* (1831), p. 476-482.

84. Notes upon vegetable tissue. No. 1 cellular tissue, *in Journal of the Royal Institution, 2* (1831), p. 264-267.

> Although ending with a note "to be continued", no more parts seem to have been published.

85. *Some considerations upon the cultivation of fruit trees.* London, A.& R. Spottiswoode. 1831.

> 24 p. 8.5".

86. LINDLEY, John *and* HUTTON, William. *The fossil flora of Great Britain;* or figures and descriptions of the vegetable remains found in a fossil state in this country. London, James Ridgway 1831-7.

> Published in parts, but discontinued after 3 volumes, containing 230 plates from drawings mostly by William Crawfurd Williamson.
> Vol 1, 1831-33; vol 2, 1833-35; vol 3, 1835-37; see p.173.
> A supplement, publishing unused illustrations, was edited by G.A. Lebour, *Illustration of fossil plants*, Newcastle on Tyne, 1877. Seen No 238.

1832

87. *An introduction to botany* ... London, Longman, Rees, Orme, Brown, Green and Longman, 1832.

> xvi, 558 p. 6 plates, 8.5".
> The plates are copper-plates numbered 1-6, and bearing diagrams drawn by the author referring to the text.

88. *An introduction to botany.* Second edition, with corrections and numerous additions ...1835.

> xiv, 580 p. 6 plates 8.6".

89. *An introduction to botany.* Third edition, with corrections and numerous additions ... 1839.

> xii, 594 p. 6 plates 8.5".

90. *An introduction to botany.* Fourth edition ... in two volumes. London, Longman, Brown, Green and Longmans, 1848.

> Vol 1, xii, 406 p. 8.5".
> Vol 2, viii, 428 p. 6 plates, 8.5".

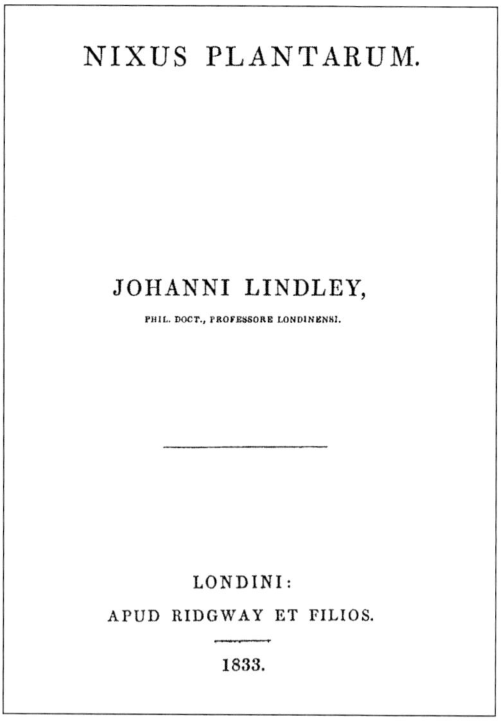

NIXUS PLANTARUM.

JOHANNI LINDLEY,

PHIL. DOCT., PROFESSORE LONDINENSI.

LONDINI:
APUD RIDGWAY ET FILIOS.

1833.

Figure 28. Title-page of Lindley, *Nixus Plantarum* (1833)

91.   On the mode of determining fossil plants *in Edinburgh New Philosophical Journal* April–Oct 1832, p. 221–228.

> This is an extract (p. xxvi line 11 to p. xxxvi, line 19) from the preface to vol 1 of No. 86.

92.   *An outline of the first principles of horticulture,* London, Longman, Rees, Orme, Brown, Green and Longman 1832.

> 72 p. 5.6".

93.   *Esquisses des premiers principes d'horticulture; ...* traduit de l'anglais et augmente de notes explicatives ou aditionelles par Ch. Morren ... Bruxelles, H. Dumont 1835.

> xviii, 180 p. 5.6".
>
> French edition of No. 92.

94.   *Principi fondamentali di orticultura* di Giovanni Lindley ... Traduzione del giardiniere Giuseppe Manetti ... Monza, Tipografia Corbetta 1833.

> 72 p. 7".
>
> Italian translation of No. 92.

1833

95.   SIBTHORP, John and SMITH, James Edward. *Flora Graeca* sive Plantarum rariorum historia, quas in provinciis aut insulis Graeciae. Legit, investigavit, et depingi curavit, Johannes Sibthorp ... Londini, Richardi Taylor, 1806–40.

> Lindley wrote the text for the last three volumes 8–10 of this work, published as follows:-

Vol 8	Part 1	pp 1–36	Plates 701–750	in 1832
Vol 8	Part 2	pp 37–75	Plates 751–800	in 1835
Vol 9	Part 1	pp 1–38	Plates 801–850	in 1837
Vol 9	Part 2	pp 39–77	Plates 851–900	in 1839
Vol 10	Part 1	pp 1–40	Plates 901–950	in 1840
Vol 10	Part 2	pp 41–106	Plates 951–1966	in 1840

96.   *Nixus plantarum*. Londini, apud Ridgway et filios, 1833.
      vi, 7-28. 8.4".

97.   *Nixus plantarum* … Die Stämme des Gewächsreiches … Verdeutscht durch C.T. Beilschmied. Mit einer Vorerinnerung von Dr. C.G. Nees von Esenbeck. Nurnberg, Johann Leonhard Schrag, 1834.
      x, 11-44, p. 8.5".
      German translation of No. 196.

98.   *PENNY CYCLOPAEDIA*. The penny cyclopaedia of the Society for the Diffusion of Useful Knowledge. London, The Society, 1833-58.
      The articles are unsigned. An incomplete list of contributors issued with the last number credits Lindley with all the 'Botany and Vegetable Physiology''. However it seems certain from internal evidence that he only contributed as far as the letter 'R' as suggested in the Dictionary of National Biography, etc. The following were reprinted under Lindley's name, but as I have only seen copies without title page, or cover, they are catalogued from the headings.

99.   Endogens (From the *Penny Cyclopaedia,* vol. *IX,* 1837, p. 395).
      4 p. illus. 12".

100. Exogens (From the *Penny Cyclopaedia,* vol *X,* 1838 p. 120).
      12 p. illus. 12".

1834

101. Catalogue of the Orchidaceae in Mr Cuming's collection of South American plants, *in Journal of Botany, 1* (1834), p. 4-8.

102. *Ladies' botany*: or, a familiar introduction to the study of the natural system of botany. London, James Ridgway and Sons, 1834.
      xvi, 302 p. 25 plates. 8.6".
      The plates are coloured engravings drawn by Miss Drake. Written in the form of twenty-five letters.

103. *Ladies' botany* … second edition. London, James Ridgway and Sons. n.d.
      xvi, 302 p. 25 plates. 8.5".
      A new impression of first edition.

104. *Ladies' botany* … third edition. London, James Ridgway and Sons.
      xvi, 302 p. 25 plates. 8.9" 1837.
      New impression of 1834 edition bound with advertisements of 1837 and usually found with:-

105. *Ladies' botany* … volume 2. London, James Ridgway and Sons, 1837.
      viii, 280p. 25 plates. 8.7".
      The plates are coloured engravings drawn by Miss Drake. Contains 25 letters, numbered 26-50. Subsequent 'editions' are new impressions of this.

106. *Ladies' botany* … volume 2. Second edition. London, James Ridgway and Sons. n.d.
      viii, 280 p. 25 plates, 8.8".

107. *Ladies' botany* … fourth edition, volume one. London, Ridgway. 1840.
      xvi, 300 p. 25 plates, 8.4".
      This and later 'editions' are new impressions of the first edition, with the omission of the final paragraphs. This edition is found with:-

108. *Ladies' botany* … volume 2. Third edition. London, James Ridgway and Sons.
      viii, 280 p. 25 plates.

109. *Ladies' botany* … fifth edition. London, James Ridgway and Sons 1848. 2 vols.

110. *Ladies' botany* … sixth edition. London, Henry G. Bohn, 1865. 2 vols.

111. *The ladies' botany of Professor Lindley;* abridged by the author, with numerous woodcuts. For the use of schools and young persons. London, Ridgway, 1840.
        xx, 424, illus. 7".
        Also issued as:-

112. *Ladies' botany;* or a familiar introduction to the study of the natural system of botany. Illustrated by numerous woodcuts. New edition. For the use of schools and young persons. London, Henry G. Bohn, 1841.
        xx, 424 p. illus. 7.5".

113. Notes upon a small collection of Peruvian Orchideae, *in Journal of Botany, 1* (1834), 8-14.
        1 coloured engraving drawn by Miss Drake.

114. On the principal questions at present debated in the philosophy of botany, *in Report* of the third meeting of the British Association for the Advancement of Science, 1834, p. 27-54.

115. Remarks on the genus Floerkea of Wildenow, *in Journal of Botany 1* (1834), p. 1-3.

116. University of London. Address delivered at the commencement of the medical session, 1834-5 on Wednesday 1st October, 1834 *in The Lancet, 1 (*1834-5) p. 86-95.
        Also reprinted as a pamphlet:-

117. University of London. Address … (Reported in *The Lancet* of 11th October 1834) n.d. 12 p. 8".

1835

118. An account of some experiments made in the garden of the Horticultural Society, with a view to ascertaining the relative productiveness of the tubers and sets of potatoes, *in Transactions of the Horticultural Society,* 2nd series, *1* (1835), p. 445-454.
        Read 4 March 1834, published 1835 (March or April).
        Reprinted with observations on the paper by Thomas Andrew Knight as:-

119. An account of some experiments … From the *Horticultural Transactions.* London, 1834. 16 p. 12".

120. A further account of experiments upon the cultivation of the potato, made in the garden of the Horticultural Society in the year 1834, *in Transactions of the Horticultural Society,* 2nd series, *1* (1835), p. 524-528.
        Read 24 January 1834, published 1835.

121. *A key to structural, physiological, and systematic botany, for the use of classes.* London, Longman, Rees, Orme, Brown, Green and Longman, 1835.
        80 p. 8.2".
        'As both the "outline of the first principles" [of botany], and the "Nixus" [plantarum] are out of print, I have determined to combine them into one work." Preface.

122. *A key* … with an appendix containing a catalogue of medicinal plants. London, Longman, Orme, Brown, Green and Longmans, 1839.
        iv, 81-96 p. 8.2".
        This appendix was issued with a title page and half-title of the whole work, which was not revised.

123. *Aphorismes de physiologie végétale et de botanique,* suivis du tableau des alliances des plantes, et de l'analyse artificielle des ordres … Traduits de l'anglais, et precedes d'une introduction par P.-A. Cap. Paris, Louis Colas, 1838.
        viii, 180 p. 8¾" x 5½".
        "J'ai reuni, dans ma traduction, aux Aphorismes botaniques et aux Alliances des Plantes, qui forment … A key of Structural and physiological and systematic Botany, l'Analyse artificielle des ordres, qui figure dans la 2nd ed. du Natural System of Botany". Preface.

124. Note upon a handsome and hardy plant called Clianthus puniceus, *in Transactions of the Horticultural Society,* 2nd series, *1* (1835) p. 519-521.
        Coloured engraving drawn by Miss Drake.

125. Notes upon some French stewing pears, *in Transactions for the Horticultural Society,* 2nd series, *1* (1835), p. 328-31.
>> Coloured plate drawn by Mrs Withers, published May 1833.

126. A note upon the Brabant Bellefleur apple, *in Transactions of the Horticultural Society,* 2nd series, *1* (1835) p. 295-6.
>> 1 coloured lithograph drawn by Mrs. Withers.
>> Read 5 February 1833, published May 1833.

127. Note upon the Cannon Hall muscat grape, *in Transactions of the Horticultural Society* 2nd series, *1* (1835), p. 169-70.
>> 1 coloured lithograph drawn by Mrs Withers.
>> Read 17 January 1832, published March 1833.

128. Notes on a collection of plants sent with his papers, by Lieutenant Wellsted, E.I.C. Marine, in *Journal of the Geographical Society,* 5 (1835), p. 206-209.

129. The results of some experiments on the growth of potatoes tried in the garden of the Society in the year 1831, *in Transactions of the Horticultural Society,* 2nd series, *1* (1835), p. 153-161.
>> Read 15 November 1831, published March 1832.

130. Upon the cultivation of epiphytes of the Orchis tribe, *in Transactions of the Society of the Horticultural Society,* 2nd series, *1* (1835), p. 42-50.
>> Read 18 May 1830, published July 1831.

131. MURCHISON, Roderick Impey. On a fossil fox found at Oeningen near Constance, *in Transactions of the Geological Society,* 2nd series, *3* (1835). p. 277-90.
>> An extract from a report by Lindley on the fossil plants of Oeningen is included on p. 288-9.

1837

132. Chrysorhöe; a new genus of Chamaelauceae. *in Companion to the Botanical Magazine, 2* (1836-7), p. 357-8, published July 1837.

133. Notes upon some genera and species of American Orchidaceae. *in Companion to the Botanical Magazine, 2* (1836-7), p. 353-7, published July 1837.

134. Notes upon some genera and species of Orchidaceae in the collection formed by Mr Drége, at the Cape of Good Hope, *in Companion to the Botanical Magazine, 2* (1836-7), 200-210, published February 1837.

135. Remarks on M. Spach's memoir on the Cistaceae, *in Companion to the Botanical Magazine, 2* (1836-7), p. 337-8, published June 1837.
>> A letter to the editor.

136. Remarks on the botanical affinities of Orobanche, *in London and Edinburgh Philosophical Magazine,* third series, *11* (1837), p. 409-12.
>> A communication to the British Association meeting, 1837, and of which only an abstract appears in the report of that meeting (p.101).

137. *Victoria regia.* Privately printed. London. Printed by William Nichol, at the Shakespeare Press. [1837.]
>> 4 leaves, 1 plate. 29".
>> Twenty-five copies only printed, published October 1837. The plate is a coloured lithograph from drawings by R.H. Schomburgh.

1838

138. *Botany* (Library of Useful Knowledge). London, Society for the Diffusion of Useful Knowledge. 1838.
>> iv. 224 p. illus. 8.4".

139. *Flora medica;* a botanical account of all the more important plants used in medicine in different parts of the world. London, Longman, Orme, Brown, Green and Longmans, 1838.
>> xv, 656 p. 8.5".

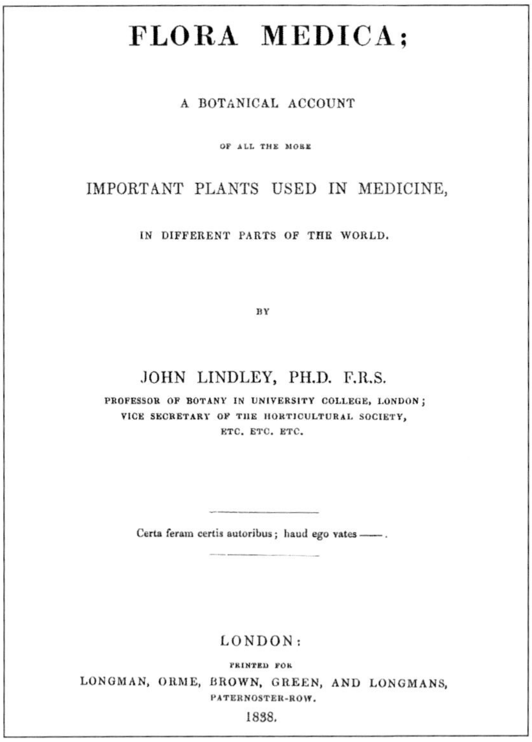

Figure 29. Title-page of Lindley, *Flora medica* (1838)

140. *Sertum orchidaceum:* a wreath of the most beautiful orchidaceaous flowers. London, James Ridgway and Sons. 1838-1841.

> 54 leaves, 49 plates, 21.5".
> Published in ten parts.
> Plates are coloured lithographs numbered 1-48, and frontispiece. They are drawn by Miss Drake –
> Front, 1, 3, 4, 6, 9, 12, 14-28, 30-39, 41-42, 44-48.
> Descourtibz, 5, 7, 11, 29.
> W. Griffith 8.
> R.H. Schomburgk 10, 29, 40.
> Schoulen 13.
> Miss M.A. Mearne 34.

Publication was as follows:-

Part	Plates	Dates	Part	Plates	Dates
1	1-5	1 Sep 1837	6	26-30★	Dec 1839
2	6-10	1 Apr 1838	7	31-34, frontisp	Feb 1840
3	11-15	1 Jul 1838	8	35-39	Jun 1840
4	16-20	1 Sep 1838	9	40-44★	May 1841
5.	21-25	1 Sep 1838	10	45-49	Dec 1841

Facsimile ed., with coloured plates: New York (Johnson reprint corporation), Amsterdam (Theatrum orbis terrarum) 1974, with add. [i★-ii★] repr. t.p. and imprint. U.S.

141. MITCHELL, Thomas Livingston. *Three expeditions into the interior of Eastern Australia.* London, T.&W. Boone, 1838, 2 vols. Lindley provided diagnostic characters for the plants collected, and these are printed as footnotes to the text on the following pages:-

> Vol. 1, pp. 54, 85, 235, 253, 286, 309, 311, 315.
> Vol. 2, pp. 8, 9, 12, 13, 20, 23, 26, 39, 41, 43, 45, 47, 48, 58, 66, 69, 70, 101, 114, 120, 121 122, 138, 143, 145, 150, 156, 164, 174, 175, 177, 178, 184, 189, 197, 200, 205, 212, 217, 249, 258, 265, 270, 275.

142. MITCHELL Thomas Livingston. *Three expeditions.*
> There are some changes and additions in this edition and Lindley's notes are on:-
> Vol. 1, pp. 54, 85, 238, 255, 285, 289, 313, 315.
> Vol. 2, pp. 9, 10, 13, 14, 17, 20, 22, 26, 39, 41, 43, 45, 47, 48, 58, 65, 69, 70, 101, 115, 121
> 122, 123, 138, 143, 145, 149, 151, 156, 165, 174, 175, 177, 185, 190 198, 201, 206, 214,
> 219, 233, 251, 260, 267, 272, 277.

1839

143. *School botany;* or, an explanation of the characters and differences of the principal natural classes and orders of plants belonging to the flora of Europe, in the botanical classification of de Candolle. London, Longman, Orme, Brown, Green, and Longmans. 1839.
> viii, 218 p. illus. 6.6".
> I have only been able to see the editions and reprints which follow, but several others almost certainly exist.

144. *School botany;* or, the rudiments of botanical science. A new edition. London: printed and published for the author by Bradbury and Evans. 1845.
> viii, 164 p. illus. 8.8".

145. *School botany;* or the rudiments of botanical science … a new edition with numerous alterations … London, printed and published for the author by Bradbury and Evans. 1846.
> viii, 164 p. illus 8.2".

146. *School botany;* or the rudiments of botanical science … a new edition with numerous alterations … London, Bradbury and Evans. 1851.
> viii, 164 p. illus. 8.5".

147. *School botany; and vegetable physiology,* or, the rudiments of botanical science … A new edition …London, Bradbury and Evans. 1854.
> viii, [221] p. illus. 8.5".
> As the text was stereotyped the pagination runs from 1 to 164 and the text has been expanded by adding pages at appropriate points, e.g. 56b and 56c between 56 and 57.

148. *School botany* … London, Bradbury and Evans. 1856. a new impression of the 1854 edition.

149. *School botany* … London, Bradbury and Evans. 1858. New impression of the 1854 edition.

150. *School botany* … London, Bradbury and Evans. 1860. New impression of 1854 edition.

151. *School botany,* descriptive botany, and vegetable physiology; or the rudiments of botanical science … London, Bradbury and Evans, 1862.
> viii [221] p. 187 – 203 = 255 p. 8.8".
> As 1854, with an extra chapter.

1840

152. Characters of five new species of orchidaceous plants from Dominica, *in Annals of Natural History,* 5 (1840), p. 115-6.

153. Characters of four new Cape Orchidaceae, *in Annals of Natural History,* 6 (1840), p. 314-5.

154. Copy of the report made to the committee appointed by the Lords of the Treasury in January, 1838 to inquire into the management, etc. of the Royal Gardens Kew, *in House of Commons, Accounts and Papers,* 1840, 29. 6 p.

155. New Orchidaceae, *in Annals of Natural History,* 4 (1839-40), p. 381-385.

156. *The theory of horticulture;* or an attempt to explain the principal operations of gardening upon physiological principles. London: Longman, Orme, Brown, Green and Longmans, 1840.
> xvi, 388 p. illus. 8.3".

157. *Grondbeginselen der horticultuur* (tuinkunst) naar het Engelsch … met bijlagen door W.H. de Vrisse. s'Gravenhage ente Amsterdam, Gebroeders van Cleef. 1842. viii, 374 p. 7.3".
> Dutch edition.

158. *Theorie der Gartenkunde* ... Uebersetz mit Anmerkungen von Ludolph Christian Treviranus. Erlangen, J.J. Palm und Ernst Enke, 1843.
>   xviii, 426 p. 8.3" x 4.9"

159. *Theorie der Gärtnerei* ... Aus dem Englischen übersetz von C.G. Wien, Carl Gerold. 1842. 282 p. 8.5". With many notes and observations by the translator. "The more interesting" of these are translated into English, anonymously, in Lindley's *Gardeners' Chronicle*, 1843, pages 398-9, 415, 487, 742-3 and 847.

160. PAXTON, Joseph. *A pocket botanical dictionary* comprising the names, history, and culture of all plants known in Britain; with a full explanation of technical terms. By Joseph Paxton ... assisted by Professor Lindley. London, J. Andrews; W.S. Orr and Co. 1840.
>   xiv, 354 p. 6.8".

161. PAXTON, Joseph. *A pocket botanical dictionary* ... a new edition with a supplement ... London, Bradbury and Evans, 1849.
>   x, 340, 74 p. 7".
>   A new impression of the 1840 text but the supplement includes the supplement to the beginning of the alphabet of the first edition.

1841

162. *The elements of botany*, structural systematical and medical, being a fourth edition of the outline of the first principles of botany. London, Taylor and Walton, 1841.
>   iv. 292 p. illus. 8.4".
>   The third edition of " A key to structural, Physiological and systematic Botany", 1835.

163. *The elements of botany* ... with a sketch of the artificial methods of classification and a glossary of technical terms. London, Bradbury & Evans, 1847.
>   xii, 242, o.p. illus. 8.3".
>   Part 2, the glossary, was also sold separately and was probably reprinted several times but I have only seen:-

164. *A glossary of technical terms used in botany*, London, Bradbury and Evans, 1848.
>   iv, o.p. diagrs. 8.7".

165. *The elements of botany* ... a new edition with some corrections. London, Bradbury and Evans, 1849.
>   xii. 142, 2, o.p. 8.7".
>   Very little change from the fifth edition in the text of the above, but part III has become volume 2, with a new title:-

166. *Medical and oeconomical botany*. London, Bradbury and Evans. 1849.
>   iv. 274 p. illus. 8.7".
>   Volume 2 of the Elements of Botany.

167. *Medical and oeconomical botany*. Second edition. London, Bradbury and Evans. 1856.
>   iv. 274. illus. diagrs. 8.7".
>   I have seen no "Elements" to correspond with this edition.

168. *The elements of botany* ... London, Bradbury and Evans, 1861.
>   xii, 142, 2, o.p. 8.7".
>   "The changes in the present reissue are for the most part verbal" – preface.

168a LINDLEY, John, editor. *The Gardeners' Chronicle,* 3 volumes, 1841-1843, continued as:-
>   *The Gardeners' Chronicle and Agricultural Gazette,* 22 volumes, 1844-65.
>   Lindley was principal editor of *The Gardeners' Chronicle* from its foundation to his death.

169. A note upon the anatomy of the roots of Ophrydeae, *in Transactions of the Linnean Society, 18* (1841), p. 423-428, published June 1840.

170. A note upon the genus Decaisnia, Ad. Brong. *in Annals of Natural History, 6* (1841), p. 52-3.

171. Notes upon the genus Epidendrum, *in Journal of Botany* (Hooker), 3 (1841) p. 81-89.

1842

172. BRANDE, William Thomas, editor. *A dictionary of science literature and art* ... edited by W.T. Brande ... assisted by Joseph Cauvin. The various departments by eminent literary and scientific gentlemen ... London; Longman, Brown, Green, and Longmans. 1842.
> viii, 1344 p. diagrs. 8.5".
> The botanical contributions were written by Lindley.

173. BRANDE, William Thomas, editor. *A dictionary* ... second edition with a supplement. London: Longman, Brown, Green and Longmans, 1852.
> viii, 1424 p. 8.7".
> A new impression of the text, with a supplement.

174. BRANDE, William Thomas. *A dictionary* ... third edition ... 1853.
> A new impression of the second edition.

175. A century of the new genera and species of Orchidaceous plants, *in Annals and Magazine of Natural History*, 10 (1842), p. 184-6; 12 (1843) p. 396-8; 15 (1845), p. 106-8, p. 256-7, p. 383-6.
> Only six "decades" were published.

176. A note on Chorozema varium; a new green house shrub from Swan River, *in Transactions of the Horticultural Society*, second series, 2 (1842), p. 478-9, published 1840.
> Coloured engraving drawn by Miss Drake.

177. Note upon Cattleya guttata, *in Transactions of the Horticultural Society*, second series, 2 (1842), p. 177-9.
> Coloured engraving drawn by Miss Drake. Read 18 April 1837, published March or April 1838.

178. A note upon Oncidium lanceanum; a new species, *in Transactions of the Horticultural Society*, second series, 2 (1842), p. 100-103, published 1836.
> Coloured plate drawn by Miss Drake.

179. Notes upon Cape orchidaceae, *in London Journal of Botany*, 1 (1842), p. 14-18.

180. Observations upon the effects produced on plants by the frost which occurred in England in the winter of 1837-8, *in Transactions of the Horticultural Society*, second series, 2 (1842), p. 225-315.
> Read 4 December 1838, published Jan 1839.

181. Note upon the Mimulus cardinalis; a new, hardy, herbaceous plant, *in Transactions of the Horticultural Society*, second series, 2 (1842), p. 70-71.
> Coloured plate drawn by Miss Drake.
> Read 4 November 1835, published 1836.

182. LINDLEY, John and others. Reports of the committee for making experiments on the preservation of vegetative powers in seeds, *in Reports of the Meetings of the British Association for the Advancement of Science* held in 1841, p. 50-52; 1842, p. 34-38; 1843, p. 105-109; 1844, p. 94-99; 1845, p. 337-9; 1846, p. 20-24; 1847, p. 145-147; 1848, p. 31-35; 1849, p. 78-79; 1850, p. 160-168; 1851, p. 53; 1852, p. 177; 1853, p. 67; 1854, p. 439-5; 1855, p. 78-79; 1857, p. 43-56. Published 1842-1858.
> The committee consisted of H.E. Strickland, Professor Charles G.B. Daubeny, Professor John S. Henslow, and Lindley.

1843

183. Characters of four new species of Orchideae from Mr Gardner's first Organ Mountain Collections, *in London Journal of Botany*, 2 (1843) p. 661-2.

1845

184. A note upon the genus Sarcobatus, Nees, *in London Journal of Botany*, 4 (1845), p. 1-3.

1846

185. FORTUNE, Robert. A further account of Weigela rosea, *in Journal of the Royal Horticultural Society*, 1 (1846), p. 189-91.
> With a note by Lindley on p. 190-191.

186. A brief account of the Naran fruit and of the attempts that have been made to cultivate it, *in Journal of the Horticultural Society*, *1* (1846), p. 199-201.

187. LINDLEY, John and PLAYFAIR, Lyon. Copy of the report of Dr Playfair and Mr Lindley on the present state of the Irish potato crop, and on the prospect of approaching scarcity, *in House of Commons. Account and Papers*, *37* (1846), 2 p.

188. A note upon the wild state of maize, or Indian Corn, *in Journal of the Horticultural Society*, *1* (1846), p. 114-7.

189. A notice of Simmon's Patent Hygrometer, *in Journal of the Horticultural Society*, *1* (1846). p. 127-30.

190. *Orchidaceae Lindenianse;* or, notes upon a collection of orchids formed in Colombia and Cuba, by Mr J. Linden, London, Bradbury and Evans, 1846, published November or December 1846.
    viii, 28 p. 8.4".

191. *The vegetable kingdom*; or, the structure, classification, and uses of plants, illustrated upon the natural system. … London, published for the author by Bradbury and Evans. 1846.
    lxviii, 908 p. illus. 8.3".

192. *The vegetable kingdom* … second edition, London, Bradbury and Evans, 1847.
    lxviii, 912 p. illus. 8.7".
    Contains a few small corrections but is otherwise as 1st edition. Pages 409-12 contain a "Supplement of additional genera".

193. *The vegetable kingdom* … London, Bradbury and Evans, 1853.
    [985 p.] illus. 9".
    The pagination is 1-908 as before and the book was printed from stereotype, the additional pages being numbered and lettered e.g. p. 144 is followed by p. 144a and 144b.

194. LINDLEY, John and PLAYFAIR, Lyon. Extract of a report of the Commissioners of Inquiry into matters connected with the failure of the potato crop, *in House of Commons Accounts and Papers*, *37* (1846), 2. p.

1847

195. HERBERT, William. A history of the species of Crocus, *in Journal of the Horticultural Society*, *2* (1847), p. 249-93.
    This was edited and published by Lindley after Herbert's death. It was also issued in pamphlet form

196. Memoranda respecting the Saa–gas–ban, or Apios tuberosa, a supposed equivalent for the potato, *in Journal of the Horticultural Society*, *2* (1847), p. 144-8.

197. *On the cultivation of the Island of Ascension*. [London, Her Majesty's Stationery Office. 1847.]
    18 p. 7.9★.
    A report to the Admiralty.

198. Report on experiments made in the garden of the Society, in 1846, with seeds prepared by Mr Francis Henry Biekes, of Mayence, on the Rhine, *in Journal of the Horticultural Society*, *2* (1847), p. 35-39.

1848

199. The dwarf cocoa-nut of Ceylon, *in Journal of the Horticultural Society*, *3* (1848), p. 258-9.

200. Notes made in the garden of the Horticultural Society upon the rate of growth of plants at different periods of the day, *in Transactions of the Horticultural Society*, second series, *3* (1844), p. 103-113, and (1845) p. 247-261.

201. Notes on the wild potato, *in Journal of the Horticultural Society*, *3* (1848), p. 65-72.

202. A notice of some species of Rhododendron inhabiting Borneo, *in Journal of the Horticultural Society*, *3* (1848), p. 81-91.

203. Observations upon the temperature to which plants are naturally exposed in New Holland, *in Journal of the Horticultural Society*, *3* (1848), p. 282-97.

204. On the arrangement of gardens and pleasure-grounds in the Elizabethan age, *in Journal of the Horticultural Society, 3* (1848), p. 1-15.

205. A short account of Col. Fielding's Coryanth (Coryanthes Fieldingii), *in Journal of the Horticultural Society, 3* (1848), p. 15-18.

206. MITCHELL, Sir Thomas Livingston. *Journal of an expedition into the interior of tropical Australia in search of a route from Sydney to the Gulf of Carpenteria.* London; Longman, Brown, Green and Longmans. 1848.

> Descriptions of the plants collected were written by Lindley and printed as footnotes to pages 31, 33, 34, 45, 56, 64, 82, 88, 91, 94, 97, 102, 148, 154-6, 187, 212, 219, 220, 224, 225, 235, 236, 239, 248, 251, 256, 258, 273, 277, 293, 298, 305, 306, 320, 342, 353, 355, 360, 361, 363, 365, 383, 384, 398.

1849

207. Memoranda concerning some new plants recently introduced into gardens otherwise than through the Horticultural Society, No. 1, *in Journal of the Horticultural Society, 4* (1849), p. 261-9.

1850

208. Memoranda concerning some new plants recently introduced into gardens otherwise than through the Horticultural Society, No. 2, *in Journal of the Horticultural Society, 5* (1850), p. 32-37.

209. Memorandum concerning a remarkable case of vegetable transformation, *in Journal of the Horticultural Society, 5* (1850), p. 29-32.

210. New plants etc., from the Society's garden, *in Journal of the Horticultural Society, 5* (1850), p. 79-88; p. 137-144; p. 192-198.

211. A short account of the more ornamental evergreen Berberries cultivated in the gardens of Great Britain, *in Journal of the Horticultural Society, 5* (1850), p. 1-21.

212. Some memoranda concerning the Melloca, *in Journal of the Horticultural Society, 5* (1850), p. 63-70.

213. Will tubers grow after the destruction of the leaves of a plant? *in Journal of the Horticultural Society, 5* (1850), p. 105-111.

214. LINDLEY, John and GORDON, G. A catalogue of coniferous plants, with their synonyms, *in Journal of the Horticultural Society, 5* (1850), p. 199-228.

215. LINDLEY, John and PAXTON, Joseph. *Paxton's flower garden,* 1-3, 1850-53.

> Descriptions of garden plants with coloured lithographs; issued in monthly parts, but discontinued after three volumes, and 108 plates (drawn by L. Constans) had been issued. The dates of publications as established by L. Garay in *Taxon* 18:711 1869 as follows

> *Copies:* NY (1853), USDA (t.p.'s dated "1850-51")

Vol	Fasc.	Pages	Plates	Date
1	1	1–16	1–3	Mar 1850
	2	17–32	4–6	Apr 1850
	3	33–48	7–9	Mai 1850
	4	49–64	10–12	Jun 1850
	5	65–80	13–15	Jul 1850
	6	81–96	16–18	Aug 1850
	7	97–112	19–21	Sep 1850
	8	113–128	22–24	Oct 1850
	9	129–144	25–27	Nov 1850
	10	145–160	28–30	Dec 1850

Vol	Fasc.	Pages	Plates	Date
	11	161–176	31–33	Jan 1851
	12	177–194	34–36	Feb 1851
2	13	1–14	37–39	Mar 1851
	14	15–30	40–42	Apr 1851
	15	31–46	43–45	Mai 1851
	16	47–60	46–48	Jun 1851
	17	61–74	49–51	Jul 1851
	18	75–88	52–54	Aug 1851
	19	89–104	55–57	Sep 1851
	20	105–120	58–60	Oct 1851
	21	121–136	61–63	Nov 1851
	22	137–152	64–66	Dec 1851
	23	153–168	67–69	Jan 1852
	24	169–186	70–72	Feb 1852
3	25	1–16	73–75	Mar 1852
	26	17–30	76–78	Apr 1852
	27	31–46	79–81	Mai 1852
	28	47–62	82–84	Jun 1852
	29	63–78	85–87	Jul 1852
	30	79–92	88–90	Aug 1852
	31	93–106	91–93	Sep 1852
	32	107–120	94–96	Oct 1852
	33	121–134	97–99	Nov 1852
	34	135–150	100–102	Dec 1852
	35	151–164	103–105	Jan 1853
	36	165–178	106–108	Feb 1853

216. NORTON, John Chalmers, editor. *A cyclopaedia of agriculture, practical and scientific, …* London, Blackie and Son 1850-1855.

      Lindley provided all the botanical articles to the end of the letter S. His contributions are signed "J.L.".

1851

217. New plants, etc., from the Society's Garden, *in Journal of the Horticultural Society*, 6 (1851), p. 52-60; p. 157-9; p. 217-223.

218. Notices of certain ornamental plants lately introduced into England, *in Journal of the Horticultural Society*, 6 (1851), p. 258-273.

219. HOOKER, Joseph Dalton, reporter. Report on substances used as food, in *Reports by the Juries* on the subjects in the thirty classes into which the exhibition was divided. London, The Royal Commission, 1852. p. 51-67.

      The Jury for the food section of the Great Exhibition of 1851 were, Edward de Lode, Sir J.P. Boileau, J.D. Hooker, Comte Herve de Kergolay, John Lindley, and Ashbel Smith.

220. *Folia orchiacea*. An enumeration of the known species of orchids. London, published for the author, by J. Matthews, 1852-55. 1859.

      414 p., 8.7".

      Parts 1-9 published at irregular intervals (parts 6 and 7 being published as one). Each genus is separately paged.

    Dates printed on the original wrappers of the parts reproduced in the 1964 facsimile edition are given below; the dates of receipt at the British Museum are cited in brackets.

1	Stanhopea, Coryanthes, Ionopsis	[48 p.] Oct 1952 [6 Nov]
	Quekettia, Zygostates	
	Odontoglossum, Didactyle	

2	Sarcopodium, Sunipia Achrochaene, Ione Erycina, Epidendrum p. 1-32	[48 p.] Jan 1853 [26 Jan]
3	Epidendrum, p. 33-80	[48 p.] Feb 1853 [26 Feb]
4	Epidendrum p. 81-97, Hemiscleria, Pinelia, Acacallis, Abola, Oncodia, Cochlioda, Cheiradenia, Acampe, Vanda, Luisa	[52 p.] Apr 1853 [2 Mai]
5	Miltonia, Brassia, Ada, Polychilos, Corymbis, Sobralia, Coelogyne, Panisea	[46 p.] Feb 1854 [13 Feb]
6&7	Calanthe, Oncidium, Lunatodis, Geodorum Title-page and contents of vol. I	Nov 1855 [6 Nov] [i]-iv [80 p.]
8	Stelis, Oberonia, Alvisia Restrepia, Brachionidium, Pleurothallis p. 1-6; Prillieux, *Observations.*	[48 p.] Feb 1859 [14 Mar]
9	Pleurothallis, concluded	[40 p.] Mai 1859 [31 Mai]

Facsimile published by A Asher & Co, Amsterdam, in 1964.

221. On substances used as food, illustrated by the Great Exhibition, in, *Lectures on the results of the Great Exhibition of 1851*, delivered before the Royal Society of Arts … London, David Bogue, 1852, p. 211-242.

222. *The symmetry of vegetation;* an outline of the principles to be observed in the delineation of plants: being the substance of three lectures delivered to the students of practical art, at Marlborough House, in November, 1852. London, Department of Science and Art. 1854.
    52 p. diagrs. 7.8".

223. LINDLEY, John and HOOKER, Joseph Dalton. Two letters to John Wood Esq., dated 9th June and 9th November, 1852, reporting methods of distinguishing coffee from chicory, and from roots etc. of other plants. No publisher or date.
    8 p. 3 leaves of diagrs ; 14 p. 4 leaves of diagrs. 12.7".
    These letters are lithographed, being written on the stone in copper-plate style.

1853

224. Plantae Muellerianae – Orchideae, *in Linnaea, 26* (1853), p. 235-243.

1855

225. *The theory and practice of horticulture;* or, an attempt to explain the chief operations of gardening upon physiological grounds … London. Longman, Brown, Green, and Longmans. 1855.
    xvi, 606 p. illus. 8.7".
    A greatly enlarged version of "The Theory of Horticulture".

226. MOORE, Thomas. *The ferns of Great Britain and Ireland* … edited by John Lindley. London, Bradbury and Evans, 1855.
    81 leaves, 51 plates. 22".
    Issued in 17 regular monthly parts between April 1855 and September 1856.
    The plates are nature-printed.
    Lindley appears to be unconnected with Moore's *Octavo Nature-Printed British Ferns,* 1859, which is a later edition of this work.

1854

227. Contributions to the Orchidology of India, *in Journal of the proceedings of the Linnean Society, 1* (1856), p. 70-90; 3 (1858) p. 1-63.

228. A note on Spiranthes gemmipara, *in Journal of the Proceedings of the Linnean Society*, *1* (1857), p. 168-170, published March 1857.

229. The Sassy tree of South Africa, *in Pharmaceutical Journal and Transactions 16* (1856-7). p. 373.
        Letter to the editor on a point of nomenclature.

1858

230. *Descriptive botany*: or, the art of describing plants correctly in scientific language. For self-instruction and the use of schools. London, Bradbury and Evans. 1858.
        32 p. 8.4".

231. *Descriptive botany* ... second edition. London, Bradbury and Evans. 1860. A new impression.

232. A list of the orchidaceous plants collected in the East of Cuba by Mr C. Wright; with characters, *Magazine of Natural History,* third series, *1* (1858), p. 325-336.

1859

233. A note upon Pseudocentrum, a new genus of Orchidaceae, *in Journal of the Proceedings of the Linnean Society*, *3* (1859), p. 63-64, published August 1858.

1862

234. Otocanthus Coeruleus, *in Flore des Serres et des Jardins de l'Europe*, *15* (1862-65), p. 53-4.

235. West African tropical orchids. *Journal of Proceedings of the Linnean Society,* *6* (1862), p. 123-140. published March 1862.

1863

236. RAVENSCROFT, Edward James, editor. *The Pinetum Britannicam*. A descriptive account of hardy coniferous trees cultivated in Great Britain. Edinburgh and London, W. Blackwood; St. John's Wood, Edward Ravenscroft, 1863-84.
        Parts 1-3, 1863 by J. Lindley.

Part 1	Picea nobilis	8 p. to be bound in vol. 2, as p. 181-8
Part 2	Pinus lambertiana	8 p. to be bound in vol. 1 as p. 47-54
Part 3	Picea cephalonica	6 p. to be bound in vol. 2 as p. 175-80
	Picea pinsapo	2 p. to be bound in vol. 2 as p. 189-90

1866

237. LINDLEY, John and MOORE, Thomas. *The treasury of botany*: a popular dictionary of the vegetable kingdom; with which is incorporated a glossary of technical terms. In two parts. London, Longmans, Green and Co. 1866.
        xx, 592, iv, 593-1254, p. 12 plates.
        The plates are steel engravings.
        "The work was planned and its superintendence, as far as the letter C, was carried on by Dr Lindley ...who had prepared a large number of notes for incorporation."

1877

238. LEBOUR, G.A. *Illustrations of fossil plants*: being an autotype reproduction of selected drawings prepared under the supervision of the late Dr Lindley and Mr W. Hutton between the years 1835 and 1840, and now for the first time published by The North of England Institute of Mining and Mechanical Engineers. London: Longmans and Company, 1877.
        viii, 140 p. 64 pls., port. 9 3/4".
        The plates are from drawings by Williamson and others collected by Lindley and Hutton and intended for publication in *The Fossil Flora of Great Britain* – No 86.

Index to Part x

CONTRIBUTORS

ALLFORD, J. MARGUERITE, Dipl. Libr., compiler of 'Bibliography of the published works of John Lindley' submitted in 1952 for the Diploma in Librarianship, University College, London, but hitherto unpublished; librarian, Royal Botanic Gardens, Edinburgh, 1955-1971.

BRICKELL, CHRISTOPHER DAVID, B.Sc (Hort), V.M.H., C.B.E., Botanist. Royal Horticultural Society's Wisley Gardens 1958-1964, Director 1969-1985; Director General, R.H.S. 1985-1993; author of *Pruning* (1979), *The Vanishing Garden* (1986), *Garden Plants* (1985); editor of horticultural encyclopedias.

BRIDGE, KATHRYN, M.A., Archivist, British Columbia Provincial Archives, Victoria, B.C., Canada; author of *Henry & Self. The private life of Sarah Crease 1826-1922* (1996).

CHALONER, WILLIAM GILBERT, B.Sc., Ph.D., F.R.S., Professor of Botany, Birkbeck College, London 1972-1979, Bedford College 1974-1985, Royal Holloway 1985-1994; author of many papers dealing with fossil plants.

CRIBB, PHILLIP, B.Sc., Ph.D., Curator of the Orchid Herbarium, Royal Botanic Gardens, Kew; author of *Manual of Cultivated Orchid Species,* 3rd edition (1991), *The Genus Paphiopedilum* (1987), *The Genus Cypripedium* (1997).

ELLIOTT, BRENT, M.A., Ph.D., Librarian of the Lindley Library, Royal Horticultural Society since 1982; author of *Victorian Gardens* (1986), *The Country House Garden* (1995) and *Treasures of the Royal Horticultural Society* (1995).

STEARN, WILLIAM THOMAS, D.Sc., Fil. Dr., V.M.H., C.B.E., Librarian of the Lindley Library, Royal Horticultural Society 1933-1941, 1946-1952 (1941-1946 in R.A.F.), botanist British Museum (Natural History) 1952-1976; Visiting Professor, University of Reading 1977-1983; author of *Botanical Latin* (1966; 4th ed. 1992), *Dictionary of Plant Names for Gardeners* (1992) etc.

TJADEN, WILLIAM LOUIS, B.Sc. (Econ.), historian of British horticulture and expert amateur grower of succulent plants; active member of the Royal Horticultural Society from 1948 and, after retirement in 1973 from the British Civil Service, member of R.H.S. Library and Floral C (Greenhouse plants) committees.

INDEX

Page numbers in bold type refer to illustrations and captions

19 Sept. 1997

Professor William William Stearn,
17 High Park Road,
Kew, Richmond, Surrey,
TW9 4BL.